THE ADDICT IN
THE STREET

❖❖❖

THE ADDICT
IN THE
STREET

❖❖❖

*Edited and with an introduction
by* JEREMY LARNER
*from tape recordings collected
by* Ralph Tefferteller

Grove Press, Inc.   *New York*

Library of Congress Catalog Card Number: 64-22976

First Printing

MANUFACTURED IN THE UNITED STATES OF AMERICA
BY THE BOOK PRESS, BRATTLEBORO, VERMONT

If you wish to alter or annihilate a pyramid of numbers in a serial relation, you alter or remove the bottom number. If we wish to annihilate the junk pyramid, we must start with the bottom of the pyramid: *the Addict in the Street,* and stop tilting quixotically for the "higher ups" so called, all of whom are immediately replaceable. *The addict in the street who must have junk to live is the one irreplaceable factor in the junk equation.* When there are no more addicts to buy junk there will be no junk traffic. As long as junk need exists, someone will service it.

—William S. Burroughs, *Naked Lunch*

Contents

✣✣✣

THE ADDICT IN
THE STREET

✛✛✛

Introduction

Jeremy Larner

THESE accounts are something different and original in the literature of drug-taking. They are neither literary nor philosophic nor sociological nor scientific. They are simply the first-person stories of heroin addicts on the streets of New York City. In following them, we learn how the addict conceives of himself and the world he lives in. Propelled by the junkie's urge to verbalize, we pass, as it were, through a mirror, into a world in which our customary sense of the social landscape is turned inside out and backward. In this mirror world we find a reflection of ourselves assembled, and our eyes are compelled to linger on that which they have seen before but never registered.

For the addict is not a phenomenon entirely of his own creation. Though he has placed himself outside the system we know as society, he has by no means left it behind: he is in fact hopelessly dependent on the institutions of society and absolutely dominated by fear of them. With the co-

11

operation of law and custom, the junkie lives in constant threat of torture, arrest, and degradation. In these pages he lets us look into his mind, where bliss melts every day into wracking need. He takes us along as he sets out once more on the trail of his body, desperately seeking to have himself back again. We are with him as he is treated and cured, escapes and is recaptured, shakes free and falls back, dreams and despairs, resolves and capitulates—always, in the end, capitulates. He has no choice, it seems; the frenzy of his suffering has gone far beyond mere will. We see him turned on a wheel, and his agonies beg us to ask ourselves: How is the wheel formed? What forces turn it? What does it correspond to on our side of the mirror?

In the popular mythology, if a drug addict can manage to kick his habit, he is cured. In reality, addicts are constantly kicking and returning to drugs again. Arrest, for example, means kicking cold turkey, which accounts for the addict's dread of arrest and perhaps for the fact that he is almost certain to go back on heroin the day he is released from prison. But there is a physical motive for the kicking-and-returning cycle which is mostly unknown to non-addicts. I am referring to the mechanism of *tolerance*, whereby an addict in pursuit of euphoria builds up his daily dosage until, simply to get "straight," i.e. to keep from experiencing withdrawal symptoms, he may need hundreds of times the narcotic that would kill an ordinary person. To get "high" the addict needs even more. According to Goodman and Gilman, in their standard text on pharmacology:

When a . . . "kick" is desired, . . . the dose must constantly be increased as tolerance develops, in order to duplicate the original thrill, dreamy state, or euphoria. . . . Heroin has greater addiction liability than other narcotics, produces more euphoria . . . requires smaller doses, and is easier to traffic in illicitly. . . . The amount of narcotic taken by the addict may be remarkably large. De Quincey in his *Autobiography and Confessions of an Opium Eater* remarked that at one time he took 133 dr (over 500 ml) of tincture of opium daily. This is the equivalent of 4.7 grams of morphine, or 300 times the single therapeutic dose.*

Thus a habit is likely to be constantly increasing, a predicament which demands accelerating activity in begging, borrowing, burglary, shoplifting, prostitution, and all the other means by which the free-enterprise addict obtains funds.

There are several accounts in this book of addicts able to support their habits by working at regular jobs—until their tolerance increased, and the resulting need for heavier dosages sent them into illegal activities. When tolerance increased still further, the addicts expressed their desire to kick, speaking urgently of the pains and humiliations of addiction and summoning up dreams of rehabilitation and respectability. I am not suggesting that their pains and dreams are fabricated, nor that they don't believe their own stories. But to understand the stories one must bear in mind the underlying factor of tolerance. If the addict can kick a big habit, he can start all over on a much smaller, cheaper dose of drugs. Social workers, and the various clinicians who help addicts undergo detoxification programs, estimate that over ninety-five per cent return to addiction.

Of course, psychological habituation as well as physical dependence is involved in addiction. Probably there are character types more readily vulnerable to narcotics and addiction than the so-called normal person. It is important,

---

* Louis S. Goodman and Alfred Gilman, *The Pharmacological Basis of Therapeutics* (2nd ed.; New York: Macmillan, 1956).

therefore, to determine what problems and attitudes the addicts who tell their stories here have in common.

To begin with, these addicts—like most addicts who are not doctors, nurses or druggists—grew up in a crowded, lower-class neighborhood where they were introduced to heroin as teenagers. Bored and delinquent at school, they couldn't face the prospect of starting at the bottom of the social ladder. College was unthinkable, and once school was left behind, there was little to do but hang around the neighborhood, and no group with which to identify but one's comrades on the corner: in brief, no place to aspire to. Small wonder that, when asked why they started on heroin, almost every one of them included in his answer the phrase, *to kill time.*

To be sure, they could have gotten jobs (all of them did at one time or another) and worked and saved and become respectable middle-class householders with families of their own. But frequently the model for such industry was missing; in almost every case, the subject reported no relationship or a negative relationship with his father. One can go right down the line: Hector's father was a brutal disciplinarian; Dom's father divorced Dom's mother and remarried; Larry's father worked eighteen hours a day and was never home; Tommy's father became an alcoholic and Tommy's mother divorced him; and Carmen—the only woman in the group— was strictly trained by her father to handle herself like a boy. In lacking a father-figure the addict misses a model of successful relations with the opposite sex as well as a model of breadwinner. It seems hardly a coincidence that heroin robs the user of sexual desire; perhaps the tension of such a possibility is simply too much to be endured. At any rate, more than one of the subjects (e.g., both Tommy and Dom) broke up marriages they swear were happy ones to return to the needle. As it happens, addicts find their friends almost entirely within a male peer group of users, and the injection itself is usually performed in company and with an elaborate fixed ritual. Contempt for women is a constant theme, typically expressed by the remark that women addicts have it easy because they can raise money by hustling. And as for Carmen Sanchez, her prostitution—like that of many other female addicts—seems expressive of an almost willful desire to annihilate her femininity.

Yet it might fairly be asked at this point, what of the bored delinquent children coming from broken homes in slum areas who *don't* resort to drug addiction? One doesn't even have to be at the bottom of the economic heap to find one-self oppressed by boredom or sexual ambiguity. No, the portrait cannot be made definitive simply by listing the objective problems which the potential addict faces. What marks the addict is the extreme style of his response.

Psychiatrists make a distinction between neurotic and psychotic illnesses. Roughly, the difference lies in the manner in which an individual denies or distorts the realities of him-self and his environment. When a neurotic is confronted with a situation that provokes anxiety his thoughts about the matter may be severely twisted, yet still they retain some reference to circumstances as they exist. If we can speak of the neurotic as fighting reality, the psychotic by comparison is fleeing reality. The psychotic withdraws from his environment in favor of suffering or bliss within a world of his own fabrication. Now what I would like to propose is an analogy between heroin addicts and psychotics. I am not saying that addicts are psychotic per se, but that their response to anxiety moves beyond neurosis toward an abso-lute escapism from which there is small hope of rescuing them.

The most striking similarity among the addicts who tell their stories in the following pages is that with each one a vast chasm gapes between his self-portrait and his actual needs and desires as expressed through the life he leads. Almost always the urgent flow of words enforces an utter separation between thought and actuality. The compulsive re-telling of their stories leads not to self-understanding but to rigid isolation.

To see just how this works, let's return to the under-privileged child from a broken home receiving an inferior education and facing an endless struggle to earn a living. This is a situation which may well create cynicism and re-bellion vis-à-vis society and its values; indeed, without some degree of negative feeling it would be impossible to maintain equilibrium in such a blatantly disadvantageous, unfair, undeserved position. Rebellion is commonplace in the slums of New York City, especially outright defiance of constituted authority. But the addict cannot openly express hostility; if he could, he would not have to become addicted. His only conscious gripe against society is that it doesn't under-stand drug addicts—and this gripe is made only after he is safely within the closed room of addiction. It is as though the addict is formed from the individual who doesn't dare to be self-consciously angry or frustrated. The addict is he who under pressure simply splits down the middle: he combines the most conventional morals and aspirations with the most completely anti-social behavior. Almost literally, his left hand knows not what his right hand is doing. He lives in the most advanced stage of alienation—alienated even from himself.

In short, addiction is a kind of cop-out. Without heroin, there would be pain and uncertainty, the empty anonymity of people on the bottom. But as nearly every subject in this book explains: *when you are high on heroin, you don't feel a thing; nothing bothers you.*

No group of people could embrace the middle-class American ideology more fervently than do the drug addicts represented in this volume. But at the same time, no group could engage in activities which by their nature more utterly repudiate and subvert that ideology. Addict after addict swears that all he wants from life is a wife and children, a steady job, a chance to provide his family with the good things of life. Marriage is sacred to him; family is sacred to him; likewise God, church, and country. I'm basically a decent person, the addict insists, though the interviewer is not doubting him. This is the way I would lead my life . . . if only I weren't a drug addict. That's why I got to kick.— And he means it.

It doesn't occur to him that through his addiction, he fulfills a wish to live by a completely different style and value. Despite his protests, he cannot abide living in a family—his own family situation repelled him. He lives instead with other men, as a rule, working in ever-shifting groups, partnerships, and alliances. Drug addicts cannot trust one another, but they are loyal to each other's company. And not, as they maintain, simply because they are ostracized from other company. They stick together because they need each other to recreate the games of hide-and-seek, cops-and-robbers they enjoyed as children, when they first learned to act in groups of male cohorts. Addicts search for money together, wait for the pusher together, take off together, go to jail together, and—like other playmates—spend endless hours talking together about their adventures. Prison, for the addict, is a place where he can exchange information and anecdotage with a wide range of lodge-brothers—find out who has what kind of stuff where, learn the latest twist in lifting, pilfering, mugging, boosting and burglary. (Addicts estimate that a large majority of the prisoners in city jails are fellow addicts, that they account for at least three-quarters of local robberies.) It's an exciting life, a dangerous life—at the farthest remove from the safety and savings-banks of the middle-classes. Addiction is a poor boy's university. One addict calls it "the Wild West," and "the New Frontier."

It seems possible, however, that if the law were willing to call off its posses and make concerted efforts in more humane directions, much of the addict's "Wild West" might be turned into ghost towns. Indeed, the continued activity on the addict's New Frontier compels one to wonder if the addict-at-large is not vital to the social and economic systems within which he operates. For certainly the most scientific methods of treatment are resisted in this country. Most people won't even permit themselves to see an addict when he is squarely before their eyes. Perhaps they feel some need to keep the addict outlawed and invisible; why else does the suggestion of clinics which might register addicts and supply them with controlled maintenance dosages meet with general indignation? More than one addict insists that if the large department stores would sponsor such clinics, they would save enormous sums through the elimination of shoplifting. But if addicts were treated clinically, the conditions which provoke addiction—such as unemployment and boredom and poverty and discontent—might press more fiercely on the naked eye. And narcotics bulls would lose *their* Wild West.

Surely it's possible to feel an irrational resentment toward addicts. As with alcoholics, the obvious physical pain that addicts suffer does not atone for their outrageous flaunting of the unspoken law that forbids pure pleasure-seeking. Most people wish to punish addicts from the same instinct that makes them bridle when approached by any sort of derelict. The syndrome goes something like this: 1) The nerve of this man loafing when I must make sacrifices and work so hard!   2) On top of this, he asks me for money, my taxpayer's money!   3) He has done this to himself—certainly

I am not responsible for him! 4) If I acknowledge his claim so much as to let him come near me, I am guilty and the same thing could happen to me. 5) Therefore I do not see him and could not possibly see him. 6) He'll get what's coming to him.

The addict exists, however, and incurs further resentment by wallowing in his unspeakable physical pain. It is easy enough to point out the masochistic element in the addict's inevitable torment. Yet for the addict himself the pain is not without reward, for it is a prelude to the high, which he may call a "cure"—as if to acknowledge the necessity of the disease. In contrast to the prescribed social model of contentment-building, the addict fills his hours, days and years with the cycle of search and discovery, need and fulfillment, cures and backslidings, despair and nirvana. And paradoxically, through the presence of heroin in his system, this most alienated of men finds himself utterly involved in his life-process. He, at least, is quit of boredom and empty role-playing. He reduces himself to a need, and becomes that need. Maybe he's even happy—as happiness goes in this best of all possible worlds. According to Freud (in *Civilization and Its Discontents*), "What is called happiness in its narrowest sense comes from the satisfaction—most often instantaneous—of pent-up needs which have reached great intensity, and by its very nature can only be a transitory experience . . . we are so constituted that we can only intensely enjoy contrasts. . . ."

The addict comes off fairly well by this definition. Few needs are more intense than the drug need when the cells have begun their journey into withdrawal—and what satisfaction could be more instantaneous than the rush that comes when the needle is inserted into a mainline vein? The discharge of the needle is like the rush of orgasm after a long, slow buildup of sexual tumescence. The addict takes happiness his own way. After the fix, he is fixed for a while. Then, as with the rest of us, the buildup starts again, and may continue until his pent-up needs reach unbearable intensity.

But the addict can't help knowing that his way is not the way happiness is supposed to be sought. The rest of us may build up and discharge, to be sure, but we are able somehow to do other things as well, to breathe easy for a space between crises and to get outside the pure needs of our cells. To go beyond our need, rather than escape into it. To sublimate, as Freud would have it; to work and love. For this the addict genuinely envies us. Work and love are what he wants too. Only, of course, he is a drug addict. And drug addiction, he repeatedly insists, was thrust on him from the outside. He did not invent it, it was brought to him by profiteers, and he is kept from defeating it by self-righteous Puritans. Yes, he knows he is weak-willed (though next time his will is going to triumph!), but still he cannot forgive the rest of us.

He is right and he won't let us forget it. The addict is an indefatigable moralizer. The only trouble is, he uses his moral invention to obscure the reality of his desires. No matter what happens, it turns out that he is doing his best but fate is against him. He is right and the others are wrong. He really wants to kick and be an upright citizen but the bastards won't give him a decent chance. One can see this most clearly in the story of Carmen Sanchez. Through her incredibly developed narrative gifts we are presented with a story of demonic self-destruction. She is, we discover, a woman who at every turn went miles out of her way to embrace her downfall. Yet, even at the end—after she has left school, brilliantly arranged her own seduction, run away from home, gotten herself with child four times, taken up drugs, returned again and again to her addicted husband, betrayed him with other men, gotten herself arrested, run away from Lexington and undone her cure, lost custody of her children, estranged and embarrassed her parents, turned to mugging, hold-ups, homosexuality, prostitution—after all this, she still describes each and every situation with absolute moral self-vindication. She was good, every time, and someone else did her bad. Not only good but the epitome of all virtue. In one of her final interviews she castigates the whores in the neighborhood who are non-addicts. How *dare* they accuse her of price-slashing! *She* respects herself; she would never sell her body for less than it is worth. Nor would she ever engage in any form of sodomy. It is those others who are ruining trade, not her. They don't have to be whores, because they are not drug addicts. They must actually enjoy being bad, and therefore they are capable of anything! What chance does a poor girl have when such people combine to run her down?

What chance indeed? Certainly the addict has a better chance if he is not hunted as a common criminal, if he is permitted to become visible rather than thrown into torture cells which only confirm his guilt and reinforce his alienation. It seems that law enforcement officers might concentrate on dismantling the international heroin cartel, instead of beating and robbing ordinary junkies, or making daring captures of harmless marijuana smokers. On the other hand, as William Burroughs suggests, the "men at the top" are replaceable, and the search for them may be quixotic. It is the junkie in the street we must seek to rehabilitate, and if we are to listen to our medical authorities rather than our captains of purity, we must be willing, experimentally, to treat him with narcotics, either medicinally or as maintenance. But this is a social problem, an existential problem, with roots deep in the psychological and historical makeup of our civilization. We cannot expect quick solutions, but it is high time we let the drug addict appear in our field of vision, that we may step toward him with some sense of shared humanity.

* * *

THE interviews contained in this book were transcribed from nearly one hundred hours of tape recordings. Naturally, transcription involved considerable selection and editing. It may be in order, therefore, for the editor to set forth the principles that guided him in the choosing and exclusion of material.

My chief purpose was to permit the drug addicts to give portraits of themselves as human beings. The questions that I hoped this book would answer were: What kind of people become addicts? How do they feel about themselves and others? What are their lives like? Consequently I tended to choose those moments of the interviews when the addicts were most aroused, most emotional, most involved; for these seemed to be the moments when they revealed their deepest feelings. Sometimes, of course, their intention was just the opposite—to hide their feelings, often with elaborate rationalizations; but their intensity of speech betrayed them. To preserve this kind of content I cut away passages of random reminiscence and haphazard anecdotage. In reality, the tone of the interviews was not always as high-pitched as it turns out in transcription; usually there was an ebb and flow of emotion.

Nor should the reader assume that all addicts are as articulate as the ones here represented. Naturally I chose the interviews which were most verbally effective, discarding about three times as many others.

In addition to passages of high emotion, I included a goodly amount of descriptive detail as to the daily routine of heroin addicts. This book therefore should provide much information about how drugs are obtained and taken, how addicts get money, prison life, hospital life, and the family backgrounds of addicts.

A certain amount of editing was necessary to make the spoken language clear on the printed page. Beyond this, I tried to maintain verbatim faithfulness to actual speech, and I think that cutting the redundancies and incoherencies of conversation supported, rather than detracted from, this end. Accents posed a special problem, but after some experimentation I found they were best conveyed by occasional phonetic spellings, which, if overdone, only distract the reader's eye and slow him down. Grammatical errors I retained, except where they made a sentence incomprehensible. Factual errors I also left uncorrected, on the assumption that the errors were more significant than the facts.

If my method has been successful, the reader will recognize several distinct styles of speech in this book, corresponding to the varying educational and ethnic backgrounds of the speakers. It is interesting to note that many of them have incorporated into their speech some high-falutin' sociological and psychological terms, which they employ freely to explain or excuse their addiction. I would conclude either that heroin, like travel, is broadening, or that jargon has penetrated to the very bottom of metropolitan society.

Except for cutting, little was done to impose continuity on the interviews, and the reader will find some of the subjects wandering in their stories. I have in practically all cases left the passages in the order in which they were spoken. It was my feeling that there was a natural development in the course of a given interview, and that to rearrange would be to distort the personality of the speaker.

Though the addicts knew that they were being recorded, the atmosphere of the interviews was such that they were more conscious of speaking to Mr. Tefferteller than to the tape recorder. In most cases, the recorder was brought out only after a number of preliminary interviews. All subjects have given written consent to the publication of their interviews. Interestingly, none refused. Nor has their confidence been abused; for proper names have been changed and identifying clues altered.

For reasons of space and pace, Mr. Tefferteller's questions and comments have been entirely eliminated from the transcription. The reader can sense them, however, and sense too at times an increasing tension or confidence in the subject's attitude toward the interviewer. Such development is particularly marked in cases where the subject returned for interviews after interludes of time—as in the sessions with Tommy Blake, which took place over a span of several years. One can see Tommy's outlook changing drastically both with his mood and with the passage of time.

It is to be understood then, that when the subject says "you" or "Mr. T.," he is addressing Mr. Tefferteller. If these transcriptions come across as they should, the reader ought to be able to visualize the social worker alone with the addict late at night in his small office, probing gently and persistently into the outlines of a desperate problem.

Preface

THE following stories of drug addicts were collected by
Ralph Tefferteller with the use of a tape recorder. The
addicts are young people, many of whom he has known since
their childhood. These and many other tapes were made over
a period of seven years, during which Mr. Tefferteller made
himself available at almost any time of day or night to addicts who sought him out at the Henry Street Settlement.

Mr. Tefferteller's eighteen years at the Settlement as Associate Director have brought him closely in touch with
thousands of neighborhood children and young people over
those years. The frankness with which the drug addicts speak
is attributable to their confidence in him. They know he is
their friend no matter how often they fail him, and they
know, also, that any small success they have will be met with
warm encouragement. What is also very important, they
know they can bring their family problems with them. Even
if they do not have the strength or self-control to deal with

the misery they are causing, the plight of a mother, a young wife and baby, younger brothers and sisters can reach into their drug-ridden minds. Older men also come to him because in the drug addict's special world, word of help travels fast and they have heard that Ralph Tefferteller might get an addict into a hospital.

Henry Street Settlement on the Lower East Side of New York has been serving its neighborhood since its founding by Lillian Wald in 1893. Neighborhoods such as ours take on different aspects as times change. During the Depression, unemployment and hunger, above all else, set its stamp on the neighborhood. Then came the war, and survival in another sense drew people together for a common purpose. As the war drew to a close and "Welcome Home" signs began to blossom on tenement fronts, the focus of the neighborhood changed again. Many of the changes coming after World War II bore down hardest on young people in their teens. We had the first peace-time draft, which brought insecurity to the eighteen-year-olds and left a higher than normal proportion of the younger teens, a less stable age group, in the neighborhood. At the same time, families were rootless in their new communities. Many teenage gangs were formed to keep intruders out, giving an impetus to gang warfare which was often further stimulated by the ethnic and racial differences of those moving in.

As neighborhoods settled down and the New York City Youth Board, the Settlements, and other agencies found more ways of meeting the problems presented by gang warfare, it became less pervasive, although violence from this source still continues in slum neighborhoods. However, while gang violence became less, a menacing new element crept into our neighborhoods: the teenage use of narcotics. It has even been suggested that we should not have tried to prevent gang violence because in doing so, gang members

became drug addicts. Aside from the fact that the drug
addict seems more often to be a loner, this is about as
reasonable as to suggest that we do nothing about unemployment, because juvenile delinquency was at a low
rate during the depression.

One might speculate as to whether the drug problem is
an aftermath of world wars, as it was in the early twenties
that youthful drug addiction played a part in some neighborhoods such as ours. The addiction of the twenties did not
reach any such proportion of youthful users as today, but it
was enough to get forty-four clinics started in different parts
of the country which were closed by 1923. They may well
have been closed as unsuccessful because we did not know
enough about addiction at the time.

We at the Henry Street Settlement first became aware of
teenage drug users in our neighborhood in 1951 through the
younger brothers of teenage experimenters who told social
workers in our Mental Hygiene Clinic of their fear of being
drawn into the same trouble.

The first teenage narcotic users in our neighborhood were
not the newcomers to the East Side. They belonged to the
older families, Irish, Italian and Jewish. It was not long,
however, before they were joined by teenage members of
the newer Negro and Puerto Rican families who had begun
moving in at an accelerated pace after World War II.
Through the joint efforts of neighborhood churches and
settlements, a narcotic information center was set up to help
addicts and their families as drug use spread through the
area. In all this, Ralph Tefferteller took a leading part, at the
same time working closely with the young boys who came to
him in those days bewildered by their predicament and un-
willing to face the fact that they were "hooked."

In spite of an increasing concentration of the problems
involved in narcotic use, we are inclined to dwell on its

negative factors, rather than on ways of meeting the problem. The low rate of cure and the high rate of recidivism shadow our efforts and sometimes seem to paralyze us in dealing with drug addiction creatively, and forever bring us back to trying to control the supply and doing little more. However, we who work with drug addicts know that the environmental factors of poverty and lack of education play a large part in making ready victims. We know, too, that the terrible momentum of drug addiction goes on, and too few experiments are undertaken, and that it is still hard to get money for the work that needs to be done.

We have not decided whether an addict is a patient or a criminal, whether the British system has any meaning at all for us, whether a doctor's "sustaining dose" can be sustained in court, and whether the doctor's reputation would be ruined in the process. Synanon House in Santa Monica on the West Coast and now in Westport, Connecticut claims to have achieved a higher proportion of success than anything so far, but we do not yet know for whom it works best. It is obvious that "halfway houses," some form of stop-over and help, are indicated on the way back from hospital or jail to the home corner. It is also obvious that the families of addicts are some of the most bewildered and tragic people in our communities, but nowhere is much help given them. Psychiatry does not seem to have found its place in the whole complicated picture, and because the addict himself is such a pitiable personality, we are apt to overlook, to some degree, the train of misery he brings with him. It is their families whom they torment, their friends whom they may contaminate, and the neighborhoods where they live to which they bring fear and deterioration. New York City's rising crime rate is in great measure attributable to narcotics users who must steal to live.

If the community stands confused and impotent to deal

with the factors present in drug addiction, think how helpless the individual addict is who struggles first and last with his addiction, but, in the process, with the police, with the courts, jails, hospitals, his family and his community—a community that has, as yet, found few ways to help him.

The stories in this book, we hope, will illustrate how different in viewpoint and personality drug addicts may be, but, at the same time, will bring to the reader some understanding of the common agony and frustration the addict brings on himself and his family.

The Henry Street Settlement is greatly indebted to Jeremy Larner for his understanding work in preparing this book.

Helen Hall, *Director*
Henry Street Settlement

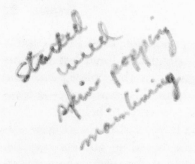

Hector Rodriguez

I STARTED taking narcotics in the Bronx, when I was eleven. I was curious, but I wasn't using them that much—I was just taking marijuana once in a while and snorting; I wasn't shooting it up, I was just skinning it then. Skinning is just where you hit anywhere in your body and shoot the dope in. That's with heroin. And snorting is where you snort it up your nose, just like if you're sniffing something. And burning marijuana, that's just like smoking a cigarette, the only thing you inhale it, you don't let it out, you just try to hold it in.

I was using it up there, and then when I moved down here, I was still using it, you know, but I didn't have no habit or nothing. Like when I started going to school, I would go to school high, and I learned how to read a little high. You know, like I wanted to learn something, the things I need in life, but the teachers wouldn't teach me. They used to ignore me, and pay attention to the other kids. Then when I didn't want to learn, they used to come and try to teach me how to learn. Like I couldn't see that; it used to burn me up. I used to go to school high and start nodding all over the classroom, get drowsy, and that's when I started staying out of school; I didn't go to school no more than three or four months in a year.

That's when I started mainlining, when I got to be fifteen; I started mainlining like a dog. Then when I was sixteen, about three or four months ago, I told my mother I was on narcotics. She started crying, but I told her don't cry, if I was another kid I would probably keep it to myself and die by myself. All I want you to do is give me your signature. That way I can go away to Riverside and help myself. The day that I was going away my mother came and gave me some money, my sister gave me some money, and my mother said, I can't see you go, and I said, well go home, 'cause I can't see myself go, 'cause I love you and I know I done one of the most stupidest mistakes in my life. My mother left crying and that hurt me, you know, but I had to take it like a man, because I knew that I stepped into something that was bigger than myself.

Then when I went to Riverside, it wasn't that bad kicking, because they give you medication to calm down your sickness, and that way you can kick in peace. I was wrapped up in a blanket for five days with cold sweats, and when they came to bring my food I couldn't eat. Then after five days I started out with soup and milk, and I couldn't hold that in my system. After that when I started eating, I started going down to my social worker, having my team meetings.

I was on Team Two. Mr. W. was my social worker, Mr. Z. was my psychiatrist; then I had Mr. P. my psychologist, and I had a few other people there that I forgot their names. I used to go down and tell them my troubles and when they asked me how come I started using narcotics, I told them I was curious, because that was the truth; it wasn't because

I had a problem or nothing, I was just curious, I played it stupid. I used to see my friends using it, I used to see them having fun, and I wanted to know what it was. When I got my hands on it I started to like it, so then it was too late to back out of it. So then I turned myself over to Riverside. They understood it, and at first they wanted to keep me six months, but I told them I wanted to come out, I wanted to start straight, see if I could get me a job, you know, to help out my parents. With a job I could occupy my time, kill time, stay away from everything. So they let me out, and every Thursday at six o'clock I got to check into the after-care clinic. I'm on three years' probation, and if I get caught with narcotics, I get taken in again, and this time they hit me with six months. And if I keep getting in trouble, they give me a year or send me upstate.

Marijuana smells like tea and olive seasoning mixed up together. Once you got it in you it makes you feel drowsy and it makes you forget about things you don't even want to know about. Or it just brings you out so you can have a gay time. If you want to jump around, you jump around; if you want to sit down and just be in a world of your own, you just sit down and look for your own kicks on it. Like if you see somebody and they come talk to you and something strikes you funny, you just crack up laughing. And you sit down, talk to a girl or boy, you know, like you got some company. You just stay sitting down in a corner and nobody can bother you, no trouble, no nothing. Since marijuana isn't habit-forming you can take it any time you feel like it. If you're in a good mood, you want to get gay, you haven't got nothing to do, you just go and buy yourself a couple of sticks, if you know anybody that sells it. You need to know the right person, 'cause you can go ask a cop for all I know, you need to know the right connection. If you get it, you just take it and there you are, in your own world.

I used to get it uptown, anywhere in Prospect Avenue, right in the streets. Like if you see a junkie and you know him, you just ask him where can I cop some pot? If he knows he'll take you, he'll cop for you. I paid 75 cents a stick, or a dollar for a bomb. A bomb is about as big as a Pall Mall and as fat as a Pall Mall. Like a regular cigarette. The other one is skinnier. I used to smoke it anywhere, like I coulda smoked it in a hallway, smoke it in my house, and if I wanted to just start walking down the street smoking it without nobody seeing me. Just cuff it up in my hand without nobody seeing me and keep on smoking it, just like if I'm smoking a cigarette. Like I would light up a cigarette and light up a joint, start smoking the joint, and everytime I would see a cop or a person coming up I would hide it in my hand or in my pocket and just take out the cigarette, keep on walking. That way nobody would suspect.

I was eleven when I started with marijuana and heroin, too. I stole the heroin off of some guys. I seen them put it up on a roof. I didn't like them because they push me around too much. And I said I don't know what it is, but the only way I can get even with them is by taking it. And I got two of my friends, you know, they were brothers; one of them was twelve and the other was thirteen, like they would shoot up and all. So I took it; since I had seen them doing it, I knew what it was already, more or less. I went and took it and then I knew what it felt like and I liked it. Then from there on I kept on using it.

When you snort heroin, you know, it got a bad bitter taste, like a taste that would turn your stomach inside out. It got some way-out taste. I couldn't snort because I couldn't take that taste; so I started shooting up. Shooting up you don't get the taste; all you get is a fast rush and a boss feeling, you know, like then you got a higher kick than marijuana. You feel drowsy, sit in a corner nodding, nobody to bother you,

you're in your own world, in other words. You ain't got no problems whatsoever, you think freely, you don't think about things you were thinking about before shooting up, like you're in your own world, nobody to bother you or nothing.

The first time I skinned, like I wouldn't hit the vein, just pick up the spike and shove it in. Skin-popping, it takes quite a while before you feel it—take a couple of minutes, but it still do the same effect. Skin-popping you don't get no tracks or nothing. Now mainlining you get tracks, and you're hitting directly in the vein. You get a faster habit and while you're mainlining you can feel the stuff faster. Tracks are marks, black marks, like a long black streak coming down your arm directly over your vein; that comes from hitting in the same place so much. Now when you skin-pop you hit all over your body; you can't keep up with tracks. You lose them; they just keep falling off.

I was fifteen when I started mainlining. I got a set of works: a spike, a whisky bottle cap with a bobby pin around it to make like a handle, an eye dropper, and a baby's pacifier. Now when you cook the stuff you just put it inside the bottle cap, draw it up with the eye dropper, tie the dropper to the spike and just shoot it in your veins. You need water to cook it up—a lot of guys carry a little bottle. You have a special spot to shoot up, that's where you have your water stashed. You measure out the heroin into the water, light a match, and cook it up in the cooker just like when you're heating up a bowl of soup or something. They got a piece of cotton inside the cooker to help them draw it all up. They put the spike on the dropper, strap their arm up and wait till the veins come up and then just hit directly. You put the spike in slow, and the only way you know you got a hit is by watching the blood come up; then you just take off the strap and squeeze it in. Then you feel that rush all over your body and you got your high.

Once you squeeze it in, the drug circulates with your blood, it will come around your system, and all of a sudden your eyes will feel like they gonna close up on you. You feel drowsy, your mouth will dry up on you, your spit will turn into cotton balls, right?; then you just start nodding all over the place, take out the works, clean 'em and hide 'em. Then you got that boss feeling, man, like you're your own boss, there ain't nobody can tell you what to do in this world.

If you're weak-minded, if you get a habit, your body will like cramp up on you, your skin'll start shrinking up, you'll start getting sick and need a fix, you'll start sweating at the same time you'll feel cold, you'll be wrapped up in blankets. You'd do anything just to get a fix. For me to get my habit without mainlining it took me six months. I just kept on using it, and I kept on getting the money, right?, so I didn't have to worry about me getting sick. When I started to get sick and I needed the money for a fix, I would go tell my Mom, look I have to buy my girl a present, this and that, and my Mom would fall for it. She would give me the money, I would run down for a shot, take off, and my body would feel relieved, feel at ease. You know, I don't cramp up, then I feel boss. Then when I had money I got my works, and anybody want to use them have to give me a taste of their junk, and somehow I kept up with my habit. Till I finally realized that I didn't want to use it no more, I wanted to straighten up, I wanted to go to work, help out my parents.

I have my own works, right? Now you're using junk yet you ain't got your own works. Well, you will come to use mine, 'cause you can't snort and you need a shoot-up. Now I'll tell you you have to give me a fix before using my works. You ain't got no choice, you have to give me a fix or go on without one. I had a bathroom in Henry Street and then I had a roof in Henry Street. Inside the bathroom they got that box upstairs, the clean water, fresh water comes down to wash out the bowl; well we just take a canful and bring it down. I had a special rule, you know: nobody could come up and get me till after nine o'clock in the morning, 'cause I was out all night. I had two sets of works—the one at home and the one I lend out to the people. Now sometimes I tell them, look, I've already shot up, I don't want to shoot up, just put a little bit inside of this bag—and I'll go shoot that home. Then we would shoot up in that bathroom or up on the roof. After that I would stash the works downstairs where nobody could see me, go home and during the night when I'm sick I have my own works home. I would lock myself in the bathroom where nobody see me and shoot up there, all by myself.

That bowl, you know, in the bathroom—I used to move it, and we had like a loose brick where I stash them; and the minute I move it back in place it look like it was built there and nobody could move it. Now before I hide them I tell my fellas, okay now go downstairs, and I start walking upstairs. They would think that I'm hiding upstairs and I would just watch them leave, and then I would just run down and hide them, go upstairs and come down through the next building. That way they wouldn't know where I had them.

The works that I had home, I used to clean up the spike and wrap it up in a piece of aluminum paper. Then I would wrap up the cooker in a piece of aluminum paper. The eye-dropper I would wrap up in a piece of bag paper, and put it all inside a box of Marlboro, you know, an empty pack of cigarettes, keep those home. Now the other works I used to wrap them up the same but wrap them up in a hanky and stash them. I kept this up till I was ready to go to Riverside, then I threw the works away, flushed them down the bowl piece by piece.

During a day I would take up two at a time; altogether it would come out to about sixteen fellas. Now you know if

I was high, I wasn't gonna shoot up sixteen times, so I say okay, just start putting what you gonna give me inside this bag; then I just used to save it all up, and the next day I have my fix. I didn't have to worry about getting money or nothing.

The others couldn't get works. I had to steal my spike out of the hospital. Like when I went to the hospital for my penicillin shot when I had the Asiatic Flu, as the nurse walked out I seen where she threw the spike, inside a big jug full of alcohol. I just put my hand in and grabbed a whole bunch of spikes. I came out and I sold a whole lot of them to a whole lot of guys. And they lost them. But I still had two of them left, and I had my two sets of works, one home and one at the bathroom. And everybody after they lost theirs started coming to me. And I just kept collecting fixes.

I kept earning, I wouldn't sell nothing out. I figured if I sold something, I would spend the money, and later on like I be sick and nobody will come to give me a fix and I be stuck right there. So I used to keep taking in but I wouldn't give none out. A bag would be about a square inch—of that bag they would give me about a third. Now I would shoot up about four bags a day, right? The rest I would save and then I would have me about two more bags. I had it in my house stashed under the bureau. Or in the bathroom under the toilet bowl. I looked a long time before I found that place.

If one of them was nervous and he couldn't hit himself, if he would ask me I would hit him myself. I hit a lot of guys in my days. Now if a fella is capable to hit his own self, I would let him, I would let him judge his own self. Now I tell you I used to hit my own self. I wouldn't let no one hit me, I wouldn't take the chance. They might be nervous and run right through my vein, and who's gonna get messed up? Me.

In the morning, that's when everybody comes out sick, you know, to cop, and that's when I used to be ready with my works, just waiting for these people to come over my way. They used to come, boom! I would be collecting right there and then. They meet me in Henry Street. I wouldn't take nobody up to my house to shoot up, because I didn't want my parents to get a bad name. If I had a bad name why mess it up for my parents? I have to clear that up in my own ways. I would wait next to La Guardia Park, let 'em meet me there. When they come on I would say okay, go ahead, you know where to meet me. When they walk I would just run ahead, have the works and everything ready. I had a short-cut and I'd be there waiting for them.

About the junk itself, it is different depending on where and who you get it from. Now if one of these big operators, you know, the brain of the gang, if he would go and cop, and if he cops a piece that already been cut, he won't have to mess around with it unless he want to mess it up, you know, to make a little more out of it. Now if he go and cop a pure piece, that piece ought to be cut six and one, but he would come down and cut it two and one, make it nice and strong. Right there and then you got good junk, good heroin. Now if he were going to mess it up to get more junk than what he's supposed to get, he'll cut it up six and four, he'll loosen it up and make it weak, like guys won't cop off of him every day. By six and four I mean cutting it one spoon of pure heroin and six or four of sugar. They say it's supposed to be six and one, but if the dealer is wise, he wants everybody to keep coming to him, and he wants to give them a nice count so they can fall out, he will go and cut it two and one, or three and one, make it nice and strong.

Uptown they had this broad, you know, she was a woman

already, she was married and she had three kids. She was a
junkie and every time she would send somebody out to cop
for her—cause she wouldn't take the chance of going and
buying for herself—they would beat her out of her money.
And she started marking down the people who started doing
that. And she lost her head. So she went and bag up a couple
of bags full of rat poison, and when the guys came, you
know, she told 'em, well I'm dealing now; and when they cop
off her she say, well this guy didn't beat me or nothing, he
didn't take my money, so she gave him a good bag. And
she say, why this guy beat me, six times, so far he got 150
of my money. Boom! We'll give him a bag of rat poison
and mess him up. Now if the guy taste it and know it's rat
poison he can't do nothing about it, 'cause he beat her. If
he shoots it up he's gonna die instantly.

I taste every bit of junk myself before I use it. I wouldn't
take the chance—somebody could be sick, and they might
want to get my money so they could get their real cure, and
they might sell me a bag of Ajax or a bag of rat poison. And
if I wouldn't taste it, if I would play stupid, I would just
shoot it up, and like I would go out. Because rat poison
cooks up. Now Ajax it cakes up on you, like it bubbles up,
and I know if it's junk or not. I make a practice of tasting
it, so I know what I'm getting and no one beats me for my
money or tries to mess me up.

I had two overdoses in my life. One of them I had in
Henry Street when I shot up, but it didn't hit me then, I
didn't feel nothing till I walk downstairs. Boom! As soon as
I hit the street I passed out. A guy took me up to his house,
to his girl's house, and they woke me up. Then the second
time I took too much, we were driving around inside a car
and we were shooting up inside the car. I wind up in Jackson
Park, unconscious, I done passed out, and the guys took me
all the way back to Henry Street, took me up to a girl's

house, gave me a salt shot, made me drink milk, forced milk down my system while I was out. Then they gave me some more salt shots and started slapping me out of it. Then when I opened one eye, they started walking me around. I was bleeding through my nose like a dog. After I woke up I thought I wasn't myself, because I was more than high. I still had that junk inside my system, and I was drowsy all over the street, I couldn't see where I was going.

It's very dangerous. If you go and shoot up someplace by yourself and you take an O.D. and you ain't got nobody to give you a salt shot, to help you out one-two-three, you'll die right there. You'll have white foam coming out of your mouth, you'll be bleeding. . . . This boy called Bobby, he died in a bathroom up here in Henry Street. He took an O.D. It was where Paul used to live. Paul came down and he was dead and Paul just stepped right over him. I know a lot of people died of overdoses.

I almost got yellow jaundice twice. I was here in Henry Street, and I was nodding. My friend came up and told me, hey, like your face is real yellow, man. Your whole body is yellow. Then when I went to the bathroom, my urinal came out like the color of tea. And the fellas told me, you know you could have yellow jaundice, and I told them no. And they looked at my eyes, made me stick out my tongue, and they said could you eat? And I told them no, and they said you got the reflex towards yellow jaundice, but we can't say for sure you got it. And like I didn't have it. I almost had it those two times, but I didn't get it. I didn't make it because I cut out in time.

I knew this Italian fellow who died of yellow jaundice in Bellevue. Like I knew George from Monroe Street. He had yellow jaundice, his eyes were all yellow; all you could see was a little black pit and the rest was all yellow. He went to the hospital and he came out all right, thank God. And a guy almost got his arm contaminated, they almost had to cut it off, because he blew air inside. He put air inside his veins and puffed them up. He was in the hospital for quite a while.

I've been walking around since I've been back, but I ain't seen none of the fellows who used to use my works. Except one, and he got popped the other day. He got picked up. I'm lucky I kicked.

Dom Abruzzi

❖❖❖

I GUESS it was sort of a lark. At that time anyway, we were all off on a kick. I was sixteen years old exactly, and I was walking with one friend on Henry Street, and he asked me, have you ever smoked pot before? I didn't know what pot was, and I had to ask him, so he told me it was marijuana and I almost fell with shock. But then he talked about it, and he explained to me it was nothing to worry about, and three days later I was smoking my first weed. Three months afterward, I started snorting heroin. I got in on that because it was so cheap—a dollar and a half apiece to split a three-dollar bag—and everybody was getting so high and seemed so happy. I just indulged, I put in my dollar and a half, and the first time I got high on horse I was sick as a pig. I couldn't see, I kept vomiting all over the place, and a few months after that I took my first shot. That was a skin-pop, and followed a week later by a mainline. But for the first few years I would say I was an oddity, because I kept myself in check;

42

I didn't get a habit. I was going out with a very wonderful girl at the time, and I wanted to marry her. But in the next few years that followed, I got arrested once, then a second time, and the girl and I broke up. After we broke up, we had money in the bank, in a joint account. I took it all out and spent it on dope, and that's how I acquired my first habit.

I didn't even know I was hooked. I was sitting on a bench right here in the Vladeck project, I was yawning and tearing and a friend came over to me and started talking to me, and said, Dom, you know you're sick. And for the first time I realized I was actually addicted. I had the habit and I had to have it. So from then on it was every day, and when I ran out of the bank money, I began borrowing. At that time, the first few years, your parents don't know anything about your taking dope and everything is so easy; money is much easier to get than when everyone knows you're a drug addict. So I did get arrested again—that was 1956—that was the third time and I went into Riverside Hospital. I spent seven months undergoing psychiatric treatment, but it was all a falsity because I wasn't really undergoing it, I was pretending my way through. I wasn't really trying to help myself. The seven months I was there I was thinking about just one thing: going home and taking that first shot of dope. In fact, all of us there were thinking the same thing. Nobody wanted to help themselves, or so it seemed to me. So I got out in April, 1957, and the first day I was out, I was out two hours, I took my first shot of dope.

And it went on for the next few months; I got another habit, and I saw I couldn't support my habit just by running around borrowing money or trying to steal money, and I started pushing. I made a lot of money pushing. I was supporting my habit, I wasn't looking to make money, but it just so happened a stroke of if-you-want-to-call-it luck,

I made a lot of money. I could support my habit, I could buy clothes, I even bought a car, and odd as it may seem I was working. I had the dope, and I could work. So it was no worry about going to work every morning, just so long as I had my tools—my needle, my eye-dropper and my heroin. I would take a shot maybe three times a day while I was at work, come home and continue selling the dope. That went on for seven or eight months.

I was young and I was a small scale, actually; I guess I coulda went deeper into it, but I was scoring in weight an eighth, and it was costing me fifty dollars an eighth. And I would buy one eighth or two, or I would get a quarter, the equivalent of two eighths. An eighth is one-eighth of an ounce. Half of it I would use for myself because I had to, and the other half I would sell, I would turn over, and it would bring me back three times the amount I paid for it. I did no cutting; the heroin I was getting was considered very good. Now it could have been cut a number of times, I could have made much more money, but I guess I just didn't want to cut it. I wanted to leave it just as good as it was. The quality was terrific and I just didn't want to be bothered. I was just thinking of my habit. I would presume it was cut before I got it with mannite or milk sugar. But considering the quality of the stuff they got today, it wasn't cut much. Today the same dope would turn over an enormous amount of money, because you don't find the same stuff anymore.

To buy my heroin, I could go to any part of the city. At that time, I knew some people on the west end of Greenwich Village. Another time I knew some people in the Bronx. Another time it was at the east end of Harlem; it was the Spanish-Italian section. It's all according to who you know at the time.

After seven-eight months of dealing I stopped it. I was really fed up. I went to a Dr. W. on 47th Street, who supposedly will take you off the habit by lowering the shots every day. The price was sixty dollars a week, double for two weeks. But it didn't help, and the disadvantage of it was that I stopped dealing, and I found myself in a hole with money and everything. I lost my car, I lost my job, and I was back in the street with holes in my pockets and seven days of beard on my face. But it is possible for an addict to kick while living at home if he wants to do it. I did it once by staying up for seven days with a friend. I told the friend ahead of time that if I want to get out of here, don't let me out. And for seven days he didn't let me out. That means I lay in bed with convulsions, jerking to and fro, and after seven days I felt very good. In fact the seventh day was on a Sunday, and I got up and to my surprise I went to church. I had to go to church because that's how good I felt. But to just show you the complete change of mind, the next day I took another shot and I was back on the road.

There is one substitute for dope you can take to help you kick without kicking cold turkey. A lot of dope addicts will try to buy them; in a drugstore with a perscription they might cost $1.75 for a bottle of a hundred. But a drug addict would give you a dollar for one pill. Because they help. I've taken them when I was trying to kick and they did help, I wasn't sick. You have to take them before you're sick and sporadically every three-four hours. I kicked my habit that way also. But being out in the street, as soon as I kicked my habit I took it for granted I'm healthy again—which wasn't true—the next day I'd be taking dope again. I guess being out in the street and being surrounded by drugs and drug addicts and this way of life, I had to take that shot.

I remember when I came out of Riverside, my mother met me at Mulberry Street, where they administer you out, and it was a warm day, we just walked along, and I talked to her, not really talking with my heart but just for the sake of talking. I remember in the back of my mind I kept looking around, wondering where am I gonna get the shot, who will I see first, where's this friend, where's that one. And then after two hours I finally got rid of my mother, I told her I'd be home soon, I went, I met a couple of friends, one who was dealing, and I bought a bag and I got high. And that night, I came home late, and although I came home very high I came home with a bottle of beer to try to fool my mother. I guess I staggered a bit to make the act good, acting out the part. But one day's not gonna do it, you'd have to do it every day, and I couldn't bring a bottle of beer home every day, not the way I was looking. So after a week or two, she found out. And when your parents find out, there's no end to the hollering and screaming and bickering. It just goes on all day.

I used to take my dope in the bathroom of the house, and my mother would just bang down the door. If I really had to go into the bathroom to deviate, she'd be banging on the door anyway. And she'd try to break down the door or peek in through the peek-hole. And she'd just scream and holler; it just got too frustrating. And in a way, psychology-wise, I found that a lot of my problems stem from my mother and I, our agreement with each other, our feelings and emotions. It's true, I did find out a lot of things from Riverside, but that's going to the second time I was there.

I got out of Riverside in 1956 the first time, I was dealing in 1957, and after I stopped dealing I tried to go down to Florida to kick my habit in December, 1957. I borrowed $200, and I still had some pills from Dr. W. It was very funny: we got at least halfway down to Florida, about 900 miles, and we were in about the middle of South Carolina. I had my father's car, and I remember driving, it was the middle of the night and I was so depressed. I kept seeing this one highway and this one white white line, nothing around me but trees and hillbillies. I just stopped the car right in the middle of the road. The friend I was with was asleep in the back seat, and I turned around and told him, Bill, we have to turn back. He was shocked, surprised, but I just told him we had to turn back, and sure enough, we turned around and came straight back to New York and the $200 was all spent on dope.

A month later I was arrested again, but it was for consorting with known criminals, the charge was dismissed, and I went on taking dope. I just went ragged, kept on doggedly, like no end to this thing, and finally it was July again, 1958, and I got arrested again. I got out on bail, I talked to my doctor at Riverside, and I told him I wanted to come back. And it seems every time I get arrested I want to come back. If I wanted to do it on my own, I guess I wouldn't. But I said let me get out of this jam I'm in. So he said, all right, come back right away. I said, well wait until the summer's over. I wanted to spend the summer on the streets. Meantime I had this case pending in court.

Sure enough, I stay out on the streets two months, and in September I get arrested again while I have one case pending. So I was up tight. But I managed to get out on bail again, which is very lucky, because I had a probation stemming from my very first case in 1954. I was on the streets three or four days and I ran right into Riverside. And they hollered in court, they wanted to put a warrant on me, but Riverside stood up and they said that we want to help this boy. The court agreed, and they said all right, we'll see how he does.

I stayed ten months that trip, and it wasn't like the first, when I didn't want psychiatric help. This time I did; I finally got down to work with my doctor and we finally started getting into my problems, all stemming from my childhood feelings, my mistrust for people, my wants. We had many good sessions, where I would just come out feeling so good about finding out new things about myself— really old things, yet I was finding them out for the first time. For ten months I underwent this treatment, and I was just getting more and more proud of myself, 'cause I knew I was just gonna make it this time. I was becoming more and more aware of myself.

At Riverside they had one head psychologist, two other psychologists, and a nurse on the psychiatric team. And each team has so many patients to see, and each week we'd have group therapy, and all the doctors and all the nurses would get together, along with the whole team—I was on team six —and we would have a group therapy session. Which I thought was very nice, because the doctors weren't fooling around—they'd get right to the point. To work with a doctor alone it's much easier to bring out things, but to work knowing that you have friends around you, guys and girls, it was very hard to bring out something. And the doctors there, at the group therapy, would try to bring up discussions about one's feelings, one's emotions, and try to get us to argue the point. And all the while they'd be observing us—this I noticed right away—and I would try my best, I guess, but I think that I had this block of some sort—I was afraid to talk in front of my friends. But you could learn a great deal from the group therapy. Only if we'd put a little more heart into it, we'd have learned even more. But then again we had our regular sessions with the doctor alone.

But to just come out and tell another person the things that have been bothering you for years and years—that's so hard, so difficult to do that most of the patients in the hospital don't want to go through it. They just don't have any trust. I didn't have any trust in my doctor, either. I'll tell you the way I finally got to trust my doctor and work with him.

My doctor, every time I came to see him, and I used to come three times a week, would say to me, Dom, what do you think of me? And he would want me to tell him point-blank, not thinking about it, not thinking up an answer, the first thing that came to my mind.

And every time he asked me, I would sit down and think about it. I would say, well, doctor, you're a very fine man, I like you, you're a good friend. And he would tell me, Dom, you're not telling me everything. You're not really coming out with it.

This went on for a month, and I finally said, the heck with it, I'm going to go full into this thing. I've got to try. And I was afraid. You'll never know how afraid I was to say something to somebody I couldn't know that well, and to put all my trust in him. But this is what he was trying to do, trying to get me to trust him implicitly.

So that day I went to him, and he asked me, Dom, what do you think of me? And this time I didn't hesitate. I told him, you're a big, fat bastard.

And he just sat there, to my surprise, and smiled, and asked me why. Like I was stunned, but he just explained: same procedure, first thing that comes to your mind.

He asked me why. And I just told him the first thing that came to my mind. And it boiled down to that . . . the reason why I didn't like him . . . not that I didn't like him, but subconsciously I cursed him out . . . was that I was afraid of him. Why was I afraid of him? It boiled down to that I thought he was gonna slap me. Why did I think he was gonna slap me? Next thing I remember that came outa my mouth was that my mother always slaps me when I do wrong.

Now when I said that I saw myself saying that, and right

away him and I saw that we hit on something. And it just came down to I didn't trust him because I'm afraid of being slapped, because my mother would slap me every time when I was a kid, when I was very young, would slap me if I said anything wrong or out of the way. And that's why I didn't trust him: I didn't want to get hurt.

Well, it turned out after that everything came out so much easier, because after that first meeting I was so surprised with myself. Because this thing came outa my mouth, it just originated in my mind, point-blank. It originated first thing that came to my mind, and after that, no matter what he said to me, I wasn't gonna think about an answer, I wasn't gonna think about something to tell him. I'd sit down, and if he said something, well fine; if I wanted to curse him, I'd curse him. But this made it all the better; this is what he wanted, this is what I wanted, and there were times when I would just fall into tears in the office. I remember a couple of times . . . because, you know, the things that came out were very hard. I just brought out things when I was a child . . . and I used to get beat by my mother; and they're divorced, my mother and father are divorced; little things, like not having anything to eat; and then being afraid of people, because of the mistrust, because I was afraid of being hurt, being slapped. And then we started interpreting the dreams.

He would tell me, Dom, I want you to interpret your dreams. I couldn't imagine what he meant; how was *I* gonna interpret 'em? But, sure enough, a month went by, and I would come in with a dream and tell him, you know, doctor, I had a dream and I think it means such-and-such and such-and-such. And if he thought that in one or two places I might be wrong, he'd bring it out to me, and I would associate again, and come out with something else. I'd walk out of the office knowing what the dream probably had meant, and what I was hiding from.

I could tell you an experience about a dream I had, if you want to hear it. All right?

I had a dream where I was fighting with this big, huge Negro fellow, and then again I couldn't tell if he was Negro, but his face was dark, I couldn't see his face. And in the dream I had killed him. And I just hid him under the bed. Now I was in a room, the same room I had at Riverside Hospital, but also it was part of the three rooms I was living in downtown. And there was a radio on top of the bed, which had wires stemming from all points of the radio going behind my locker, behind my bed, behind the radiator, about six or seven wires. Now after I killed this huge man, I proceeded to try to tear out all these *wires*. And I couldn't tear them out. I teared a few out but I couldn't get enough out. And next I knew it was a knock on the door. And I was afraid. And I heard my mother and my brother's voice. Then one of them went to answer the door. And I was peeking out, and I saw the door open and it was a friend I knew, standing there. And in the hallway behind him, there was a . . . a sort of a . . . wooden . . . a wooden dummy. No face, just a plain dummy, and all I could see was from the waist up. The dummy was on a slant, and the rest of the dummy was hidden by the door. And that's all I saw of the dummy. That was the end of the dream.

I brought this in to the doctor, and this is what we figured out. Now the big fellow that I was trying to kill was, in reality, or could be, the doctor himself. Because he told me that it's true that when we dislike or distrust people, when we dream of them we don't dream of them as their true faces but disguised as somebody else. So this was supposed to be him, I was killing him, trying to get rid of him. The radio was a means of communication. Now being that the radio's a means of communication, here we are, the doctor and I, talking. Now our talking is a means of communication. Now this radio, right here, could represent this talking, and all these wires were the new ideas, the new things I was finding out about myself, which *hurt* me, which I couldn't stand to find out. Which was very true, I was learning things about myself, and I was trying desperately to pull these wires out. I didn't want to learn it, because it was too hard, too hard, too much to learn. I was trying to pull these wires out. The knock on the door, my mother and brother, and my being home was my great wish to want to go home. Now when the door opened here was a friend that I knew; here was another wish, that I could be with my friends. And the dummy, the dummy . . . I was lost: I couldn't imagine why the dummy was there, the wooden dummy. So, I had my eyes closed while I was with the doctor, telling him about the dream, and he told me, open your eyes. He said, Dom, you remember you saw the dummy only from his hips up. I said, right. So he said, Dom, open your eyes. I opened my eyes. So he said, Dom, take a look at me. So I looked at him. He said, how much do you see of me? I looked, and it took a few seconds but I saw what he was trying to get at. I took a very good look, as he was sitting behind his desk, and all I could see of him was from below the hips up. And he said, there again, the dummy was me; it represented me trying to bring things to you. You couldn't get away from me, I was always there, he said.

And after we ran this dream down, I walked out of there with my mouth open in awe. It was so understandable after it was explained. And I helped explain it, and he helped explain it; and it was so understandable that I think I must have been for three days wondering, you know, amazed at the fact that this thing could come about. And every dream I had after that, I never hesitated; I brought it to him, and we got down to it.

After ten months of the psychiatric treatment, I felt that

this time I was going to make it. I really and truly felt it. I went to live, though, with my father this time, and his wife (he had remarried). I went to live with them in the Bronx. And for the next eight months I did not use dope. I might have used a little pot, marijuana, here and there, but that was it. I would drink, once in a while a little pot, but all in all, nothing. I was going to the mountains with my father, I was enjoying myself, I was healthy, tanned, ate a lot, was working, and for eight months I lived a normal, routine, average life. I was a normal citizen again. And I was happy.

I was working in a lingerie place; they made petticoats. I was packing, sending packages out and whatnot. I wasn't making too much, but I didn't care, just as long as I had a job. I was working and I was having a good time.

But I think at the end of eight months I might have took too much to heart, or I took too much for granted, like I've said before. I guess I underestimated the first shot. Years before, my clique—drug addicts—would always say the first shot, forget about it, you're hooked after the first shot. And I would tell them, well I don't think so. I thought it was baloney; I knew the first shot could not hook you physically, it was impossible. And mentally, I felt that if you had strong will power, it wouldn't hook you. But I underestimated it, and I think it's very true: if you have a weak will power, that first shot will hook you mentally. Because after I took the first one, I felt well, I can throw it away any time I want, I don't need it, I can stop. I decided to take another one a week later, and a week later another one, and a week later maybe two shots. Then maybe three the following week. The following month I found myself taking off every day, and I was hooked again.

I ended up moving out of my father's place and living with a girl. We were living common law; she was working, and I was taking dope. Well, I had a roof over my head and

I was running all over Manhattan and the Bronx, just taking dope. In between that time I got another job as a typist, which I really liked. This job had opportunities. But at the time I got that job I started taking dope, and these two things, the dope and the opportunities, impinged, and once that happens, one has got to go. And it wasn't the drugs. So I ended up losing the job, and in July, 1960, I got arrested again.

I spend three weeks in The Tombs, and was sentenced to go to Lexington, Kentucky. I went to Lexington, Kentucky, and stood only ten-eleven days. After the three weeks in The Tombs, when I went before Judge M., my mother was there, you were there, Mr. T., and my lawyer stood up and asked the judge to help me go to Lexington. And I was very grateful to you for standing up for me. It was a year's suspended sentence if I went to Lexington for treatment. I left the next day for Lexington, but I had gone down there with the intentions of undergoing psychiatric treatment again. Now Lexington, Kentucky, you don't see a doctor too often, being close to three thousand patients there. It's almost like a prison, actually. Of course many fellows there are doing time. And I couldn't get enough treatment. I wanted the same treatment I had gotten at Riverside, three times a day. You can call me greedy, but I wanted it, I needed it. I mean three times a week, that's right, excuse me. I wanted it that badly. And over here I might have gotten it once every week, or once in two weeks, and for the five-six months I had to stay that wasn't enough. So after ten-eleven days I signed out, with the idea of going back home to New York and signing into Metropolitan Hospital, where I heard they had good doctors and I could be treated more often.

I got out, and I was out in the streets, and for the two weeks I was out in the streets I must have took only three shots of dope, which I felt was very good. I got a job as a typist down on Fulton Street, and everything was working very well, and after two weeks, I got arrested again.

The girl I was living with in the beginning of 1960 was very devoted to me, supposedly, and she loved me, but I had no feelings for her. But, you know, as a friend I liked her. Well, the one day I had between getting out of jail and going to Lexington, I was supposed to see her. I told her to call me up, and I'd be home. She had to go down to a pay booth to call, and it just so happens she saw me with another girl, just walking the streets, mind you, with no intentions on my part. Right there we had a big argument, and she herself broke it off. Which I'm glad she did, because I didn't have the heart to break it off. She broke it off and that was the end: I figured I'd never see her again. But I went into Lex, got out of Lex ten days later, and when she saw me she was very surprised. In the two weeks I was in the streets, every time I saw her she had this murderous look in her eye, like this emanating of hate for me. I didn't say a word, just didn't bother her. In fact, I don't know how true it is, they said she started taking dope, but that could be just some fallacy on somebody's part.

The day I got arrested I was going to the mountains and I was coming up my house for my valise-case. I went into my hallway and two narcotic agents came in and started searching me. And I said, whaddya want? Why ya picking on me? And they said, well, we got a tip on you, and somebody's complaining. I couldn't imagine who was complaining because I wasn't doing anything, I took dope maybe three times in the two weeks, and they said, we want to search your house. I told them they were very welcome to search my house, because I knew deep down in my heart I had no dope up there. I had been living with my father, then on my own, and I had just moved back into the apartment that my mother and my brother had. They came up, and they took a little dabble here, they looked under an ashtray maybe, behind the door, but with no heart. Then finally they went straight to the bathroom, went under the tub, and they pulled out four bags. Of heroin. They pulled it out and showed it to me and said, what's this? And I was shocked: my eyes opened up the size of half-dollars. I turned to my brother and I started accusing him, as low as it may seem. I was even suspicious that he might have started taking dope. He swore that he never put it there, and my mother started blaming me for trying to hold back—you're lying, you put it there—my brother started getting suspicious, and the ironic thing about it, it wasn't mine. For the first time, I was innocent.

Finally the officers threatened to take my mother and my brother and I down to jail, arrest the three of us. Well, that I couldn't have happen, so I told them, all right, I'll take the four bags, you can arrest me. Well that's what they wanted.

Now a few days before that happened the girl that I had been going with had come up my house, for no reason at all, because my mother and her were not exactly on speaking terms. She said she just came up to say hello, she had to go right down, her friends were waiting. And my mother said she stood in that house for fifteen minutes, and of that time a good eight-nine minutes must have been spent in the bathroom. Then five minutes talking and she went right down. Now also, someone in the neighborhood had saw the two cops in a car, and saw in the back of the car the head of a girl, very low in the back seat. They were parked on Montgomery Street in view of my doorway, so probably when they saw me walking she just pointed me out. That's him. Because they never knew me from Adam, but they came right to me.

On August 31, I went to court and I waived my rights; I wanted to be sentenced right away. Now normally I would get a year in jail—because just two weeks earlier I had gotten a year's suspended sentence to go to Kentucky. But my lawyer explained to the judge, man to man, that I came out because I wanted psychiatric treatment. The judge went over my whole record, which is a record of eight arrests, and the judge looked at me and said, all right, six months—which was a break, believe me. Out of the six months, I served four months—which is normal for anyone with good time. While I was at Riker's Island, I worked as a clerk-typist in the school at night, and in the daytime I was going to the school itself. I went to school and I acquired a high school diploma by taking a high school equivalency test.

Riker's Island is not as bad as The Tombs, because you have a job. The biggest thing you have there is the work you do; otherwise it's pretty boring. Weekends are very boring. The food is lousy; the chicken we got on Thanksgiving and Christmas was raw and still had the feathers on it. I had to give mine away, but I laughed at it. It was all a joke. There is a hospital there, where they'll treat you if you're physically sick or hurt yourself, but only the inmates doing pen bits, one to three years, are allowed to see a psychiatrist. And then again, they don't see them too often, because there are very few psychiatrists and too many patients; there are close to three thousand inmates in Riker's Island.

I'd say about sixty to seventy per cent of the Riker's Island population was dope addicts, and I'm not exaggerating, because I asked around. Mostly they all go in for petty larceny, possession of a bag of heroin, possession of the tools, burglary. Most of them are doing six months. Riker's Island is not conducive to helping drug addicts; it's a jail, and we all know it's a jail, and we just bide our time till we get out.

Three-quarters of the time out there we'd talk about drugs. Maybe the other quarter of the time we'd talk about old love-lifes and money that we made stealing and whatnot. But three-quarters of the time it was drugs and how one pushed, how one was sick, how one was running around to look for money: that's all that's talked about. I myself just got into a corner and got three guys and started playing cards. All my free time, if I wasn't working, I was playing cards, playing whist or bridge.

Most of the drug addicts will get out of there and go right back on drugs again. It would surprise me if they didn't. In fact, the three weeks I've been home I've seen four-five guys that were on Riker's Island with me, and they're now back on drugs again.

Why does an addict go back to drugs? Well, just to get away from this daily routine, this hunch on his back, this great responsibility that society has given. Which every normal person takes as it comes along, and goes through life not taking drugs, and takes the responsibilities. But a drug addict knows the feeling of drugs, knows the great sedative it can be, and how mild and complacent it can make a person. Once you're high you don't have to worry about anything, I must say truthfully: just sit back and all your problems are gone for a few hours and that's it. But to go look for a job, or to go pay money for rent, or to give money to people. . . . I guess just working alone, work is a big problem. I think most of us are afraid of people, can't associate with anybody; I guess that stems from our childhood. But as teenagers and before we took dope, we had a clique, and running around. And while we take dope we still have a clique, although they're new faces, colored, Spanish, white—we still have this little group of drug addicts, and we stick together and are basically afraid of people.

Only two that I know of have kicked and stayed off for

the past two years. One is living in Staten Island, is married and has a child—which is my godchild—he's working and is doing very well. In fact he has his own house—five rooms, beautiful furniture—he pays on time but he's happy. The other was in Riverside with me. He got out in June '59, and since that time he hasn't taken dope. He also took his high school equivalency test, acquired his diploma, and is now going to New York University.

Yes, the drug addict is as intelligent as other people, but only through going through the life, through these years do they acquire this intelligence and wisdom. I would say that maybe at sixteen or seventeen years old, compared to a fellow that's going to college, the addict might not be equipped, then. But going through the life of drugs, this certain way of life, you just acquire wisdom, you pick up knowledge, you mature much faster. In the first few years you progress so fast that I would put the addict next to any person going to college then, and say that he could sit in the same class for the same four years and do just as well.

I would look at addicts as poor, disillusioned people. When it comes to force, I'd say most drug addicts are afraid to use force. They'd break into a house, stealthily, or go boosting in a grocery store—that way, yes, but to use force in any way, I have never, in the eight-nine years that I have taken dope, seen one drug addict use force. They're all very meek people, very meek and very humble, and very afraid. People have the wrong idea. If they would see us as we are, we're more amicable than some other people I know. And we tend to have a kind of heart, when we have the dope in us; drug addicts will give their right arms to give helping hands. If people could stop seeing us as stereotypes, it would be a great help, we would have taken a great step toward understanding our problem. They'll just have to realize that we don't have horns on our heads, that we don't carry a tail around behind, but instead are very afraid, and afraid of all the people around us, and very weak. I'm not making any excuses for us; I'm talking of what I've seen. They are very weak, and they need a push. It's harder for them to do things on their own than it would be for normal human beings, even if they're off drugs. They need a helping hand, they need friends, they need people they can trust. Of course before they can find a person they can trust, a drug addict has to put his trust in a person first. Which is the hardest thing, like I explained to you with my doctor. But once they find that, I doubt if they'll let it go. Because friends are the thing we need now, and we need many friends. . . .

Can we trust each other? Well, under the influence of drugs, if there are about five or ten of us sitting around, and we're all high on dope, we'd be sitting and talking all friends, all good friends, and you'd never believe we're under the influence of drugs. But you get the same ten, sick, without dope, then you have a vicious group, who don't trust each other at all and go out each for himself. When a drug addict is sick he will go out and just worry about himself, to get his money, to get his dope. Once he has his dope, he goes back to his group, sits there, and mingles.

The first few addicts I met of course were in my neighborhood, my own friends. But going away to jail, and to Riverside, and to Lexington, I met a great many more, which enables me to go into any part of New York City and buy some heroin. I can go to the Bronx, Brooklyn, Long Island, and everywhere I go I find the dope addicts huddled together in one corner, talking shop. They talk who's got good stuff and who's got bad stuff; they try to get the best. Once they have it . . . in the wintertime, for instance, if it's too cold, they'll take their shot, go up and watch television, and not bother a soul. Give them the dope, they'll work eight hours a day, and you would never know the difference.

Of course, after a while the effect of the heroin gives them a normal look. At first when you take dope, you're able to get high, you start getting sleepy; but after acquiring a habit you're just sick, and you need it just to become a normal human person. You can work and nobody know the difference. I even used to work overtime.

It would be so funny sometimes, I'd be working on a job, I'd be typing, and the people around me would bring up the discussion of drugs. And oh yes, drug addicts this, drug addicts that, and I'd be sitting there high. I had the stuff in me, only since I was taking it every day I wasn't nodding or anything like that. And I would discuss it with them, as if I were a square. And maybe five minutes later I would be going into the bathroom to take a shot, so I could work the rest of the day.

At one time I was taking four to five five-dollar bags a day, which was costing me twenty-five dollars a day. That was one reason I might be working, plus I was living with this girl and she'd be giving me money out of her salary. I'm afraid I left her quite broke. I'd try to get my dope in quantity, so I could take it to work, and have my tools with me, my works, and my heroin, right at work, so I'd have no fear that I'd be getting sick. Because there've been a number of times when I've gotten sick on the job and walked right off, regardless of how they needed me. There were many times I've taken advancements of pay. The first week I was on this job as a typist, I was hardly known there and I took an advance of fifteen dollars. I needed this money to get my dope and be able to come back to work the next day. It kept me going.

I remember working for my father in his shop, a couple of times I was so sick I was seeing double, I was weak and I couldn't work with the machines. I just told the boss over me I had to leave—and I'd just walk right out, not telling

my father or any of the bosses. I didn't want to hear their
tongues wagging. I knew I had to hear it the next morning,
but I said well I'll worry about that when it comes along.
Sure enough, I went out, found money, if not in the shop
somewhere in the streets, got my dope and was satisfied.

I remember one time I walked off the job and didn't
come back for three days. I came back limping, with a cane.
Of course it was all a fallacy; nothing was wrong with me,
but I made up the excuse that I had got hit by a car. I
didn't want to lose the job. I loved the job, I really did. And
I came in limping, I said I was hit by a car but I'm willing
to work, I'll make the big sacrifice. It was so pathetic; here
I am lying like a fiend and these people are good enough to
take me back.

When there's a call for drugs, and you have to get it—
you could be a surgeon in the middle of a big operation—
you must stop and take your shot. Because you just can't do
anything without it. You can't continue to work, and if you
do try to continue, your work will be terrible. It will come
out weak, and with mistakes.

But when you're high your work will be as good if not
better than anyone's. I remember many times, working
with my father, I used to go into the bathroom three times
a day to take off, and I'd come back whistling and copious
with things to do, things on my mind. I'd be working all the
harder, 'cause I was content, happy, I had the shot in me,
and I found myself working harder, more vehemently, wanting to get these things done, get this work out. And I can
say that with the dope I could work just as well, if not better,
than if I had not been on dope.

As soon as you take your shot and it rolls into your arm,
you have this great relief; you feel the sickness leaving your
body. You're able to sit back and relax and let out this
great whoosh from your mouth, like at last! When you're

sick, I remember too well the kicking and jerking of your body; the blood cells being so used to having this coating of drugs around them, the body is emitting all this energy now that was covered normally by drugs. All this energy now is let loose, and it jerks your body to and fro; it's frustrating, you can't keep your body still. You have to throw up, you have convulsions; and your back hurts—you have such a pain in your back! It's too terrible to explain how your back hurts—I dread even thinking about it. That's why you get this great relief: everything leaves when you get your shot. Before that you feel ragged, like you're just hanging up some place. You feel totally out of place, like you're out of this world, you don't belong. You just want the shot so you could belong, and get back into the routine, the cycle of things.

Being high just brings you back to normality. And I think you observe things a little more deeply; you have a little more perspective on things around you. Because actually you're going through a lot—you're going through being sick, hiding from cops, getting arrested—and each shot gives you a little more perspective, a little more knowledge.

When you get up, the first thought in your mind is do I have any money? If you don't, you got to get it. And that means keeping up a lively pace. Now I'm so used to walking fast, if they would induct me into the Army, it would be nothing to walk twenty-five miles. Because when a drug addict has to walk—especially when he has just enough for dope and no carfare—he might have to walk the equivalent of eighty-five blocks to get his fix. He might have three-four guys around him. You'll find a lot who'll just leech on you, and who'll get something out of the next dope addict who does have money. Now this I find happening a lot: if I have money, this next man is sick—I take him along and give him half my stuff. Then the next time he'll get me some.

Then he might give somebody else some. Each drug addict has his good days and his bad days, just like in regular life.

It's this constant pace, this quickening pace—when it slows down, you're at a loss. That's why I said it's a way of life. It's such a quick way of life, to and fro and not really getting anywhere. All you're really doing is the same thing you did the day before: getting money to get high. But the idea is that each day brings up a new quest. I've gone as far as Tarrytown, in upstate New York, just to get money.

Most drugs are bought right in the street—in hallways, in cellars—and the next best place would be a house, the pusher's house—a house connection, we call it. You go up to the house, knock on the door, get so many bags, and that's it. But they're more susceptible to arrest, being in one place; one man can rat you out in a minute. A street connection is looking around, sees more things, and takes less chances. So that's what we mostly find.

Most pushers are drug addicts. Actually, there was only two times in all the nine-ten years that I've been taking dope that I've gone to men who didn't take dope themselves but were just pushing it for profit. Now all the pushers in a local neighborhood, any local neighborhood, they mostly go to people who are also taking dope to get their supply. Maybe the next man up might be a man who doesn't use it, but then again he will not be a *big* man. A drug addict will never see the big people in his lifetime. The people who deal drugs for a profit in millions want nothing to do with drug addicts. Drug addicts are known to be weak, and might rat you out for a shot of dope. The big people sell through lesser people, and the lesser people sell through still lesser people. Until the one man that sells for profit somewhere has to meet up with one man who does take dope, but before you get to that spot the dope has passed down a chain of about ten people. The drug addict will never reach the top.

Now as for the cops, sometimes when they are given some money they will not arrest a user, or they'll keep his name off the books at the precinct house. But what always frustrated me and irked me is that here you have the narcotics bulls going out to make their certain number of arrests and getting their drug addicts when they all could be pooling their power and their brain power to try to get the big people, the people who are pushing for profit. There was one time when I was walking from the neighborhood, I had the bag on me, in my hands, and someone ran up behind me and held me by the arms, so I couldn't reach up and swallow the bag. I dropped it, and I heard somebody hollering, he dropped it, he dropped it! I looked up and there was a car, right across the street, with two more inside. And then there was another bull across the street walking, and there was another one behind the one that got me. So actually there were five narcotic bulls. And I told them, when I got in the car, all right, you got me, you got my bag. But why did it take five big husky men like you to get little me?

I told them this; it got me mad. Takes five men to get me? I just wanted a shot of dope, and that's all I wanted. Took five of 'em, and meanwhile some bigshot is sitting behind a desk and making a lot of money. But he's probably paying off.

They have to make their number of arrests, you know. Each narcotic bull has to make a certain number of arrests to stay in good with the top men at the narcotics bureau. They even told me that. And of course the drug addicts are the easiest to arrest, since they stay in the street and take so many chances.

Law enforcement could be improved here; it's a flam as it is now. But in my opinion you'll never be able to stop

dope coming in to this country. There's so many ways it
can be brought in. All they can do is stop a few here, stop
a few there, get into the papers, pacify society, and like
show that they're doing their work. But actually what are
they doing? They're not doing anything, because in order to
really do something beneficial they'll have to stop the whole
flow altogether, which they'll never be able to do. Stopping
it is something they should forget about—unless, of course,
they're gonna have a man on each foot of the United States
coast.

I feel that most of the heroin comes from Italy in Europe
and Red China in Asia. I know by the laws in China it used
to be legal to take dope, but now it's illegal. This is fact, I
believe. The first time you take dope, they give you warning
and let you kick it. The second time, I believe they give you
a fine and they might imprison you. The third time, they
kill you.

Drug addicts have the will power to go into clinics for
treatment. On their own? Definitely. I've seen many drug
addicts do this. They see how down and out they've gotten,
how it's getting harder to get money every day, how roguey
they might be getting, dirty and filthy, without any care for
their parents or friends. This provokes them right away to go
into a hospital on their own, and many people have done
it. It's not unusual at all. I'd say three-quarters of them
would do it.

Psychiatric help is another thing altogether. They go in
to kick physically, so they can get rid of this thing on their
back, put on a little weight and become healthy again; but
they'll shy away from psychiatric treatment because of the
work involved—it's too hard. Probing deep within the mind
and letting out all those problems—it's too much for them,
I guess.

I heard there were clinics for drug addicts in the early

1920's. But I heard that the neighborhoods around the clinics deteriorated, because the drug addicts started to hang around. Well, I don't know how true it is, but I always felt deep down that clinics would help if they only would try to give the drug addict his dope for a minimum amount of money, and let him be off on his own way. It would put an abrupt stop to most of your crime. But then again you have the problem of the drug addict who might not be satisfied with the shot they give out, might want more, and couldn't possibly get more. I still think there would be a black market.

Compared to others in the population, a drug addict doesn't have a good chance of getting hospitalization. I've heard of the waiting list at Metropolitan. For the thousands of drug addicts in New York, the only beds open are in The Tombs, and then on Riker's Island. We need many more hospitals. By the way, they say there are twenty thousand drug addicts in New York City. I've run across many people who believe—and I believe myself—that there are forty thousand drug addicts here. So I doubt very much that there are hospital facilities to treat addiction. They need many more hospital beds—and I'm wondering how they're gonna do it.

I think the teenage years are the ripe years; those are the best time to get addicts under psychiatric treatment. But it's also the hardest time to get them under treatment. I remember myself; I was wild, I didn't want to have any- thing to do with authority—I thought it was a bunch of baloney. So I think that's your biggest problem. If you can get them at that age under psychiatric treatment, it's very good. But I doubt if you can. Maybe I might be a little pessimistic, but I think drugs does that to you. Makes you a little pessimistic now and then.

That second time I went to Riverside, I was a little older

and a little wiser. I wanted to try, because at that time, the end of '58, I had been on drugs five years, I had six arrests under my belt, and I felt that I had just about had it, and I wanted to make it this time. I was twenty years old, going on twenty-one. Like I said before, with age comes wisdom, and with drugs—that gives you a little more wisdom, a little more insight, and a little more wanting to get away from this thing. But also as you get older, and the more you take dope, it's much harder. If I had this insight when I was younger, it would have been a different story.

They say that if you take dope up to the age of twenty-four, you'll never stop. I don't know how true it is, might be just some rumor. . . . But I used to talk about it as a teenager, friends of mine saying, yeah, if you take till you're twenty-four, forget about it, you're gonna take forever. In fact, all of us used to say when we got that age, we'd stop—thinking that we could. And I turned twenty-four on Riker's Island, and on my birthday I just stood there and said to myself, well, here I am twenty-four years old. . . . And that's why I've been trying to keep clean. I'm sorely afraid to go back on dope. So I'm trying to hesitate on that, forever.

I made that one desperate try—it lasted eight months. This is my second desperate try.

TWO YEARS LATER

It's been ten years now. I almost have it down to the date. On May 29, I think it will be ten years. I'm twenty-six years old, so I had just turned sixteen when I started.

I got married last January—1962. She's from the Northwest, and more or less a country girl, a good, clean girl. She had come over from Idaho to visit a friend, and I met her through another friend. I was taking stuff at the time. But I'll tell you one thing: the first day I met her, I told her I was taking stuff. I did not hold it back from her. I told her point-blank where it was at; I wanted to see if she was afraid. She could have walked away, she didn't have to have anything to do with me; I wanted to make sure of this first. And it didn't mean anything to her; I mean, concerning our feelings towards each other. We picked it up from there, and we started seeing each other more and more, and before we knew it . . . I don't know what to call it . . . we just fell in love and we wanted to get married.

Now before we got married I knew I couldn't take stuff. So I . . . I stopped taking stuff for about a month. I kicked cold—well, not cold, I had dolophine pills. I had a doctor right up here on 14th Street—he was giving out dollies and goofballs to everyone; in fact, he got arrested. I got dolophine from him and it helped me out a lot.

I was clean for seven days, and after that I was on my own—without the dollies. I stood clean one month, then the month we were married I was clean, and almost another month afterward: a total of about three months. Then I fell, I started falling. I didn't tell my wife, but eventually of course she found out. I lost my job and I went on from there and started taking stuff again. And once she found out, she's stuck by me ever since. She hasn't walked out, she hasn't thought of walking out, she just wants me to go to the hospital, she wants me to kick, she wants to see me clean, she wants to see me working, she wants to see me do a number of things *without drugs*. So ever since that time she's been by my side, and I gotta hand it to her, 'cause she's taken a hell of a beating, mentally.

She makes about seventy-eight dollars and change. She works at a scientific institute as an assistant editor, steno, secretary, and whatnot. She's worked her way up; in fact, she's getting another raise soon. She's a pretty smart girl. She brings home money all right, which I don't like. It's a lousy feeling not to be working.

At first, she didn't know a thing about drug addiction—very naive, ve-ry na-ive, and she—jesus!—in fact, I had to laugh sometimes at her naiveness. I had to teach her a lot of things, I guess. But today, it's a different girl. Like she's learned so much. I classify her now, when I speak of her, I say she's *hip,* she understands now. What I go through, the things I say, she understands—everything. You would never believe it was the same girl as a year and a half ago. It's a complete change. I don't know if it's for the better or the worse, but she's grown up a lot since she's been here. In fact, she's only nineteen; she won't be twenty for a few months yet. This is still her first job: when she came to New York she started working and she's been in the same place ever since.

She's a budget-minded girl. She pays everything on time —food and whatnot—but with only one of us working, of course, that doesn't leave much money. And any money that's left over I'm always taking or grabbing it for myself.

The tensions are awfully strong. I'd say that we argue . . . oh, I can't take 'em, I tell you these arguments that we have sometime, they get so bad, that I'm surprised that she doesn't say she'll walk out on me. Lately I find that the arguments are getting a little worse, and a little worse, and I don't want 'em to get any worse!

Money: that's the main argument. Just a recent incident: her last six dollars, her *last* six dollars. Woman gets paid every two weeks, she needs carfare and whatnot. I wanted the six dollars, because I was sick. She needed it for carfare and food. And I couldn't see why she couldn't give me this money, 'cause here I was sick. And she tried to show me the other way round about it, and I didn't want to go out stealing, I definitely did not want to go stealing, because the chance I take . . . I wanted to have the money instead, you see . . . because to go stealing is not my line. And anyway, she gave it to me. That's all we argue about—money, money —and it's always concerning drugs. Any other arguments, not concerning drugs, are very small. In fact, I welcome them. They're a pleasure to have.

So tension will mount up. When she gets paid I'm always at the doorstep, looking to get money. Anything not to go out stealing. She gives me some of it, all the time. Of course, every time I ask, there's always a little argument, but she always gives me the money—most of the time out of fear, 'cause she knows what I have to do. She's afraid for me, and she doesn't want me to get arrested, either. When she can't afford it, she gives it to me, all the time. She's never failed me in that way.

She hardly buys any clothes for herself. And as for the apartment, when we first got married we were lucky enough to get some money from my father, and I was clean, and we got the things we have in the house. But anything else we need, we can't get, it's impossible. So we have to be satisfied with what we have now. Which isn't very much.

Of course the drugs will make me incapable at times to have any sex at all. So I would say more or less we've had less than the usual young couple will have. So this alone has built the tension, too. This is something I should have realized. Although at times this is not half as bad as I thought it would be, because being hooked, I don't get as high as I would get normally. Normally when you get high, you just nod out, and you have this utopia, you're just incapable to bringing yourself about to have any sex. But I'm hooked; I take the shot just to be normal. I don't nod, my eyes are not closed or anything like that. I'm just normal, and I find that sex is not a thing that's too bad to argue about. I do have it more than I thought I would, behind drugs.

Where do I get most of my money? Stealing, of course. Stealing's the utmost thing in my mind right now. I just walk the streets at nights, and I look at cars, and if I see there's anything in the car worthwhile, I'll try to get into the car, cracking the part of the window where the little handle is, take it out, and either hock it or sell it to a fence. This is how I have to go about every day, and it gets on your mind after a while. You're in constant fear of getting arrested.

I used to go boosting also. This was stealing meats out of supermarkets. After a certain amount of time I had the same feeling I have now. You're in a state of *ennui*, like you just don't want to, you're tired, you're just *tired* of it, you don't want to do anything anymore, you want to just take it easy, you wish like you didn't have to bother with anybody. In fact, you just wish you weren't taking stuff; you wish like maybe you were sitting by yourself somewhere high on a mountain, didn't know anybody.

When I started boosting, it was just mainly to get five dollars a day. I was living uptown at the time, on my own; in fact, this happened after we first talked, in 1961. Immediately afterwards, in fact, I started boosting. I had never stole before. Now when I went to that first store and took meat for the first time and walked out, I realized how easy it was. Before I knew it I was taking more meat—and getting more meat I was getting more money and of course I was building up my habit. At the end it was coming out that I was taking five bags a day; in other words I was spending thirty dollars a day. So in order to get the thirty dollars I had to boost sixty dollars worth of meat, because I would get half price for the meat.

I boosted mainly steaks and roasts. I would have to go to about three or four stores, and in each store I would have to take about five or six pieces of meat. This was wrapped around my body, inside my shirt, big overcoat over it— wintertime's your best time—close the overcoat and walk right out.

At first I didn't know anybody; I took the meat either from door to door or store to store. The people that I found that bought the meat kept asking for more; they wanted it, because this was a bargain, they were getting meat at half price. Before I knew it, I had a certain clientele. Every day I had a different person to bring my meat to. They wanted more; in fact, they couldn't get enough. Fine, I brang 'em all they wanted.

Supermarkets close on Sunday, and on Saturday I had to boost twice as much to make up for Sunday. I used to have to get $120 worth of meat. So I had to double my efforts, and the meat gets very heavy, let me tell you. Sixty dollars worth of meat is heavy enough, but in the wintertime I can't forget just carrying these shopping bags full of meat. I was cold, I was freezing, and I was actually near to tears, 'cause I had something that just had to get done.

Funny thing is that during this time I was working. I was working nights, in a hotel. And I was making sixty-five dollars there. I took that sixty-five dollars, whatever I got left of it after taxes, and I did like this: I said, well since I get paid on Friday, I'm gonna take one day off from boosting. And like this was such a pleasure to me, to know that I wouldn't have to go out boosting. It was a holiday, every Friday was a holiday; I could spend my pay and I wouldn't have to take any risks. Sunday was also like a rest period for me.

But I was working from eleven to seven. Now, I'd get home at seven o'clock in the morning, I'd take my shot and go to sleep at eight. I'd be up at twelve noon, because I had to go to the supermarkets in the afternoon. This is every day, every day—four hours sleep a day. And six bags a day. Now when you lack sleep and you take drugs on top of that, you just fall into a state of . . . lethargy. You could say I was hypnotized. I used to get up from my bed, four hours sleep, I was dying to sleep, but I knew I hadda go out, I didn't have much drugs left. I'd get up, I'd take another shot. Fine, I'd feel good, but the lack of sleep and the drugs mixing. . . . Before I knew it I was downstairs and walking towards the subway. . . .

I'll never forget one day, walking towards the subway, I had my head down, and I couldn't think straight. I was half asleep, but I was high from drugs and I just didn't care. It seemed the subway was miles away, though it was only two blocks. I got into the subway, and like I was so *tired!* I got into the train, I fell asleep, got off at my stop where most of the supermarkets I hit were, I started walking up one block, and I stopped . . . I stopped, and I had to sit down. I had to sit down because I was so tired, and fed up, and scared that I didn't want to go in the store. 'Cause I was so messed up. I sat down, and I just put my face in my hands and fell asleep. For about fifteen minutes. When I opened my eyes, I realized I hadda go, and I started back to the stores. Again before I went into the stores, I purposely went into a candy store, and made like I was making a phone call. But I wasn't; I just wanted to sit down someplace. I went into the phone booth, picked up the receiver, and made like I was talking to somebody. Leaned my head against it, and just tried to rest for five minutes. Anything to prolong, to put off going into the stores. Of course, when I went into the stores I woke up right away, because here I was taking a chance of getting arrested. I had to be very aware of what I was doing, although at times I found myself not caring, not giving a damn. When I'd get meats in the basket I'd have to go someplace where no one could see, to stuff them in my shirt. But

I found times when I didn't give a damn at all: there might
be people in back of me, in front of me, but I was so tired
and fed up I'd just open my shirt right in front of 'em and
put 'em in. I didn't care. And I walked out.

When I got my meats, I sold them, and then I'd go up to
the neighborhood. I was living near 145th and Broadway at
that time, and was scoring up there. I'd get my six bags,
eleven o'clock at night go to work, and the same routine all
day.

I kept the job about four months; I boosted about six
months. After six months' time I couldn't take it anymore.
Near the end of it, when it was telling on me, you could
just look at me and see that I was just falling apart. I couldn't
even bring myself to bathe, I was so tired. It took great
effort to get into the bathtub. I was living up at 113th Street
with another fellow, both boosting together and he was
working also. He was just as bad off as I was. And you know,
misery loves company. We had guys sleep there, 'cause they
didn't have no place to live—junkies, and they slept on the
floor. We didn't care. The rent was only eighteen dollars a
week—one large room—and we always managed to pay the
rent on time. But I tell you, we didn't eat right. Even though
we boosted all these meats, one thing I never did was take a
piece of meat home to cook for myself. I more or less ate in
restaurants, and that was very seldom.

When I got bad, very, very bad, that was when I went
down to 14th Street to see that doctor, and I got these dollies
from him. And I finally kicked, with the dollies. Kicked, and
well, I started taking again but not as much. And then I
moved down here—that was the summer of '61—and I met
my wife.

One thing I don't want to do again is boosting—bad
enough I gotta do these things with the cars. I find it's not as
bad, but the same thing is creeping over me, the same thing

of not wanting to do it, of wanting to stay away. I'll do anything to put it off. If I knew I could get six dollars right away begging on street corners, I'd do it. In fact, funny thing a few of the fellows are doing—subway begging. They would approach a person and tell him they lost their carfare and get fifteen cents. I tried it one time with this one fellow—and we got six dollars up in less than an hour and a half! Now, mind you, I was so surprised I never did it again, 'cause I can't bring myself to asking people for fifteen cents for carfare. And yet these fellows did it every day, and every day they had their money.

I'm the clumsy type about entering cars; I just crack the window, push the button up and enter the car. There are many other ways to do it, but I don't know them, 'cause I just started this. It's only been two-three weeks, since my habit got worse. And I'd like to catch it before it gets worse yet, 'cause eventually I have to get arrested, I know, it's the law of averages.

When I was boosting, I got caught twice, in the store, by the store detective or one of the workers. But what they did is sign me out; in other words, they catch you, bring you in the office, and both times I signed a paper stating that if I'm caught in that chain of stores again, they could get me right on the spot and arrest me. Of course, I never went back to those stores. Now, you can't even do it anymore; they got hip to it. Other guys have gone in and just burned it out. Tell you the truth, I'd rather do this thing with the cars. I feel less people staring at me. Especially at night. It's not as bad as going in a store and knowing that you've gone in that same store who knows how many times, constantly, every other day, and you know these people know you already, they've seen your face.

The best district I hit was Sutton Place; like Sutton Place was the best. And I think I got away with it simply because

I looked like an eccentric. They thought maybe I was somebody who had money. I walked in with sneakers and a pair
of blue jeans and a raincoat, always a book under my arm—
I made sure of that. I looked around at people shopping
there, and they looked just as eccentric as I did. So right
away they took it for granted that maybe I was one of the
people living there. I used to walk out without buying anything, but I found out that this was wrong. So I used to push
my basket around, get my meats, fill it up with all kinds of
groceries, and when I got my meat stashed away, I'd take out
maybe a ten-cent piece of cake and walk to the counter.
Leave the basket in back, take the ten-cent piece of cake
and stand right in line, filled with meats, and buy your cake
and leave.

Some guys will burglarize houses, some cars, like me, some
go boosting. Each to his own. But more or less it doesn't vary
too much from those three. A lot of guys just deal to try to
support their habits. Me, if I had the choice, I would deal
in a minute. If somebody said, look, you work for me, I'll
give you a dollar or two on each bag you sell—fine! I would
take that chance over stealing—I think any guy would. Right
now there's a kid not more than eighteen years old, and he's
dealing—simply because he has a hard time getting money.
But he's happy with what he's doing because he doesn't have
to run around. He just takes it easy, he's got his stuff, and
that's it. I would do the same thing, and I think any drug
addict would do it. I'd do it for only a dollar a bag. As long
as I knew I could get high every day, and I didn't have to
get involved with the hassle of stealing and lying and cheat-
ing. I wouldn't have to ask my wife for any money, that's
for sure.

And you know it's pretty cold now—very cold. And one
thing I can't stand is the cold weather. We have a hard time
at times finding somebody with stuff; sometimes you have to

wait. Just picture waiting on the street corner in five-degree ten-degree weather. It's freezing, and I'm standing on a corner with six guys—on the other corner, another six guys. I mean this is torture. The other day I was dancing around, trying to keep warm, and this alone looks suspicious. The other day the cops were kicking everybody off the streets. Well, who was left, hanging out on the corners? In the summertime you can get away with it, but not in the wintertime. I've had times when I waited three hours in the cold weather. And one fellow who was dealing—very cheap fellow, he was dealing for somebody else—but anyway, I had $5.90; I was ten cents short. He refused me the bag on account of that one dime. Now I was sick. And he sold the bag to somebody else; it was his last bag. He had to wait two hours before he got another load. And I was sick and I got mad; we almost started fighting. I just controlled myself because this man deals; I said to myself, I don't want to get in bad with him, I can't afford to. I have to eat shit, in other words, off of him. And it was cold and I was sick. I waited over two hours for him to come back, and it was just pure suffering. I stood in a hallway near his house, but the hallway was void of heat, and it was just as cold inside as outside. I was bundled up, I had my hands under my legs and two hoods around my neck, gloves . . . and I was just trying to get up in a corner, get a little warm. But it didn't work; I had to wait it out. And when he finally came, when I saw him and got my bag, it was like worth it. You know you got your bag, you know you're going home and it's warm in there, you know you're gonna be high and not be sick anymore. So you forget it, and more or less you say it was worth waiting and suffering for.

These are the consequences of the game, the cold weather, the hard winters, the stealing, the arrests. I don't know how many times I've wanted to scream and say the heck with it.

As if I could turn my back on it—I wish I could. Walk away from it like it was a rotten egg. But I'm stuck with the fumes; I need it, I can't walk away.

So I went to the hospital one week in August, another week in October, and each time I got out I was clean, but I was so anxious, so mentally disturbed at the idea of getting off, that I was actually nervous. Do you know that guys actually get *sick*, even when they're clean? As soon as they hit the streets, they'll get butterflies. And before you know it, it's on your mind. And of course you have this damn habit, this mental thing you've built up for years and years. You're so afraid—you want to stay away from it but the first negative thought in your mind, or somebody coming over and approaching you about it, that's it. You forget any idea of kicking. You forget it completely, whatever you've said in the hospital about staying off—all this is forgotten. The nervousness is gone, it goes. You start to pace again, and you're running to get it, and you're gonna do something. The nervousness goes, everything leaves you, and you know you're doing what's in you, what your body is used to and your mind is used to. And of course this is the habit to break. And I don't know how to do it.

If somebody should come at that time and offer you drugs, you're through. But more or less it's you. A lot of times nobody would come over to me, but a negative thought would just sow its seed, and it would just grow. And before I know it, that's all I'm thinking. I don't want to know nothing else. People could be dragging at my tails, begging me not to, not to, but if I have this negative thought already, I'm not concerned with them anymore. I wouldn't give a damn. I just have to go and do what I have to, what's been planted in my mind. You just can't get it out.

It's so hard to understand for me. Like before I might be thinking, I'm gonna stay off, stay off. Then I might start thinking a little shot, one little shot. And it grows bigger; it's a gigantic thing in my mind now. You can't push out that negative thought. You can't even budge it an eighth of an inch. It just stays in your mind. It's so powerful. It just rots right there. And by rotting it drives you on. It just rots right there and you have to go on and rot with it and there's nothing you can do about it.

If the President and the Pope came over to me and said, don't do this, you're thinking wrong—they couldn't do anything. I don't think anybody can help at that moment, when you have your mind made up as to what you're going to do. Last time I came out of the hospital I was clean a day and a half. And my mind was made up. I was sitting in the house with my wife and brother, and we were laughing and everything . . . but in my mind I was thinking of how to get out and get money for the shot. I was scheming all these things while sitting there joking around. Outwardly I was laughing, it was all right; but inwardly I was scheming. My mind was made up: I had to do it.

Now if I blew my cool—if I got up and said I was going and they knew what was happening—they couldn't stop me—my mother, my brother, my wife, anyone. If they didn't know, that was better, I could get away with it that much more. But if I got up and they knew it, and they started screaming and hollering, I'd probably lie to them, and they couldn't stop me. I'd go right out and do what I had made up my mind to do.

Riverside is dying now; they're closing it up—I was sorry I went there in October. But it meant a great deal to me that second time I went in 1958. That was the best ten months of my life, at least in the last ten years. I learned a lot about myself there; I learned a lot about other people. I was so open-minded I could take everything in. I saw a lot, and I was more receptive to anything that was told me. I was on the *Riverside Journal,* and was editing the paper, I was taking up an instrument, I was in dramatics; and then seeing my psychiatrist three times a week. And the people there were wonderful. They're the greatest people in the world, because each and every one of 'em wanted to see you do good. And I got along with all of them, the nurses, the doctors—down to the janitors. Everybody was just wonderful, and this gave me such hope—seeing my doctor and being helped through psychiatry—I was so clear-minded when I walked out of that hospital ten months later. I knew what I was going to do, I definitely knew I was going to do good. And I did. I did good for eight months. And after the eight months I fell, and since that time it hasn't been the same.

That was the longest period of time I stood off of drugs: ten months incarcerated on the inside and eight months in the streets on my own. It was nice, I had a nice time. I guess I lived it up, tried to make up for lost years. I had sort of a ball. I was clean, I went to the mountains vacationing, swimming, tennis, basketball, going out with girls. I was going steady with one girl, and oh I was having a ball! And at the end of eight months, when I had to quiet down—you know, the ball has to end—and settle down to reality, I think I settled down too fast. It punched me right in the windbasket. I think I also took too much for granted. I knew I was doing all right; I said I can make it, nothing to it. So when that first shot came, I said I can take this shot and leave it. I took that shot and I didn't leave it. That was the end.

When I kicked while I was married, I actually did it for my wife. But the first person you should do it for is yourself. I wanted to see her happy, but I think because I wasn't thinking of myself too much, that's why I fell so soon after—less than three months. If I'd felt like I did when I got out of Riverside, I coulda kicked longer. I could have conquered the world, I felt so good.

In eight months' time, how many times I must have been approached! You want a shot, Dom? You want to take off? And each time I told 'em no, definitely not, because I knew what was good for me. And by the end of the eight months nobody came over to me: I did that on my own. I decided by myself that I should take a shot.

You know, we have a way of joking about guys, amongst addicts; we say, you love stuff too much to ever stop. And they used to say this about me, before I went to Riverside. So they were very surprised when I came out and started doing good. But I must say this for some drug addicts, friends of mine: they were very happy that I was doing good. Sincerely happy, and they really hoped that I would keep it up. I think that in me they saw themselves someday maybe cleaning up. Because I know when I see a guy clean, I envy him. I want to be in his shoes, to stand up straight and not worry where my next penny's coming from. Not worry about jail, not worry about being sick, not worry about where to score, how to score, or about the cold weather, or sleeping enough, or falling apart at the seams. When I see a guy clean I say good luck, and I wish it was me.

But I tell you the truth, lately I haven't seen too many guys clean. I mean I know a couple who are. But in this neighborhood, no. Haven't seen anybody. But there are two I know from Riverside who have kept clean. As long as you know it's possible, you try not to give up hope. I don't want to resign myself to the fact that this is my life.

As long as you make an attempt—even if you only kick for three days, or one week, or three weeks—as long as the attempt is there, there's still a chance that one day you're gonna make it. I'm not giving up hope, definitely not giving up hope. As long as I know in my mind I want to try again. If I fall again, I'll want to try again, until one day I'll make it.

I want my marriage to be successful more than anything

else in the world. I want children, my wife wants children. That's one thing, though, we will not have. As long as I'm shooting dope, I don't want to bring any children into this world. If I'm clean, we've agreed that I have to stay clean for two years before we try for any kids. Because I'm taking stuff, I'm putting a curse on them. They'll be stuck with their mother.

Have I ever been tempted to get her on dope? No, sir. Definitely not. I'd kill myself first.

This does happen. It's happened many times that a husband brings a wife into drugs. Of course, for a woman it's much easier to get money, 'cause she can go out and prostitute herself. And this makes it easy for the fella. But if I ever thought that my wife even read a book on drugs! All she does is shiver, man, she's so scared of it. I want to keep her scared. As long as she's scared, fine. Once she gets curious, that's when we'll start arguing. But the truth is, I don't think she ever will; she's got a brain in her head.

FIVE DAYS LATER

I COULDN'T go down . . . because it's too crowded there in the morning. And I didn't have no drugs, and I *can't* sit down there when you're sick, you just can't wait, you can't wait fifteen minutes. I tried it once before, and I know I couldn't last. So when my wife got me up this morning, I made like I was gonna go to the hospital, but I knew I couldn't make it. And I didn't go, because I would have been too damn sick. I just blew the appointment.

Well, you have to have something in you to be able to sit down and wait. Last time I went to Manhattan General, that's what I did. I went early in the morning, I was there about three hours, but I was *high*, I could wait, I sat and waited and it was nothing. It was crowded . . . and smelly, but I didn't give a damn. Otherwise, when you're sick, boy . . . I don't know, it doesn't look right. You have dry heaves, and whatnot; I don't think anybody could do it. I haven't seen one guy down there waiting that wasn't high. Just *can't* do it . . . it is impossible. And if I had to wait, why . . . it's just a vicious circle, you just can't do it. You gotta get high, and in order to get high you gotta go out and get the money. By the time you do that, it's too late to go down there.

So you got a vicious circle and you just can't get out of it. The only way you can do it is have the money ahead of time, score a few bags ahead of time, one to carry over at night and the next day in the morning you take off again another bag, and go down and sit and wait, and just hope to high heaven they take you the same day. That's about it.

Why didn't I have any stuff? Well, first of all, the other day I was near getting arrested. I was trying to get into a car, and I think somebody musta saw me. It was an awfully odd coincidence, because police cars came from both directions. I started running. I didn't look back to see what the heck was happening, I just ran into a building, went through backyards, and lucky enough I got away. It scared the hell out of me and I haven't gone near a car since.

So yesterday I . . . happened to have the key to my mother's house. I went in, and I got my brother's coat and my mother's jacket, hocked the coat for five dollars and I *sold* the jacket for five dollars. And that's . . . that's stooping pretty low. I never did anything like that before in my life. To hock something is all right, because you can always get it out, but to take something out and actually *sell* it, where you can't get it back: I've never done that before. And the reason I did that was because I was *sick*. And when I'm sick

I can't think of anything. Like I don't give a damn. All I can think about is getting off, getting my fix, and I just don't have the patience to sit down and think it out. I never did anything like that—to sell something where she can't get it back. And I just stole it right out of her house.

I don't know. . . . It's just getting to be so bad, because it's so low, man, when you gotta steal something off your mother. And like, it's one thing that I held in esteem: not to touch anything I could steal off your mother, anything like that. You know, I mighta borrowed something, hocked it, but never anything like that. When we were living together, I took my own stuff—a victrola, a radio and whatnot—and recently my brother's coat and whatnot. But a couple of times I told my brother ahead of time and he said all right, take it out, as long as you take it out of the hockshop in a couple of days. Which I hope to do with my brother's coat soon. Now, in fact. But my mother's jacket I can't get back 'cause I sold it. And she's mad. There was a big argument last night. And I had my brother on my back, not too much, 'cause he sort of understands, he went through it. But my mother, my wife—you know they're all on my back. I try to get them to understand and they can't grasp it—that when you're sick, you just don't think. It's not that I want to do a thing like that. I don't, I hate to do a thing like that. It's just that I have no other alternative.

I was too scared to hit a car. I don't want to get arrested right now. It's a bad time, you know, 'cause my wife it would break her heart and my mother and everything. I want to get into the hospital to avoid all that, and I'll be clean and everything.

Well, I took the stuff out. Nobody was home. Now I still needed a few more dollars and I had to go begging for quarters and dimes. And anyway, I went home, I had my stuff, I took it, and I get a phone call. It was my mother.

And it just so happens to be she noticed the stuff was missing. I was hoping she wouldn't. Started screaming over the
phone. Started cursing and screaming me, and I just said
all right, all right, I'm coming over. And on the pretense I
was coming over, I hung up. And I didn't go, and she kept
calling me. And I wouldn't pick up the phone. I did not want
to hear her, that's all. Now I waited in front of my mother's
house, about five o'clock, for my brother to come home. When
he came home I explained to him what had happened and
what I did. I told him, I said, look Nicky, I did something
lousy. And he looked at me, he said, you took my coat. He
knew. And then I told him about the jacket. And he was
awfully bugged. The coat he didn't mind, because the kid
understands. And I promised him I would take it out.

My mother must have called my wife at work, because
when she came home she said, if you think I'm gonna give
you any money to take out the coat, no-good. . . . She was
mad, and I had to hear it from both ends. So I just walked
out of the house, to get away from it. I just walked the
streets, and walked and walked and thought. I felt lousy, I
felt like I was the lowest, what am I doing? I went into the
neighborhood, Avenue C, and I didn't have any money,
because I had spent the money already. I saw a friend, a
good friend of mine. And he looked at me, and I don't know,
it must have shown all over my face. He must have felt bad,
and he offered me half a bag. And I felt so rotten I just
wanted to take as much as possible so I could get into the
deepest nod and not even think about it.

So that night I think my mother calmed down just a little
bit. But today! When my wife woke up and she was waking
me up to go to the hospital, she says that my mother found
another jacket missing. Now this is a jacket I had taken a
few months ago. There were two of them my mother bought
my brother and I. My brother didn't like his and never wore

it. I still have mine. I took his and I sold it, 'cause I knew my brother didn't like it and he *offered* it to me, said you want the jacket, take it. So I felt I was in the right. But we don't like to mention this to my mother, 'cause even if it was like legal, she still gets angry behind this thing. So we never said anything, and she just noticed it 'cause she was looking at all the clothes, since I stole something. And she found out about that, and she's mad behind that too. But I happen to have the other one, and I'm gonna have to lie to her. When I talk to her tonight, I'll say mine tore, and Nicky offered me his, and I'll bring it back. When she gets angry and starts yelling, it just gets on my nerves; in fact, when I was seeing the psychiatrist, it was a big, big thing, the relationship between her and me.

You know, it was causing a lot of things I do today, her screaming and her yelling. Actually, the slap in the face . . . just by screaming, I'd be getting slapped in the face. It goes into intricate things. But my doctor always told me, look, when you get out of Riverside and go home and you're on your own, go to live with your father. It will be the best thing for you. I mean I love my mother, but the things she does, the mental things, hollering and whatnot, bother me and caused me to do a lot of things. And I didn't realize until I saw my doctor and talked it out for ten months. Well that time I moved away, but these things still bother me, and when she hollers I know what's happening, I realize that it just bugs me *so much,* I just want to get out of it. I wish I could get on a slow boat and travel to the end of the world. And just make like you don't have nothing to do with nobody.

When I was a kid, it was the beatings then, but of course when I grew older she couldn't hit me. But when I was a kid I remember she broke a broom over my head one time. Many times I used to run under the bed to hide from her when she was mad and screaming. And she used to come with the broom and poke it under the bed to try to get me out. And I would just hide under there in the dark. Another time I was downstairs and she was on the top floor, yelling Come on up, Dom! I said no, I wanted to stay down. And she just *yelled,* you know, screamed COME UP HERE RIGHT NOW! And from four flights down I was so shook behind that, that automatically, like a robot, I just came right up. I knew I was gonna get hit, but I had to come up.

When I got older there were no more beatings, but the screaming and the nagging . . . and she'd always find something to argue about. It's not her fault, you know. She can't change, it's too late for her to change. She doesn't realize what she's doing. But, you have to live with it. And today, like when she hollers and screams, it's just like I were a kid and as if she were hitting me. Only she's doing it verbally. And this is the thing that was bugging me, and that's why I had to get out of the house to help myself.

I always told her we should sit down together with a doctor and talk it out. She got insulted. No-oo! Right away she thinks a psychiatrist means like a bug doctor, you're supposed to be crazy or something. The best thing I had to combat her was that I learned that when she yells, just don't pay any attention to her. Don't argue back; don't give her fuel to feed the fire.

My father was entirely the opposite, the greatest man in the world. I think maybe he spoiled me a little bit. He used to get me anything me and my brother wanted. We weren't living together, I mean they were divorced. I think I must have been about five years old when they separated, and eight years old when they divorced. So I can't remember too much of my father living with us. Just my mother, me, and my brother. But he might have felt guilty behind that, 'cause he bought us everything, everything we wanted; he saw us three times a week and did everything for us. I think if it had been different, if they had been living together, it might have been different today for me. But they couldn't live together. They weren't suited for each other maybe. I know if my father had lived at home, a lot of things that happened would of *never* happened. He would have seen to it that a lot of things were done right.

My mother is not the smartest woman in the world, and a lot of things she did wrong, and we were wild kids. Like a lot of mothers tell their kids not to cross streets, to watch out, but my brother and I, we'd cross streets, we'd run around. . . . We could be seven years old and we'd be up-town, getting on the subway. Of course my mother cared. But she was young when they got divorced and she's only human. She went out with a couple of men, and one time she almost got married, but it didn't work out. I don't know what happened. I guess she was thinking a lot about herself, too, although she tried to think of us.

Now we didn't eat right; I mean we ate, but there was never a set time for lunch, dinner or supper, and sometimes we'd just eat hero sandwiches for supper or just go out to the deli's. We didn't mind this as kids, we enjoyed it, my brother and I, we had a ball. But when we got older, I remember I was going to Junior High School and I realized what was right and what was wrong. I told my mother, look, we've gotta have breakfast, lunch and dinner at certain times, and certain plates gotta be set out, and *meals,* regular meals. And since then, she's always done it. She needed somebody to tell her, I guess.

I don't know; she needed a lot of help. My father was giving alimony—about $24 a week. At that time that was a nice sum; we could get along all right on it. Of course my father bought all the clothes for us—toys and everything. My mother just had to take care of the food and rent. And as far back as I remember, the rent was never paid on time. There were always bills in the house, debts to be paid. And I was always borrowing money. My mother was always getting money from her sister, my aunt. In fact, her sister used to buy us furniture every couple of years—buying us a bedroom set or a living room set. Even two years ago—I was living uptown and my brother was living with my father— we were all separated. My mother decided we should get together again. I didn't have any money, and my aunt bought the complete bedroom set, living room set and kitchen, for the rooms we live in right now. She was supposed to pay it, but she passed away and the debt went to my mother. My mother's having a hard time; my brother's helping out as much as he can. I can't. But she pays a few dollars every week.

They were hounding her and everything. I told her, look, let them take it back. Because I know they're not gonna go and take used furniture back. She just gets too scared. She's very *shy* with people, like she doesn't talk much in front of people, and she gets frightened over little things.

And there's always debts. I remember when we were kids the phone used to be closed every few months. And a few times we neglected the electric bill and lived by candlelight.

I didn't do too well in school. Of course, I was always playing hookey. After junior high I went to the High School of Performing Arts, but . . . I was scared. Through my own shyness I quit the High School of Performing Arts and went to Metropolitan. That's a terrible school. And most of the times I wasn't even in the school; I was playing hookey.

Finally I quit and I went to work. My father has a machine shop up in the Bronx. I worked for my father when he first opened up the business. And I worked, and I brought home the money, and I was doing all right. Even when I started taking stuff I wasn't taking that much, I was working, doing good. Every once in a while I'd be out of work two months, but always fell back. Then when I started getting in too deep in the drugs, that's when I started neglecting working, and I was more out of work than in work. That's how it's been ever since.

My father bought me a car when I turned eighteen years old—he got me a '50 Pontiac in 1955. I was eighteen, a teen-ager, and you know, it was great—a car and everything, and working for him at the same time. And money in my pocket, and I was going out with a nice girl. This is before I got my first habit; I was using stuff but I wasn't hooked; it was still half-ass. Healthy, you know, and feeling good.

I got arrested. And I lost the job, the car and the girl.

When I lost those three, I said the heck with it! I started taking stuff every day, stuff stuff stuff. I got my first habit, got arrested again, and went into Riverside. First trip—that was seven months.

I can keep a job only by having junk in my pocket. Being able to take off every morning and during the day at work. If I don't have my junk, I walk out sick and I lose the job.

This doctor on 14th Street—he saved me that time by helping me kick with the dollies. And after that, every time I got hooked I went to him and kicked with the dollies. All right, so maybe I started again. But it helped me, because I was making an *attempt*, I was trying, I kept trying. And everybody I saw in his office was all trying. There were a few, of course, who got the dollies because they were hooked on dollies. And a few that went in for dilaudids, just to get high. Now I might have done a wrong thing by telling a lot of people about him, but I did it for a reason. Each day I would send somebody to the doctor, and sure enough, they would get the dollies and they would try to kick. Even if they didn't make it in the end, they tried—that's the main thing. They made an effort, I saw that they wanted to make an effort. And I saw a few of them that went all the way, and stood off of it a few months, because I helped 'em out. I felt good that I helped them out.

Times I wish I could do much more. I'd talk to all kinds of people and scream and just tell 'em, show 'em, that they're being misled and they could understand so much more if only they could take the time out to stop and listen. Because most drug addicts are not like they visualize, with horns and a tail. They're very meek, timid, like they don't want no trouble, they just want their drugs. I myself am like that. They just want to be understood. People have a wrong idea of them, and if people saw them in a true light it would help out a lot.

Sometimes I wish I could help by telling somebody, but there's no one to talk to but the wall. And you don't get no answers from a wall. When you start getting answers from a wall, you're pretty up tight.

Of course there's some who will never be off drugs. Definitely. Even when they say they want to stop, you might mean it, but they know . . . maybe fooling ourselves, it's really gonna go on for the rest of our lives. It's gonna be the same life, on and on: getting arrested, going to jail, coming out, shooting stuff, sick, stealing, going through miserable winters, cold, freezing weather. After a few years—eight-nine years—you never get used to it, but you know: this is the game, this is the way it's played, and I have to pay the consequences.

Nick Abruzzi

✦✦✦

I STARTED nine years ago with marijuana. I started off in a poolroom. I used to go in the poolroom when I was under age, and the Spanish fellas used to be smoking marijuana there. Before you know, a couple friends of mine started, and I started too. I followed them. From there I went to snorting heroin and then using the needle. We all switched together, after about six months of pot and six months of snorting. I guess we just got tired of marijuana and were looking for a higher high. It was always a group, at least two or three of us together. We used to shoot up together, in hallways and on rooftops.

About two years ago I caught syphilis from a dirty needle. I was just cured about a year ago.

Since I was fifteen and started using drugs I've been pretty lucky. I had an older brother always chasing me away and trying to keep me off drugs. By him always chasing me away, I never used that often. I still got a small habit, which we call a chippie. I never got real bad because my brother kept

93

on always pushing me away and always hitting me when he seen me around drug addicts. So he kept me from actually getting hooked like he was and going to jail. I didn't get busted till 1959.

When I quit high school, I worked for a year in my father's machine shop in the Bronx. Then in 1956 I wanted him to teach me more about the machines, but he never would take the time. I joined the army and stood there for two years. After I was in the army for five months, they shipped me over to Korea and I ended up using drugs again. This time it was opium.

Over there you didn't have to use a needle to get this certain kind of a high. You can smoke it. You can fill up four cigarettes halfway for two dollars and smoke them and get the same high as you would taking a needle over here for five dollars.

It was the Koreans themselves who sold this opium. It was being sold all around Korea—I never saw so many drug addicts in my life. A lot of GI's who'd never used drugs in their lives started there in Korea, because everybody was just smoking, and to them smoking was nothing. They didn't know that smoking is just as bad as the needle, when it's opium.

For the first year there I smoked opium on and off and didn't get a habit. But after a year, I bought a needle in a Korean village. I had a hard time getting it. I got tired of smoking opium just like I got tired of smoking marijuana here. I used the needle, and with the opium the high on the needle was something else. Tremendous—it was too much!

I only did it for four months, because my time was up. When it was time to catch my ship to go back to America, I was pretty sick on opium, so I turned myself in. I told them I was using drugs, and I stood there a little more than a month in a hospital. Being I admitted it and turned myself in, they still gave me an honorable discharge from the army.

Danny Stern

I'M twenty-three years old and I've been on narcotics for about six years. It was in vogue at the time; everybody was doing it. There were four or five of us; one boy had been doing it for quite a while and said, would you like to try? This was at a sweet sixteen party at the Clinton Plaza. To prove a lot of fallacies wrong, it was heroin and it was a mainline shot from the very first. The boy who'd been taking narcotics staked everybody to a free shot, and administered it and made a big adventure out of it. He said that we could try it once and not get addicted, which I can say, so many years later, was the truth. He explained that you can steal and carry on all kinds of perverted things to get it, but at the time you're not concerned about what's going to happen later; it's what's going to happen now and the feeling you're going to achieve. And the feeling was so overpowering that it clouds your mind to any idea of going to jail, breaking society's rules, stealing or anything like it. You don't believe it.

Of the kids who took a shot at that party, all of us became addicts—only one didn't. He was what we considered a weekender. He partied and partied until he finally got married and settled down. Then he felt that it was passé; it was out of style, and he quit. Of the five who took shots, four of us are still addicts today, that still keep in touch and see each other, and try and play this big game of not getting caught by the police.

I just came back last November from doing a hitch at Elmira. It was June 26, 1957; I was out with a boy and we decided to buy some narcotics up in Harlem. We took a fix, I was feeling kind of good, there was nothing to do, we were just walking around enjoying the sensation, and we decided to take a taxi ride home, all the way back to Queens. We took the taxi without the driver. We took people around, and we pretended that we were hacking this cab. We didn't take any of the money—just a weekend prank. I was sent to Elmira for zip-five and I did forty-eight months. And upon my getting out, the first thing I did, the first day, was look to secure some narcotics. To see if, was this forty-eight months worth it? And now that I took that fix, I feel that no amount of keeping anyone incapacitated will cure it—if you want to do it, you will do it.

I wouldn't consider myself honestly a criminal. This was done in a clouded mind, as a prank. It was an out-and-out robbery, grand larceny, but I don't think that I'm a criminal at heart. I'm disturbed to a degree, because I like narcotics and I wouldn't want anyone to sway me from the thought of narcotics. But I was subjected to perverts, wise guys, guys that had much more time than me. They send a guy that has zip-five—that's a maximum of five years—in with a guy that has twenty to life. And that boy who has twenty to life, he's lost hope to a certain degree. He doesn't care how much aggravation he causes you while you're there. You run into so much difficulty; you have to be a fighter and you have to fight back. And it makes you hard. You come out, you resent people, and you just want to go into a shell. And that's only another reason I went back to narcotics. I forget the past. I don't want to remember that forty-eight months; it was the most horrible forty-eight months in my life. I don't think anything could have done as much harm as Elmira. I don't feel narcotics has done any greater harm to me.

It taught me things that I didn't have any need to learn, like how to steal a car. It graduated me into the higher crime bracket. It gave me telephone numbers of people to look up when I got out, more connections, more criminal activity. Narcotics is very easy to get, once you're in Elmira. You can get synthetic drugs. It's very easy to go to the hospital and get seconal or miltown or tranquilizers of all sorts. Dorazine, paraldehyde, achloral hydrate . . . I could go on and name more. Heroin, I will concede, is very hard to get in, but there have been cases where it has been gotten in. It's rough treatment; you're not treated like a human being, you're treated like an animal. And the only thing that you can do when you're treated like an animal is fight back. And there's no weapon. There's no weapon that a young boy that wants to help himself can fight back with other than his hands and his feet. They say, and I believe this, that the only person you hurt when you fight is yourself. But you're too blind to it, you can't see it.

The whole subject of narcotics has been gone at the wrong way. Everybody says you're a criminal. Basically I think that a narcotics addict, if he's under the influence of narcotics, will not bother anyone. If he's not under the influence of narcotics, and he's trying to secure his fix, he *will* bother you, to a certain degree. But it's not because he wants to bother you; he's not a violent individual. It isn't as bad as this gang warfare, believe me. They're out there causing trouble just for the sake of trouble. For the sole enjoyment of aggravating people, picking on somebody. We're doing it for a reason. We need narcotics, that's all.

After speaking to numerous addicts in the jail at Elmira, in The Tombs, and in the street, I find this: that when the dope addict needs money, he doesn't want to hurt anybody; he just wants the money. He will take your money and run. He's meek. He's the meekest of all people there is, because he's sick. Everybody says he's a killer, but he won't kill you. He's afraid. If you scare him, he might do it out of fear and not even know what he's doing. But that's not his goal. I've went on numerous things to get money, and I knew in my heart I didn't want to hurt anybody. And thank God, to this day I haven't hurt anybody.

An addict is very yellow. Once he's hooked, he's very afraid of withdrawal. So what he does, he steals from people he knows will not send him to jail. That takes in your own immediate family, your mom and pop's friends. People that like you, that you know will try and help you and say, well, it was a mistake. That is the first step in stealing for a narcotics addict.

Second step is boosting. That's going into a department store and walking out with two pair of pants. It's easy, it's tempting, and you learn very easy. Once you do it and get away with it, there's no stopping you from coming back and doing it a second or third time.

The third way is selling fake narcotics to other addicts, to fool them. In other words, you take a cellophane bag and fill it up with any white powder that looks like heroin. And when you see a sick addict that comes strutting down pounding the pavement begging for a fix, you sell him this. It's very cutthroat, you rob from one another. There's no honor among dope addicts.

Or you tell a fellow you're a gopher. You know the pusher and you'll gopher narcotics. The addict is from another neighborhood, but he knows you and he doesn't know the pusher. So you promise him: give me your ten-fifteen-twenty and I'll go look for the pusher for you. As soon as I score the dope, I'll bring it back to you. What happens then is you take his money and you buy the dope, but you never bring it back to him. You take it yourself. It's too overpowering. It's like being very sick, and a doctor says one shot of penicillin cures you. It's the same thing. Narcotics is mental; it's physical. One shot cures you.

You see, it works like this. Every boy in his teens, in his growing years, idolizes somebody—usually a tough guy. It's like the kids today watching TV—they idolize the Capones, and the Roaring Twenties, and the Untouchables. They're all glorious, picturesque characters. In my stages of growing up, there were certain boys in the neighborhood that were the big shots, the strong arm; everybody respected them. Now, we realize it's a false respect. At the time, I wanted to be so much like him. And when I realized he was taking dope, I said, well, if it's good for him it's good for me; he's the big shot. Now, today, when I see this boy, I know he's not a big shot.

But what I try and do is, being I'm taking narcotics, I try to keep it to a minimum, where I can control it. I don't ever want narcotics to control me again. And I feel that if it's done rationally, with a realistic mind, to a certain degree you can control it. Unless it takes over your body. Mentally, if you're strong and have a good will power, you can control it to a degree.

When it really comes down to it basically, everybody wants to be recognized. Everybody. Now these boys that stick with it—the reason they stick with it is narcotics brought them a new way of life. It's an adventure. Let's face it: if narcotics was easy to come by, there wouldn't be half as many addicts. To take narcotics right now, it is cloak-and-dagger, it's spy work, it's something out of television, believe me. You have to walk the street, you have to secure a pusher, you have to locate the money to buy this narcotics, you have to check in dark hallways, on roofs, go through cellars, all this running about, all the time keeping one eye out for the police.

All this. This is an adventure for a young man. And when you finally get your narcotics back to your pad where you can use it, you say to yourself: man, I did it, I beat the fuzz. I made the scene. And you feel relieved.

Then the second stage is to take it. And that clouds your mind. You feel content just to sit there and not be annoyed and let the world go by. Just leave me alone, I'm happy the way I am.

When people see these glorious characters like Buggsy Siegal walking around with Rolls Royces and diamond stickpins and bodyguards and throwing money around with all these fine-looking broads on their arm, it gets you wondering. I know myself, I'm from a pretty well-to-do family, I have never been in want of anything in my whole life, except narcotics. Anything I asked for, I got. I had broken rules—when I was sixteen, I had secured an automobile. Through a forged birth certificate. It wasn't completely legal, but I drove around. I was a big shot in the neighborhood. Everybody looked up to me. There goes Danny in his big Buick convertible!

Everybody wants to be recognized. And to be recognized as an Al Capone, it's a great thing for these people. It gives them a chance. I have a cousin who's been to college six years; he's gonna be a psychiatrist. I talk to him; I think I'm of an intelligence to understand some of the things he tries to explain to me. And right now I'm a common laborer—I'm a painter by trade, I paint apartments in housing projects. And I make $127 a week, union scale. I'm bringing home more money right now than my cousin who works for the Board of Education as a clinical psychologist! Those are the things that warp the youth today; that's what's warping me. This false sense of values—everybody has a price. That's what children are taught today.

Recently in the papers there's seventeen boys from well-to-do families in Queens arrested for 500 burglaries and fencing. Now these boys were offered help by a psychiatrist. Now I know this case personally; I know all the defendants in this case. I know all the parents. To my knowledge, this is a shyster move on the part of the families, pooling their funds to secure this psychiatrist, who's head of a clinic in Forest Hills. He is probably going to say all these boys are mentally disturbed, and offer for a dismissal of the case, pending that they have psychiatric treatment. Which will last for approximately a week. I have had the same circumstances for myself. I've had a shyster psychiatrist say that I was not well, and after everything was dropped he declared me sane again. And the probation officer dropped the case. That's what the youth today learns. How do they expect them, when they send them to institutions to be helped for narcotics, to be helped?

When you get in the hospital the first thing they do is give you sedation, they put you to sleep, they keep you in a state of complete obliviousness for a week. And then they tell you you're cured of your narcotics habit, go home. When you go home you're not really cured; all you do is tell all the boys in the neighborhood about, man, what a hospital this hospital was! I went up there and ate steak, and lamb chops, and milk! Which some of these boys don't eat when they're home. They're getting it the first time in the hospital, and talking about, man, free dope! This isn't solving the problem. There has to be another way to do it.

It got to the point once where I wanted to quit. I'd gotten to the stage where I felt I would go out and commit a robbery of some type. I knew I was on the verge of violating a law. So I went to my parents and asked help. I explained the situation, I was a dope addict. At first everybody got excited and nobody knew how to handle it, so I tried to help. I explained to them that there's only one right way to do it, and that's cold turkey. I explained that I would like everything removed from my bedroom. My father and my uncle and two cousins much older than I came in a bare room—all it was was a nine by twelve room, with nothing in it, a bare floor. I was told I could secrete on the floor, I could vomit—anything I wanted to do. Just stay in here. And I asked them to please not let me out for at least four days, and if possible to keep me there a week. This went on for five days. They stayed there around the clock. They changed shifts like changing of the guard at Buckingham Palace. And I kicked my habit.

But I found one thing. What that did was open a door to me. You see, kicking the first time is the hard one. I didn't know what to expect; I heard so much about it. You die, you're in agony, you suffer, you carry on something terrible. I admit it: I carried on something terrible, I suffered, I vomited, I threw up, I sweated, I chilled—I did everything that all addicts do when they kick. And I had been on some strong narcotics at the time.

But—it's like a kid. When you take a kid, and he beats you up all your life, you're afraid of him. And when you beat up this kid, you flex your muscles every time you see him. Because finally you beat him. And it's the same thing. I had feared withdrawal so bad that when I finally accomplished complete withdrawal—conquered the physical aspects of it—I felt very good and I was flexing my muscles. I was ripe right then to get addicted again. Because I knew, well, I know what it is to kick now, and I think it's possible. The human mind is an irrational mind at times like that. You say well, I got it beaten. I won, I'm not dead. I can take another beating, it won't kill me. And that's the way I looked at it.

I stayed off it approximately a month. And I was running around with the same boys. It was a test of will power to myself. I did this on my own. I hung out with my old cronies, I carried on all the scenes they made: I went to the dances—they blew pot, I refused; they shot up heroin, I refused. I refused everything for one month, and at the end of the month I said to myself, Danny, you have the will power. Now it's up to you. If you want to do it, go ahead. But in my heart I knew that anytime I wanted to, I could stop.

Physically, I find now that it's impossible. Eventually, you do get hooked. You get hooked physically. Mentally, the aspect may take twenty-thirty years; you may never get cured. The mental outlook is a very hard subject to go into. But to institutionalize people is very wrong in a narcotics problem. It won't help them. It only makes them bitter.

I don't want to condemn Riverside, I've never been there. I have been to Lexington, Kentucky, at the federal hospital. And I found that, speaking to people about Riverside, it's a home away from home. The boys say, look, man, let me get high. Let me catch a habit. Who cares? What's the consequences? If worst comes to worst, they send me up to North Brother Island, I kick my habit, I eat good, I come out sixty-five pounds heavier, I look like a million dollars with a sun tan, and everything is great. I'm healthy again, and I'm ripe to start again. This is what it is: it's a big merry-go-round.

The boys don't want to get off. It's like a child with sex. You ask a little boy what he's gonna do. Go out and play with the girls? No no no, I wanna play with the boys, I don't want to be with the girls. But when he comes into his teens and he finally has an experience with a girl, sexually, all he does now when he sees girls with big fannies, he's out after girls and running after girls. He's had his taste. It's the same thing with narcotics. Once you have your taste, you just keep running and running and running.

I have a cousin that had been an addict since 1949. He got out of Lexington, Kentucky, in February. He got married. He died two months later, in April, in Miami Beach, Florida, of an overdose of narcotics. Now this is in my own family. I should sit down and feel terrible about it, because we were very close. We were more or less junkies-under-the-skin, so to speak. But I know that he played the game, and he paid. Because he played wrong. The idea is to be careful. I'm careful now. I don't want to hurt anybody; I don't want to hurt myself. I just want to achieve the better things I can out of life.

Today, the world is in such a turmoil that the pressure on youth, and the people not understanding us, it's just terrible. The boys have nothing to do; they're bored with themselves. You take a boy nineteen years old. His friend has a car so he buys a car. And the first thing you know the car gets him in trouble. He's joy-riding all hours of the night, drinking beer. It's the same thing. Some boys find that narcotics is a lot cleaner and easier than alcohol, because if you take whisky you have to drink for hours. Whereas if you take narcotics you feel the effect within a few seconds. That's the easy way.

I've taken about six overdoses. One overdose I've taken was on Rivington and Avenue D. I was out for thirteen hours; I thought I died. But when I woke up, came to, and all these boys was there, I really felt indebted to these fellows for not leaving, for sticking to me for thirteen hours. Now thirteen hours when you say it in numbers is nothing. But in reality, when you're unconscious from an overdose of narcotics, it's a lifetime. I died and was born again in that time. And I feel that I owe these boys something.

I was on a landing in a hallway, one landing down from the roof. I was injected with salt into my veins—I don't know if that has any effect at all, to be honest—and rubbing and massaging, trying to keep the blood circulating through my body. They inject the salt water with the same needle they use the heroin with. It's just that to call up an ambulance and to say there's somebody up here took an overdose of narcotics, we know the treatment that's gonna happen. The ambulance takes three hours to get there. The police come, they'll beat your brains in. They're liable to find you and say they found dope in your pocket. Which we know isn't true. If a dope addict is unconscious from an overdose, there's nothing in his pockets. Because addicts today do not take off by themselves. Everybody wants somebody there, just in case, because there's been an epidemic of bad narcotics. And everybody's afraid.

I took an overdose, and upon being out and coming to, I felt that this was it. I was quitting. But when you go out, everything is so white and pure. The world goes by. You don't care about anything, you have no worries. You're not thinking about Mom paying the telephone bill or your wife being sick. Everything is so great. I want to do everything for everybody. I may act a little spooky and groggy, and appear to be not in my senses, but really I'm in my senses, more so than a lot of people believe. Nothing goes past your hearing; everything is extra-sensitive as far as your hearing goes. The only thing that's numb is your thinking mind. You can't think abstractly, you can't think of the future. You just think for now.

About cops and bribery, I wouldn't like to talk about what other boys tell me, because I don't hold too much to a narcotic addict's word; a lot of it is fantasy. I will say this has happened to me. There is a neighborhood cop, he knows what I'm up to, he knows I'm an addict, he knows that I do things in the neighborhood concerning drugs. He watches me every time he sees me; he'll tail me for hours. Twice he stopped me. And I was sick both times, in dire need of a fix. And he looked in my pocket, and there, sure enough, he found an eighth of heroin. Which I know was not there, because I know at the time he "found" it, my goal was to secure narcotics. The agent had put it there, and he threatened me.

Another time I was stopped in a brand-new car. It was my own, I had bought it from my hard-earned money. It had nothing to do with narcotics; I have never peddled narcotics to that extent. I have peddled narcotics among my own friends, in my immediate club. If I had bought $40 worth, I could afford to sell $20 to my friends, and save them a trip up to Harlem. But what happened was I got stopped, and at this time I had about $300 in my pocket. A narcotics agent took the $300 and said it was money I had earned pushing dope. He refused to give it back, and said if I put up a big stink I'd find myself in the seventh precinct. So, of course, being a narcotic addict and not wanting to be arrested, I gave him the money and never said anything about it. Because my word is nothing. I'm the bad guy.

This one policeman told me, he said, look, Danny, you just come home. I have this circular, I got the wire on you, you're here, I know what you're up to. You're still an addict, you're still associating with the same people. I'm gonna catch you. It'll take me a week or two, and you bastard, if I don't catch you, I'm gonna frame you. You're going back anyway. So get out of the neighborhood; don't get into trouble.

Now things like that, where there were no grounds for it. . . . All right, I admit, I might have had narcotics hidden on me. But he didn't find them. That does not give him the grounds to call me guilty. He's supposed to call me innocent till I'm proven guilty.

This Harry Anslinger, the head of the Federal Narcotics Commission. I had two of his agents come down to the precinct and question me when I was arrested. They offered me a deal: they told me if I gave names and places, I would go home on a *state* robbery charge. It just shows you how the two agencies work hand in hand. The federal agent promised that if they had the names, he could sway the state into dropping the robbery charges. It doesn't give a guy the sense of values that he's supposed to have. It shows you that there's graft and corruption.

Two fellows get arrested; one fellow has $800 in his pocket. Who goes away? Of course, the boy that had no money. The boy that had the $800, he doesn't go to jail; he gets a boot in the pants and get home, and don't let me see you in the neighborhood. This has been going on, but nobody believes it. It's the same cry all the time: aah, he's a junkie! He's looking for a way out, so he's making the police a patsy. But it isn't so.

The police, they're undermanned. They're going about apprehending narcotics addicts. They should leave the darn addict alone. Don't get the addict, he's helpless. Get the pusher. Not the pusher that's selling it so he could get a fix. He's not really a pusher. He buys ten dollars' worth of narcotics and takes an eighth and cuts it into two sixteenths. He sells you a sixteenth for ten dollars, so he gets his fix free. He's not a pusher; it's the guy dealing in the ounces— $350 an ounce, $475 an ounce—these are the businessmen.

They don't take narcotics themselves, but they sell it. They beg you to sell it for them.

It's not like it used to be. They give drugs on consignment these days. It's been offered to me on numerous occasions—take three ounces of pure heroin. It's not pure—it would come out about eighty-six per cent on a police meter. Anyway, I could get a good grade of heroin—three ounces for $750. That's the bargain for buying the three ounces in a batch. Now I can bag this up into five-dollar bags, and I can turn over exactly 340 per cent over the price I pay. So even a small nobody, a nothing like me, a street dope addict, if I had the initial money, I can have that big car and those three-hundred-dollar suits and all those pretty girls and the money to burn. But the consequences are great.

You're working with neighborhood police, who know who's doing what, but don't say anything because it's bigger than them. They can't fight it. They're joining it. They'd rather accept the fifty dollars under the table to forget this bar and forget that there's junkies hanging out in the bar. They're not in there to arrest them. They know where they hang out; they're there all the time. We're not stupid, we know their cars. We know twenty minutes before they're in the neighborhood that they're coming, so when they get there they don't find anything. But I give them credit for the arrests they do make, if they're honest arrests. Because the dope addict will fight back; he fears going to the city jail, because that means kicking cold turkey right there.

From meeting them and seeing them, I'd say that out of every ten dope addicts, three are girls. Girls are a big factor in making boys dope addicts, believe it or not. Let's face it. You take a quiet guy, a little backward and shy, the potential raper, the guy that has trouble getting a girlfriend. He's slow and awkward with girls; he doesn't know the female sex. He's the type of fellow that will snatch a little girl in the street and rape her. Or force a lady to do things that are perverted. You take a guy like that, and you get one of these real, so-called "hip chicks," a swinger that knows the score. She's a hustler, she's been around, she turns tricks. She'll do anything for a buck to secure her fix. She has an outlet. It's easier for a girl to secure a habit and to keep it under control, because all she has to do is lay down on the bed and there's ten dollars. She can put any price she wants on that, see? Because she's a woman, and men will buy women. Those girls take a plain ordinary joe that doesn't know too much, and they say, look honey, you can sleep with me and live with me and I'll take care of you. They give this guy his first taste of sex. And believe me, he's at their beck and call. They'll make him anything they want to make him. They'll make him a dope addict, eventually. Girls are the biggest factor in making dope addicts.

My sex drive, before narcotics, was so great that upon having intercourse with a girl, I would achieve my climax almost immediately. And I noticed something. That upon taking narcotics, it killed my sex drive. But on drugs, I was able to have sex for three-four hours at a time. Which made me feel superior over the girl. The girl was always begging me to stop, she couldn't take it, when it used to be the other way around, when I used to tell this girl, you're wearing me out, honey. I never reach a climax when I'm under the influence of narcotics, but mentally, I feel that I can satisfy the woman I'm with.

Any girl that has sexual intercourse with a dope addict will never be satisfied by a normal person. Because there are very few normal human beings on this earth that can have a sexual intercourse for three-four hours, without achieving a climax. It's almost an impossibility. Heroin will help you achieve that effect. And you'd be surprised the effects when you have a few girls running after you, talking about your powers as a lady's man. It does something to your ego, and your super-ego, and you get all excited and you go out and you do sillier things to prove it.

I don't know the figures on narcotics addiction in New York City, but I will say that of the narcotic addicts that I know personally, I found that eight out of ten have never been arrested and are not known addicts. So therefore, whatever figures the state and the federal might have, the number of addicts is actually five times larger than that. You have a minority who get the blame for everything.

My parents were very hurt by my addiction, because I never asked for anything in my life that I didn't get it. They're trying to trust me now, 'cause I'm fresh home from Elmira Reformatory, but other than that. . . . There's the sneaky look at my armpit, to see if I have any new marks. It's where ya goin?—it's eleven o'clock! I'm a boy of twenty-four and that bothers me, that annoys me. I'm not a baby, I want to be a man. I feel I'm strong enough to take care of myself right now, even though I use narcotics. I use narcotics that I feel I have control over. I've proved it to myself on numerous occasions. When narcotics have gotten the best of me, I went into seclusion for a few weeks, staying away from the neighborhood and my old friends.

But it's not that taking a boy out of his environment will keep him from using narcotics. That's wrong. I lived on the East Side all my life. While using narcotics I have met boys from Queens, Brooklyn, Bronx. . . . Now, no matter where I go, I can pick out a dope addict. You can take me to a strange neighborhood where I've never been, with people I don't even know, put one dope addict in the crowd, give me twenty minutes and I'll pick him out. It's like a brother club. One junkie knows another junkie. You smell each other.

It's not a matter of take him away. I was taken away. They moved me to Queens, in one of the most exclusive parts of Jamaica, Long Island. And I find narcotics addicts. I might not find the type of narcotic addict I find on the East Side now, because of the big migration of Puerto Rican and Negro into the neighborhood. The older addicts are Irish, Jewish and Italian. But I find dope addicts. If I don't find a C.P.A. that's a dope addict, I find a lawyer, I find a sculptor, I find them all over. These are the lucky few. They have never been to court, so they're not considered addicts, they're not statistics. But they do exist.

Living out in Jamaica Estates, I migrate to Harlem to get my narcotics. Harlem is the center-point for narcotics in the New York area. From 100th Street to 140th Street is narcotics row. Narcotics can be got very easy, it's not too much trouble, most of the policemen are paid off, and the ones that aren't—they're not out for the big people. The big people pay too much. The big people are covered. When they do a business that turns in twenty thousand dollars a week, they're not letting a little patrolman—a nothing that makes $5,800 a year—arrest them. They pay him. They give him a thousand dollars. A thousand dollars is gold to this officer, I don't care who he is. It's very tempting.

I have worked for this lady up in Harlem, around the corner from the Park Palace. I have been there one night when there was a raid. I was up there for the purpose of securing one-quarter of an ounce of heroin. I wasn't up there to buy weight, so-called, ounces. As a personal favor from this girl to me, she was giving me a quarter of pure heroin. It was a raid. The cops came in, money was passed, the cops walked out. Nobody was arrested. When I came downstairs I seen what they did. They had arrested two junkies on the street—street junkies. Poor, helpless creatures. They didn't arrest her. She's probably still in circulation to this day. Because she pays, and she pays big and to the right people.

I feel that if they legalized narcotics to a certain degree, that would kill half of the narcotics problem. If you look at the crime statistics in New York City, they say that crime is up 50 per cent. And the crimes are committed by dope addicts. We don't have a big crime rate in New York City, we definitely do not—it's the dope addict, the guy who boosts a pocketbook from an open car, he takes a camera or he goes in a candy store and boosts a box of candy—or something. This is what makes a big crime rate. Of every five thousand burglaries, all but three hundred are by dope addicts that couldn't help themselves.

If they had some sort of system where narcotics could be administered free of charge, or for costs, it would kill the black market trade. We're not strong enough to kill it otherwise; it's run by a lot of people with a lot of money that runs into millions and billions, and they're not letting anybody push them out. They like money. They smuggle in dope on planes and on boats—with their merchant marine friends that I know bring stuff in.

Now you open up a clinic and you take away the main incentives of a dope addict. You take away the adventure in it. There's no more adventure; it becomes hospitalization. Dope addicts thrive on this adventure of running around and going to buy it and getting off without getting caught. And then sitting and being with all the boys and *talking* about how it felt. That would be taken away. There wouldn't be all this scariness, and all the worries. It wouldn't get to the point where you would get addicted—and even if you did get addicted, it could be controlled to a degree. If a dope addict can be maintained so that he will not get sick, he will not commit a crime. He will be content not to be sick.

What they do is they make it hard for the dope addict to get dope, they make the prices go up and the business illicit, and the addict has to steal. He has to do something to keep up with it.

So I feel they should have some sort of a clinic, where you can come in and get fingerprinted if you want to be a known addict. Let it be known! If you want to be an addict, don't be ashamed of it. Take your card, go in, get your thing to keep you happy. It would kill the crime and they'd live a happy life.

There would be a few that would want more than whatever the clinic would be administering. If the clinic was giving just enough to keep them satisfied and not on cloud nine, they'd want a little extra so they could get up to cloud nine. That kind of illicit drug trade you can't stop. But taking the adventure away would kill a lot of the drugs. It would stop a lot of these young schoolboys that are ripe for picking. There wouldn't be anything interesting to them; it would be just a bore.

Take any kid. You just walk up and say, you want to be a junkie? I'll get you a fix. But you gotta go down to Joe's Hospital with me. He wouldn't want it. What is it to walk into a hospital? It's a cold institution where somebody sticks a needle in your arm, you get a fix and you go back. They don't want that.

The teenagers today are standing on the street corners and sitting in the luncheonettes. They're talking baloney. *Nothing* to talk about—they're beat for conversation. They're not intellectuals. They ain't even pseudo-intellectuals. They just stand there. And when somebody offers them a cloak-and-dagger game, it's like taking a kid and giving him cowboys-and-Indians, or let's-play-soldier. They enjoy it. It gives them something to do, it keeps their mind occupied.

How to beat the cop on the beat? How to beat the narcotic agent who's sneaking up on you in the hallway? You think at the time that your mind is working. Your mind isn't working—I know that now. But I feel that I can't be helped, because I have found in drugs something to keep me calm, collected. I'm happy with the knowledge I have; I think I can make my way in the world. But I want to be an honest citizen. I don't want to hurt people, I don't want to bother anybody. I'm just content—like somebody comes home and has his five beers, I want to come home and be able to smoke marijuana, take a shot of dope.

I find marijuana never to be habit-forming. I feel that the only reason they don't legalize marijuana is that the liquor industry and the A.B.C. [Alcoholic Beverage Control Board] would go crazy. Let's figure it out. Take a couple, they go into a bar. It takes eight dollars to drink before they feel a little giddy. Where marijuana, with sixteen cents for one stick, puts you in the same state as twenty dollars' worth of liquor. And it has no after effects. I've had two occasions to drink—once I drank rye and once I drank scotch. And I had some head in the morning; I had a hangover, I was sick, I was nauseous—all the works. I smoked three sticks of marijuana, I was loaded all night, I woke up in the morning and never even knew I did it. Everything was good.

Marijuana made my senses more alert—more so than heroin. Heroin calms me down, more like a tranquilizer. Whereas marijuana made me lively, like whisky. It made me a little boisterous. Everything is funny, whole world is a big joke.

And I feel the only reason they never make it legal is the A.B.C. My ideas may be warped, I grant you that. I need help, I know I need help. I want to help myself; I eventually will, in time. But fighting people with a lot of money, you can't.

Carmen Sanchez

❖❖❖

I'M twenty-five and I've been using narcotics for five years. I have two brothers twenty-four and twenty and they both use narcotics. The younger one hasn't used for two years, though. He moved out of the state where there weren't any drugs.

My mother and father, I'm very proud of them. They feel bad that their children have started using drugs. Because we all come from a very good family, and some of us in the family are very important people. My mother and father don't use drugs. And the little that my mother knows about drugs is because my father explains to her, because he does a lot of reading on narcotics. And he has explained to her the symptoms that we feel when we are on narcotics.

My father always has worked on the waterfront. He drives big machines to carry the lumber from the ship to the pier. He was a boxer in Puerto Rico, then he moved to New York when he was very young. He thought he could make more money on the waterfront. He stopped boxing. He was one

of the champions in Puerto Rico. I was born in Puerto Rico
and came here at the age of seven.

My mother used to work, but that was fifteen years ago.
Since then she's been a housewife. She cannot read or write,
and she cannot speak English. She worked in a clothing
factory, separating the dresses that had holes in them. It was
a very hard job that she had, plus it was very dirty. She used
to blow her nose, and it was dirt that she used to blow.

My father and mother, they're very strict. One thing my
mother has never gone into is a movie. All her life she's been
in the house, taking care of us children. She's been brought
up like that, in the house. Her mother was very strict with
her and all her sisters. They was always kept in the house.
Always sewing, cooking, and taking the clothes to the laun-
dry. In the wartime in Puerto Rico, my mother used to sew
the clothes for the mens that were in the army.

My mother has been married three times, and now with
my father, that makes four. She had three girls before me,
and then me with my father, and then three baby boys, but
the three boys all died. One was born dead, one died from
a heart attack at the age of four months, and the other one
died from one of those attacks where you bite your tongue.
I was small at the time but I seen it and I was the one that
called my mother to the crib. These two brothers that I live
with now are not my mother's sons.

After I was born my father left my mother, and he went
and took this woman away from her parents and he eloped
with her. After he married this woman he went into the
army, and when he came back to visit her, well my father's
mother told my father that the woman was not good: that
while he was away, she did not stay in the house. She used
to go out with mens, and do bad things with these mens.
She was double-crossing my father. My father did not like
that, so he used to beat her up. But that didn't change

nothing; she got worse. After all, he was beating her up because she was doing a wrong. He got a divorce, and in court they gave him the two sons that she had for my father. Those are the two brothers that I got.

He left my mother completely with me. I was small at the time, but I never forget. My mother never brought a man into the house. That's why I'm so proud of my mother. Because she waited for my father. She told me when I got older that she always had a mind that he'll come back to her and ask her for forgiveness. The reason he came back was that he seen that she was a good woman. While she was separated from him she did not have a man, ever! All the time she was praying for my father to come back to her and me.

I never forget it the way he was begging for her to take him back. She started crying, and she told him, Benny, you don't have to beg me and you don't have to ask me for forgiveness. You made me suffer a lot, but you are the father of my child. And since I never wanted no man only you, I'll take you back gladly.

And he kiss her and he kiss me, he put my mother and myself into his arms, and he started crying. He said, I never would believe it. That a woman like you would wait and take me back. And I had no right of leaving you, because you was very good.

My father came over here and worked and made some money and got a very nice apartment. And then he wrote my mother, I got a job, and I found an apartment for you; it's in a very nice neighborhood. I would like if you would come to New York and live with me. I still love you very much, and since you know that you took me back, you got to be my wife. You have to be together with me and our child, because she's the only girl that we got, and I would like to have her with me, so she'll grow up respecting me.

A couple of months later we received a letter from my father's mother in Puerto Rico. She said, Benny, this is urgent. I would like very much if you could see what you could do about your sons. I'm getting very old, and I'm sick; I cannot handle them any longer. You know very soon I'm gonna die, and they have to live with you and learn to respect you.

So my father told my mother, I know this is asking for too much, and I have no right to ask you, because I did a wrong to you. But now I'm begging you: please, can you take care of these two sons that I have from this other woman? Please don't let me down.

My mother says, look, whatever happened with that other woman is forgotten. It's good that your boys and your girl be brought up together.

So my father got happy and jump up and kiss my mother and says, I knew you were always an angel. There's never been a woman like this in my life. A woman like you will live many years, 'cause you're good.

So my two brothers came to New York City, and my mother brought them up.

The older one was always nasty to my mother. And I don't like that. He's the only one on narcotics now, plus me. He's married; he's got two girls and one boy. My father got him a job on the waterfront, but he left that job—he's been in jail twice—he left that job in order to be with his friends using drugs. He didn't think right. Now, his wife is on Welfare. And he can't live with his wife, because they're going to be investigating, and he better look for a job. And since he doesn't like to work, he better not stay in his wife's house, because she will lose the help she's getting from Welfare.

My first school was P.S. 177, and they put me in the third term of school, because I was very smart. I had a very clear mind, the teachers told my father. I was a very good student, and I always respected my teachers. I have always respected my elders: that's one thing my father and mother have always taught us. I went every day, and my mother used to make sure we went to bed early. My father used to help my brothers and me do our homework. I was always getting a lot of homework, and I loved school very much.

I loved my teacher, Mrs. C. I liked her a lot because she always gave me a lot of attention because she always seen that I was very good with her. When other boys and girls used to scream at her or throw chalk or crayons at her, I used to get up in the classroom and scream at them. As you can hear, all you people that are listening, I have a very heavy voice. I used to get up and open the door and tell the kids, well, youse want to get smart? Youse want to get fresh with Mrs. C.? Well, I'm gonna teach you a lesson. I'm going to get the principal right this minute. And everybody used to shut up right away. Some of them went right up to the front desk and told Mrs. C., we're very sorry and we'll be very good from now on. And every time someone gave her trouble, I would put in my two cents and help the teacher. And every time she would say something, I would put down my pencil on the paper and pick up my head and listen. And everybody respected me in that way. Everybody started doing the same thing that I did.

From there, I asked my father if he didn't mind if I go to a far school for high school. He says, you're a girl, you have a beautiful body, maybe you come late from school and something happen to you, because you never travel by yourself. But since you want to go to this school, I'll give you the permission. You don't do nothing wrong; I don't have no complaints from the parents around this neighborhood. They say that when a boy touch you, you start fighting with them, fist-fight like I told you to, to defend yourself from boys and mens. That's one thing I don't have to worry about—you don't let nobody put a hand on you.

I went to Washington Irving High School, which is all girls. And I got along wonderful. The teachers would always help me, and if I didn't know anything I stood right up and asked.

I started hanging around with this crowd of boys and girls in a candy store on Broome Street. I met a boy there, his name was Johnnie. The same night I met him, he asked if I mind if he walk me home. I was living in Baruch projects. I told him well look, Red asked me before if he could walk me home. So he asked Red, and Red said, okay Johnnie, you can come along. Instead of taking the elevator, we took the stairs, and we were talking about a gang we were gonna make so we could go fishing, swimming, and dancing in the settlement. When we got up to my floor, Red said, excuse me, Johnnie, I want to say something to Carmen. And Johnnie went one flight down.

Red told me, Carmen, would you like to be my girl friend?

I say no, I can't be your girl friend. My father would kill me if he knew I was going out with boys. Get yourself another girl, beautiful girl, your complexion, too. Because I was ignorant, I figured that if I would start going out with this guy who was lighter than me, people would start laughing at us. That's why I told him no.

I told him I can't keep my mind on two things. As soon as I put my foot in high school, I made up my mind. I said to myself, Carmen, it's either school or your friends. And believe me, I don't want my parents ever to walk with their heads bent down. I want them to walk with their heads high. I said to myself, it's school I'm sticking to.

But then Johnnie came upstairs, and he told me Red was waiting downstairs. He says, would you like to be my girl?

I says, Wow! What is it that I got? This morning it was two other boys, now it's you and Red?

He says, well, Carmen, I love you. The moment I saw you I went for you.

I says, look, I don't want to have no more trouble with people asking me if I want to be their girl or marry them. Okay, Johnnie, I don't even know you—it's the first time I see you in my life. All right, I'll be your girl friend.

He says, Wow! Is Red gonna be mad! I hope the boys aren't gonna be jealous—they'll probably throw me out of the club now.

I says, no, they won't throw you out of the club, because I'm the leader. You didn't know that? Tonight there was a meeting, and they elected me the boss of the gang. We were the Black Diamonds. I had a black jacket with white letters on it. It was for boys and girls both. The boys said I have a lot of guts. They said, your father taught you how to fight like a man.

I could put on boxing gloves and box with anybody. Even now that I'm twenty-five years old I still remember my tricks. I'm a very good boxer—I should have been born a man, that's what my father says.

I started going out with Johnnie. And then one time six or seven months later, I was talking to Johnnie in the street, and I forgot about the time. It was fifteen minutes past nine, and I had no right to be out that late. So I turn my face around, and who do I see? My mother. I was sitting on top of a car, and Johnnie was standing next to me. He wasn't close to me and he wasn't touching my body whatsoever. My mother just came up to me and she slapped me in the face in front of Johnnie, and she says, so this is what you're doing!

So I says, I'm gonna tell Daddy you hit me! You know he doesn't hit me, and he doesn't like for you to hit me either!

Unless I do something wrong! That's the only time Daddy told you to ever hit me. I'm going right upstairs and I'm gonna tell him you hit me right in front of this boy that's a friend of mine!

She says, a friend of yours! Look at that—it's a disgrace! And it's fifteen minutes past nine!

I got mad at my mother and I answered her back—very first time that I ever answered my mother back. Because I got heartbroken at the way she treated me in front of that boy.

So Johnnie says, I'm gonna go right upstairs, lady, and I'm gonna talk to your husband.

My mother says, you better not go upstairs, 'cause my husband's gonna kill you! No wonder she hasn't been doing her homework lately! No wonder she's just standing looking out the window all the time! 'Cause you've been bothering her! Why don't you leave her alone? Don't you think she wants to be something, when she grows up? She wants to work in an office, she wants to be somebody important. And you, a tramp like you, a no-good bum like you, that you don't even work! I seen you hanging around the corners every time I go shopping. I know you: you're one of them little gangsters!

He says, well, look: I love your daughter and I'm gonna talk to your husband man-to-man.

I said, Johnnie, please Johnnie, don't go upstairs! My father will *really* kill me now! Please, Johnnie, let's just break up and forget it. You can wait for me till I finish my school. I got two more years to go, please wait.

So Johnnie says, no Carmen. 'Cause your mother's gonna be always slapping you in front of everybody like that, that's not good. That's not good. You're a good girl and she should be proud of you. You're a good girl. Because if you would have been a bad girl, you would have run out with me already and we would have done bad things already, which you haven't done. We only kiss and that's all, and we don't even get close together. So I'm going to see your father.

He took the stairs. He didn't want to take the elevator with me and my mother, 'cause he was scared she would start slapping him too. When we got there, Johnnie was there knocking at the door—and it's eight flights! He really love me, you know, and I love him too.

My mother opened the door with the key, and she said, Benny, you got a visitor. It's one of them gangsters that we always see in the neighborhood. He wants to marry your daughter—ain't that something big? He's the one that's been bothering her all the time.

And my father says, wait a minute, take it easy. Don't talk like that about the boy. Just because you see him in a group don't mean that he's a gangster. You haven't seen him killing nobody. The guy probably doesn't even carry a knife, and you insulting him like that!

Johnnie says, thank you very much Mr. Sanchez. But you have no right to defend me. You should talk like that about your daughter. Your wife just called her fresh and all kinds of nasty things, calling her all kinds of ugly names in the street, plus your wife dare slap this girl in the face without Carmen and me doing nothing at all. I wasn't even near her body! You got a wonderful daughter and you should both be proud of her.

So my father say to him, thank you very much. You don't have to say that about my daughter, 'cause I know that she's good. That's why I trust her, and that's why I let her stay with boys. And I thank God that he send me a woman like this to this house. Lucia, don't ever insult Carmen again and don't ever slap her. You know I don't like nobody to hit my daughter. She's fifteen years old and you should have more consideration for her. People who seen you slapping her will make fun of her. Even the people in the windows, what will they think? That she's not a virgin and that she's a bad girl.

My mother started crying. She said, look, I don't want her to get married! That's why I did it. Put her in a home, Benny! Put her in a home! Don't give her permission to go out with this boy—you're gonna kill me if you do.

But my father said, look, Lucia, it's better that she learn what's good and what's bad. If this boy wants to see her, and they love each other, it's better that she sees him here than in the street. After all, it's the first time that our daughter says she loves somebody. And she's a good girl and you know it. She's always helping you in the house. Sometimes she doesn't do nothing because you don't want her to do it, so that's your fault. She just sits around reading and doing her homework because you don't want her to work in the house. That's not her fault; that's your fault.

So my mother says, okay, Benny, do whatever you do, but if something goes wrong, don't say that I didn't tell you!

So my father says to Johnnie, you say you want to go out with my daughter? Okay, I'll give you permission. But please, please, have respect for me and for my wife and for my daughter. Do not wait for her on the corner, and do not take her to school, and do not hang around the school building she goes to. You can see her three times a week from seven to nine o'clock. You don't take her out of here unless she goes with her older brother. You gonna take her to the movies, I'll give her two brothers the money to go along. But I don't want to see you hanging around with her in the hallways. That's a bad reputation for her. See her only in my apartment, 'cause I don't want people talking bad about my daughter.

So that's the way he did it. Then one day, eight days before my sixteenth birthday, my mother told me, Carmen,

I'm going to be outside the school building waiting for you today. I want to buy you a dress for your birthday.

I was so happy she was going to buy me a beautiful dress. She buy me clothes to go to school, but it was so long she didn't buy me something extra expensive and extra beautiful. And she told me she was going to give me permission to wear a little bit of high-heeled shoes. First time in my life. I was so crazy—ooh!—I was very happy.

But Johnnie and I had started sneaking out on my parents. He couldn't bear to see me only three times a week at my father's house. He used to walk me to school. He was working and he was going to buy me my wedding rings. He came up and give me my engagement ring without consulting my father, and my father was mad. He said, I never should have given him permission to come up here! You're so stupid; you have no respect for me, after I've been so good to you! And I had some girl friends and boy friends up there at the time in the next room, and my father scolded me so loud that they could hear him! He talks louder than I do.

See how good Johnnie was: he said to my mother, since you're her mother, you put away the wedding band.

Two or three days later, that's when he walked me to school. We started walking to school, but I see the time and it was too late for me to go to school. So I says to him, I cannot go to school, Johnnie, I have to skip my day, because if my father sees one lateness on my report card, that's it! So I can lie in school about where I was, and then when I get my report card I can erase where it says one day absent. Then when I take the report card back to school, I can write it back, 'cause I know how to copy the teacher's handwriting.

So we went to the movies, and I forgot that I was supposed to meet my mother at school. Oh wow, I didn't know what to do!

I said, I'm not going home, Johnnie, I'm scared. You and I better get married right now, that's what I told him.

He says, are you crazy? I promised your parents that I wait for you two years! You want your father to blow my brains out with a gun?

He took me by the hand and he started pushing me to take the bus to come back home.

I said no, no, I'm not going home.

But we did go to my house. It was nine-thirty; my mother had already come home and was crying—she told me that later. Johnnie was forcing me up the stairs, and I started crying.

I said, you don't love me. I want you to marry me right away, Johnnie. So please, let's do something wrong so my Daddy can say nothing and they have to marry us. 'Cause I know if we do something wrong, my father's gonna marry us. He's not gonna do like the parents that let their kids go to school and not get married. Not my father! He says if I ever do something wrong, I have to pay for it by getting married. Either this guy goes to jail that does it to me, or he marries me: that's the way my father is.

I says, you willing to marry me? Come on, let's do something wrong, Johnnie!

Johnnie says, Carmen, I don't want to do it. I want you to have the chance to finish school. Since I didn't finish school because my parents were poor, I want you to go and be the smart one of the family. So when we have children, they can be proud of you, Carmen. So please Carmen, let's wait for two years. Let's do it right.

So I say, okay, Johnnie. If you don't want to have intercourse with me, then I'll get somebody else. I'll get Red. I'll do intercourse with him, because he still wants me. You didn't know that? You want to be stupid and lose me? Then lose me. But I'm not coming back to my house. Because they're very strict with me. You yourself know that they don't let me go noplace, they don't let me have parties, I cannot wear lipstick, I cannot pull my hair down, I cannot wear high heels, I cannot put on a tight skirt or a low-cut blouse. What's the matter with them? They treat me like if I'm a boy, like if I'm some kind of animal or something? No, sir! I'm fed up. I've been a good daughter this far, and they don't want to believe me or trust me, well that's it! Either you have intercourse with me now, Johnnie, or you going to lose me. Because I could run out of this stairways and you could not stop me, and you know it. Because if you try to stop me, I'll start screaming and you'll be in trouble. I'm gonna get Red, and I'm gonna make them beat you up. Either you have intercourse with me now, or you don't love me.

He says, Carmen, that's the reason I don't want to do it, because I love you. You're young, you're beautiful, you got a beautiful shape: why don't you think, Carmen? Think, you're making a mistake, Carmen. I'm a man, I'm holding myself back because I love you. I want the best for you. Your parents don't let you go to parties because you're going out with me. Your father told you, if you go out with a man, that's the man you got to respect, you cannot be in gangs no more. What else you want? Don't you got me—you have to be in parties? No, Carmen, we're going to wait.

I make believe that I was going to run down the stairs, and he held me. He slapped me and he says, you're gonna be treated like a dog, baby! You're gonna go upstairs to your house. A virgin like you, that's the way I met you and that's the way you're gonna stay. I'm not going to take any chances of raping you, and then your father probably won't let us get married. He'll put you in a home, where I won't be able to see you no more. No!

Then he slapped me four more times. He says you're gonna go upstairs!

I says, all right, but you're gonna kiss me good night.

I was crying. He says all right. So he kiss me, and when he kiss me I started teasing him around, put my hands in his pocket, and I started, you know, getting very sexy with him. I started touching his back, and his ears, and I started putting my tongue in his ears, and he just couldn't stop himself. We sat down in the stairs, we started kissing each other, I sat down in his lap, and that's when we did intercourse.

So he said, Carmen, you're going to get me in so much trouble! Why did you let me do this? Oh God, Carmen, something wrong is going to happen!

I said, come on, don't be a sissy! Let's go upstairs and tell my parents that we did something wrong and we have to get married right away. You'll see, Johnnie, everything is going to work out all right.

He says, I think you're crazy! I'm going to end up in jail doing five years on account of you, and you're going to end up in a home and probably pregnant.

My mother opens the door and says, you are a disgrace to your father and me! You have no respect for us! Look at yourself: you look like a piece of garbage! I'm gonna put your brother to call up your father right this minute, and you're gonna go to a home! It's five past ten! And you show up with this no-good bum!

She jump into Johnnie and try to slap him. And I jump in the middle and say, you put a hand on him, so help me God I'll kill you! You're not my mother anymore! I was mad, I was like a savage! I don't love you—I hate you, I hate you, I hate you! I love Johnnie. I love him more than you love Daddy, and I'm going to marry him even if I have to kill everybody in this house!

My mother says you better shut up before I'll kill you. She took a stick to hit me and I held the stick. We started dragging each other with the stick from one side to the other side. That's one thing—I would not hit my mother or put a hand on her, but I put a hand on the stick to stop her from hitting me. Because she went crazy. She knew what happen already, I think, because after all it was late. I told her, Mommy, you got to marry Johnnie and me. Something happened. Something went wrong with us.

She said oh my God, my daughter! My daughter! My daughter's gonna have a baby! Oh Johnnie, why do you do this to me? Johnnie, don't you know that I love her? We gave you this break to be her boyfriend, why did you spoil her life?

I says, Mommy, don't talk to him; he had *nothing* to do with it. It was me, I forced him to, or else I would have gone with any man in the street. I don't want to stay in this house no more. I'll go crazy in this house! You people don't treat me the way you're supposed to treat a girl when she's sixteen years old. Girls in school are always making fun of the colors of my clothes and the colors of my shoes. You want to bring me up the way your mother brought you up, and that's not good. I'm through with all that.

She says, okay, Carmen, I'll marry you, Carmen. But don't go; stay here. Please, Johnnie, Carmen only listens to you. Johnnie, tell her to stay here, Johnnie. So Johnnie told me, Carmen, stay here; wait for your father. I'll be back tomorrow and I'll talk to your father tomorrow.

My mother got in the middle of the door so I couldn't go through, and Johnnie was outside in the hallway. My two brothers were hugging me, and I went crazy. I started screaming, Johnnie, don't leave me, Johnnie! You got to marry me now, I'm gonna have a baby from you, Johnnie! Don't leave me, please don't leave me! And I started crying and crying and I told my mother, please, Mommy, let me go, let me go to Johnnie! He'll never come back to me, Mommy, I love him, Mommy, no use spoiling my marriage. Now he'll never marry me. Now he's getting a chance to break.

Johnnie heard what I say, so he says, Carmen, I love you! I'll wait for you. I'll come back tomorrow and speak to your father. I'll marry you. I'll do anything for you, Carmen, but please trust me. I'll see you tomorrow.

He went, so I say okay, Mommy, I'll stay and wait for Daddy. So I went into the bathroom and I washed myself, because I was bleeding a lot. The inside of my skirt was stained with blood. The sides of my legs were dripping with blood, and so was my bloomers—they were very filthy with blood. So I took them off and I washed them before my mother would see it. I cleaned my skirt and I wash up very good. Then I went into my room, I pick out a pair of white socks and a head kerchief, and I put a whole stack of bobby-pins inside the head kerchief, because at nighttimes I always fix up my head with rollers. I put a comb in there, and I made a note: Mommy, I love you, please forgive me. Daddy forgive me too. I'll be back if you give us permission to marry.

I read the note and it broke my heart, so I broke it up and threw it down the toilet bowl.

I went into the kitchen and my mother was watching to make sure that I don't go out of the house. I says, I only want a glass of water, don't worry, Mommy, don't get up, I'm not gonna go out the door. She says, okay, Carmen, okay. I still love you, don't make me suffer. You're gonna kill me, she says. You wait for Daddy. I'll tell him to let you marry. I promise I won't send you to the home.

I took a glass of water, I went back into my room, and I took the kerchief with the socks and a pair of bloomers and a brassiere inside of my jacket. And I go out and I see that my mother was sitting down. I open the door and I say, I love you, Mommy, but I'm going to Johnnie!

I went down the stairs so fast! She called to my brothers to run after me, but I'm a fast runner and they couldn't catch me. I ran through the streets near the project and I was running fast, real fast! I couldn't fall down or nothing, 'cause I made up my mind to get married and to run out of the house, or else I'd go crazy. I was jealous of other girls having freedom, and I didn't have any freedom, being a good girl like I was. So I kept running, running. . . .

I whistled for Johnnie and he came down with a sweater for me and we started running. My father came by in his car but thank God he didn't see us! We ran all the way to 14th Street. We didn't have any money on us, so we walked to 23rd Street and Eighth Avenue; Johnnie had some friends there. As soon as I saw these boys, I didn't like them. I knew what they were. They were drug addicts and crooks.

They used to give people holdups. They used to beat up mens. But even though I didn't like them, they were very good to me. And I seen that no matter what they were, they were human beings like I am. And they were the only persons that helped Johnnie and me.

This block that we were in, they used to call it Korea, because there were always fights and killings there. This boy Georgie used to live there in a furnished room. He had a very small bed only one person could sleep in. But he told Johnnie it was the best place to stay in until he could find someplace better for us. He said, right now you could not go into the street, Johnnie, because her father is looking for her and you, and he might kill you. And he might even kill his own daughter, because for a man to lose his only lover, the only love that he's got in his heart, his daughter, the only daughter that he's got, he could kill anybody. He'll be so blind with madness that he won't know what he do at the moment.

So we stood in that room for two days. We used to have intercourse on that bed, and sometimes we'd end up on the floor, because the bed was so small. We used to have pie and milk, that was the only thing his friend could give us. Because he didn't have no money. After all, he had a habit of his own to support. I didn't know nothing about drugs at the time. I know now what he must have gone through. He didn't have no money, but he didn't let Johnnie and I go to bed without something in our stomachs. He even paid the rent for us.

Then we went to a friend of Johnnie's who was hiding out from the police because he just finished cutting a man's face. He liked Johnnie very much and didn't want my father to find him, so every day he paid five dollars rent for that hotel room we were staying in. Plus the food he gave Johnnie and me.

So Johnnie went out and found a job in the same place he used to work when I met him. He started working in the garment center, making forty dollars a week. He didn't want to leave me alone in the hotel with his friend—he didn't trust his friend, he said that his friend was a sex maniac and that his friend was looking at me too much. So he got in touch with this Cuban woman that his family knows. This lady liked me very much. I was ashamed, because I was the only one dark inside her apartment. Everybody was white and I was dark-complexioned, and I felt embarrassed and ashamed of myself. 'Cause I was very ignorant at the time. I didn't know that white people care for dark people. I thought they didn't like us.

But this lady treated me like if it was my own family.

She even trusted me. She went to work, everyone went to work, and I stayed alone in the apartment. The second day in the apartment I tried to cook. I did not know how to make rice and beans, because that's one thing my mother never taught me. My mother treated me like if I was queen of the house, and I had freedom in the house, except no parties, and no freedom for me to go into the street. My mother wasn't bad at all; it's just that they were very strict. And I don't blame them: with the shape that I had, any father and mother would be jealous of their own daughter.

So the second day I try to make rice, and it was like glue. And the beans! They were so hard that when Johnnie put one in his mouth he say, you spoil this for them! And blap blap! he slapped me in the face. He say why do you start cooking if you don't know? Don't you see that's the only food these people have?

When he finished hitting me, my lip was broken, I was bleeding a lot. I say, that's the first and last time you're going to put a hand on me, boy, 'cause I'm leaving you right now. I don't take no beatings from nobody. My father never put a hand on me, and my mother, the only time she ever put a hand on me was when she found me talking to you on the corner, remember? Well you made the biggest mistake of your life, hitting me like that for nothing. *Now* I know why my mother didn't want me to marry you! Now I know why she wanted me to keep to school so I could learn to do things better, instead of making a mistake on a lousy mess-up of my life. You have no right to hit me. You'll feel sorry.

So I started to leave, and he hauled me back and started to cry, asking me to forgive him, like he didn't mean it. He started screaming Carmen! I love you, don't leave me, I'll never hit you again as long as I live!

While he was begging me, the lady from the apartment comes in. Carmen! You're bleeding! Oh my poor child! She put her arms around me, and she slapped Johnnie in the face, and she says, I'll never love you like a son as long as I live. This girl was good enough to leave her school, to leave her parents for you, and you gonna treat her like a dog? You should be ashamed of yourself. Beautiful lips like this woman has and look what you done to them!

So we made up and we went back to the hotel room. On my birthday I called my mother, because on that day in 1937, she suffered a lot having me. She said, you're a wonderful daughter. Please come home; I'll marry you. I forgave you already; seven days ago I forgave you.

Johnnie said, what you did? You called your mother! Five years in jail! You know she's lying to you! She's gonna put you in a home and she's gonna put me in jail!

I said, listen, Johnnie, I know my mother pretty good. I ought to: I spent more time with her than my own father has. Nothing is gonna happen, you'll see.

We took a taxi and we went down to Baruch projects. When we got out from the taxi, my mother jumped on Johnnie and me and started kissing both of us and crying. She even invited the taxi driver upstairs. She talked to the man in Spanish and invited him up to have some coffee. The man says, me no have no Spanish, me no Puerto Rican. She says, thank you, thank you, God bless you for bringing my daughter and my son safely home. My mother was crying, Johnnie was crying; they got me crying, too.

I said, all right, I'm back; now what's going to happen? I'm going to a home?

I was nasty to my mother. I put the book on the table right away. I told her, Johnnie's been very good to me. Don't lock him up, Mommy, please. You could put me in a home if you want to, because after all, I lied to you. I was a virgin. Johnnie and me did not have intercourse whatsoever. Johnnie hasn't put a hand on me. He has slept in the same bed as me but he hasn't touched me. I lied to you: I told you Johnnie and me had intercourse to see if you would marry us fast.

I thought my mother was not going to marry us, so that's the reason I told her Johnnie had not put a hand on me. I told a lie, because after all, it's not his fault what happen. It was my fault; I was the one that forced him. It was very nasty of me to do something like that. Because after all, I was a very good girl.

I don't know what happened to me, that I acted the way I did at the time. I behaved like a prostitute. There must have been something terrible wrong with me. I don't know what it was, and I don't even want to know. But I think if my parents had not been so strict with me, it would not have happened.

I had it all planned. I ran away from home eight days before my birthday, and on the day of my birthday I called up my mother and came back home. The next day we went to City Hall and we signed all the papers, we went to this doctor for blood tests and we paid the doctor twenty dollars. A judge married us.

When did Johnnie start on narcotics? I remember one time when he was my boy friend his mother visited my mother. Johnnie's mother told my mother that she found a brown paper bag with a bunch of long, skinny cigarettes. Johnnie's mother didn't know what it was because she was very stupid, and at that time I didn't know what it was, but my mother knew because my father always reads the papers and my father told her, that's marijuana; that's drug. So I figure that's maybe why my parents didn't want me to marry Johnnie, and that's why they didn't let me go to no parties with him. Because maybe they figure I start using it, too.

Johnnie was nineteen years old when he started with marijuana. Then, after we got married, I didn't see him using any drugs until we moved to this building on Clinton Street. He used to bring all his boy friends upstairs, all his partners. They used to stay in the toilet half an hour sometimes, three or four of them inside the bathroom. And then they used to come out scratching, or jumping up, or screaming, or cursing. Some of them used to come scratching in the middle of the legs, putting their hands inside their zipper, and I used to say, don't do that in here, because I had my little daughters with me, you know. And Johnnie said, why don't you shut up and mind your own business?

I told him, look, Johnnie, I don't like what you're doing. Every time you go in the toilet with your friends, either you're having intercourse with them or you're using drugs. I don't know what drugs is because I never seen it, but I seen the way people that use it act. And you and your friends act the same way.

So he slapped me one day, and he said, don't you ever say I'm having intercourse with my friends!

I say, well then you're using drugs, right? Don't deny it, you can't deny it, 'cause look at your face. Look at your eyes. You can tell that you're using something, and it's not whisky, honey, 'cause I'm too damn smart. Goddammit, stop lying to me; tell me what you're doing! You bastard, what do you think I am—a piece of garbage from the street? You have to respect me or get out of this fucking house! You no-good bum, you!

So he told me, look, you son-of-a-bitch, I'll kill you if you ever speak to me like that. You want to find out what it is? Why the hell don't you use it yourself? Try it! I have a bag here. This is heroin, you see, you black bitch, this is heroin! You want to use it, go ahead use it! Try it yourself, you no-good bastard. (*Weeping.*) It's good! Use it and you'll find out how good it is! You'll feel so good, Carmen, use it, go ahead, I'll show you how to use it.

And I ran away from him. I said, no. I'm not gonna use that; I'm not that stupid. I love you, but I'll never use that in my life, so help me God!

He says, one of these days you'll use it. You wait and see. Because it's good, baby; you'll have a boss time. If you're scared of a person, when you use drugs, you're not scared of that person no more. If this person that you're so afraid of tells you to fight with him, you take a shot of drugs and you'll fight. You won't be scared.

Then every day he started talking a little more about it. Then one day I gave him my arm and he shot a little bit of stuff in my arm.

And since that time, here I am. I'm a drug addict. (*Weeps.*) A mother of four children! Four wonderful children and wonderful set of parents!

I've been through a lot. When I don't have drugs, my arms start to twist and my arms they stretch on me, and my legs they stretch on me. It's very painful. I start sweating, and all of a sudden I get chills in my body and I throw up and I get a sour taste in my mouth.

If I don't have the money to buy a bag of heroin, I'll steal it. I'll break into people's apartments, and I have given holdups. If I go into apartments and I don't find money, I'll take a radio, a watch, men's suits, ladies' dresses—anything that's good to sell. Another boy and me will do that, because sometimes I need help to break into an apartment.

Sometimes we don't find money and we don't find nothing good to sell. What do I have to do? I have to go into the street with this cold, with these chills, throwing up, I can't even take a bath, I can't even wash my teeth. I can't comb my hair; I just put my hair back and make a line in my eyebrows because I used to shave my eyebrows off. I put a scarf on my head, put on two or three sweaters and two pairs of pants, socks, warm shoes and go into the street. If

I don't find a man in the street, I'll go into a man's apartment that I know, even if he's a friend of mine, or a husband of a very good girl friend of mine. I'll tell him, look, I need money—can you lend it to me? I need six dollars. If the man says no, I'll tell him please, I'll give you my body. I'll give you a good time. So please, I need the six dollars badly. Please, don't let me down. Please.

Sometimes the man—these lousy bastards, they have no consideration for a woman like us drug addicts—dare to tell me, look, give me a piece of your pussy for three dollars. That's all I got, three dollars. Come on! I'll do it fast, I come fast. Take the three dollars; you don't need the whole six dollars—you can find three dollars someplace else! Three dollars I give you and three dollars someplace else makes six. Come on, baby, give me a good time—give me a piece of your ass!

That's how these bastards dare talk to me! I don't have to go through all this. That's the reason I came to you for help. It's over four months already I don't give my body to a man. I cannot do it anymore. I rather go steal and give a person a holdup, then to put my body in a filthy bed, to a filthy, no-good man that don't deserve me.

Sometimes I get regular customers. They tell me, every Tuesday night you come here, Carmen; now don't let me down. I'm not going to bring another girl. I only want to see you, because you're very clean and you're a very good woman and you know what you do. You got a beautiful body, I want to see you again, Carmen. I never met a woman like you in my life.

Sometimes I know they're lying, because I'm not beautiful at all.

They just talk to me like that so they could get what they want, and to see if I could do the things they want me to do. But I don't do nothing else besides slipping down with them into bed, having intercourse and that's it. The reason I stopped going out with mens is because a couple of my own steady customers have *dared* to tell me to do one thing I'll never do. I won't say I will never do it, but it will be to the person I know and the person I love; who knows, I can not ever say, from this water I will not drink. Because from that water, sooner or later, I have to drink. That's the reason I say I can never do it. Not to these bums in the street.

I got for regular customers some Polacks, one Chinese, three Jewish mens and three Puerto Ricans. Some of the Polacks are very careful with me. It all depends on how you treat them. If you try to tell them to hurry up and come fast, they get mad and say, go away, I'll get somebody else. Sometimes they want to stay with you three or four hours. They think you got all night for a miserable six dollars!

Because that's what they pay. It would be a miracle if you find a man that would give you ten or fifteen dollars. It would be a miracle! Because a lot of girls in this neighborhood have spoiled it. Some of them are not even drug addicts. They're girls that just hustle for the pimps. They lay down with men for just two or three dollars.

Some of these women come to the luncheonette and they start saying that we, the junkies, have spoiled this neighborhood. Knowing that they are the ones who have done it bad, they're saying that we, the drug addicts, are selling our bodies for fifty cents or three dollars, because that's the exact amount of money we need to get our drugs with. But they're wrong. I know, because I go to a man who wants to go out with me and I tell him it's ten dollars. He say, you're crazy, ten dollars for a piece of pussy? He say, last week I went out with this beautiful woman and she only charged me three dollars. I say, well, show me that beautiful woman. He says, I'm not lying. I wish this woman could pass by right now so I could point her out to you. I say, I wish she could, 'cause that bitch is gonna get a beating!

A filthy bitch, for three dollars sell her body! Doesn't matter who at all, that's a *pig!* That's what we call them in the neighborhood, you know, pigs.

FOUR DAYS LATER

THE Black Diamonds hung out in a candy store. There were only two girls in the gang, and six or seven other young little girls who would only buy candy and stick around for a little while to play the jukebox and dance with the boys.

We did get in a lot of fights. For instance, some girls used to be troublemakers. They would say, one of them colored niggers from 4th Street got fresh with me in school today. And he said that the Black Diamonds are full of baloney, that his gang could beat us up any time. They could wipe us out completely, because the spics aren't worth a cent. That's what they would say to the girl. And the girl, she's young and ignorant; instead of keeping it to herself, she would tell all the boys in the gang, and she would tell things that never even happened. And the boys would say, you're my girl, and we're both Puerto Ricans, and we ain't gonna stand around to let no lousy nigger call you a spic. Because you are our woman, and just for that we're gonna burn them out. We'll prove that we're not scared of them!

The boys usually used to tell me, well since you're the wisest girl over here, and you know how to fight like a boy, and you're a pretty good runner—we'll let you carry the pieces for us. We had B-B guns and hand-made guns. Grown men in the street would make guns for the boys.

They would say, look, I'll make you two guns in a week or two, if you will get me a portable television or a typewriter that I need for my daughter or steal a suit for me. I want an expensive suit, you hear?—exactly this same suit that I'm gonna show you in the store—and I'll make the zip guns for you.

Nancy was a troublemaker who would tell the boys someone tried to rape her and get them to go out and fight. She did not belong to our club; she only used to come to the club to look up the boys. Matter of fact, she was not a virgin; she would lay down even with old mens. They would give her two dollars and she would lay down in bed with them. She was thirteen years old. Her mother was always in the street, and she didn't have no father. Her father left her mother because he found her drunk with this other man in the house. The boys finally told Nancy to leave the candy store, or they would tell her mother, but she said, huh!, that's a fine person to tell! Go ahead, baby, tell my mother anything you like. She's worse than me!

So the boys got me to run Nancy out of the candy store. I didn't beat her up or nothing, because I felt sorry for her, and after all she was a girl just like I am. I have always used my head, except now that I made the mistake of using drugs. I called her, and I said, look, baby: they're gonna elect me the leader of the gang. I'm gonna be telling the boys what to do. And you know they respect me because I'm a good fighter. I don't want to see your stinking face around here again. You come to the candy store, buy what you want (*clap*), make it out. Or else baby (*short whistle*), I'll have to wipe you out completely. And you know what I mean by that: no guns, no knives—I'll use my fists on you. I'll beat you up, so help me God. Don't come here making trouble, because I'm trying to keep these boys from fighting with the colored boys. I don't want the Sportsmen or the

Viceroys fighting with our people. I want all of us together, like human beings like we are. You tease the colored boys, and that's why they try to kiss you and start trouble. You with your little happy shape, you think you own the world. So don't complain, and don't tell any more stories, because they're not going to listen to you.

We were Black Diamond Debs. Sometimes the police would come into the candy store, and would put the boys against the wall, and search them. Sometimes they would even push the boys and slap them around. And they would give us girls a kick in our asses, and throw us out of the candy store, and send us home to take a bath and help our mothers do the cooking. We would laugh at them and start running, 'cause we were a little afraid of the policemens.

If we did not carry the guns for the boys, they would call us chickens, and throw us out of the gang, and even would beat us up. The boys themselves would gang up on the girl that said no, I'm scared. We would put the pieces inside our waistlines, inside our dungarees. We would tie them there with our garrison belt. And knives, we used to carry them with the handle of the knife right below our bust-line, inside the brassiere, and the part that cuts was loose down to our waistline. In case we have to give the knife right to the boy, we would only have to pick up our blouses or our sweaters, and take the knife by the handle and hand it to the boys.

Sometimes the other gangs peace-talked to our gang, and they would say, let's straighten this out. That girl over there started everything. She called one of our girls a bad name. Why don't you throw that girl out of the gang, and the three gangs could be together and work like brotherhood. It seems that the only trouble that we get into is because of the girls. The girls get into an argument, and instead of the girls fighting with each other, we boys end up fighting with you boys. We have been so stupid, all of us: every time a girl comes to us with a story, we listen and we start fighting, instead of putting them to fight. They keep their nice behinds nice and clean, and sometimes we end up in the hospital.

Just because of that diddleybop walk, there were always fights, too. They would come through the neighborhood making a little jump every time they take a step, making their leg jump. The diddleybops would come from 4th Street and they would walk in doubles or triples, walking tough, diddleybopping, and they would talk loud and wise sometimes. And that would start a fight.

A couple of times when I went to school at P.S. 177, I used to run back home with my braids loose because some colored girls used to take my ribbons off. They used to pick on me because I didn't know how to speak English. And one day my father was coming from his work and he was passing by the school building in his car. He stopped when he seen a bunch of colored girls beating up a girl, and he saw that it was I myself that was getting beat up. They were trying to take off my coat, either to take it or to get it dirty. He pulled the girls away and he took his belt off, and he said to the biggest girl in English, listen, you're the biggest one here and I want you to have a fight with my daughter right now. Because what you're doing isn't right. Why don't you ask your mother for ribbon and ask her to fix your clothes nice? You got to pick on her all the time? This is the last time. Because you're going to have to fight with my daughter now, and if you don't fight with her I'm going to take this belt, so help me God, and I'm going to beat you to death!

And he said to me, in Spanish: Carmen, you're going to fight with this big girl. And you better win, or else with this belt that I'm holding, I'm gonna kill you!

I started crying. I was begging him not to make me fight, 'cause I was really scared of those girls.

He says, you're not my daughter if you don't fight with them. I'll send you away.

My father *pushed* me against this girl, and the girl threw a punch on me, and then she pulled me by the hair. My father started telling me in Spanish, hit her with your left! Hit her with your right! Hit her in the stomach! In the stomach with your left! In the face now with the right!

And that's how I learned to defend myself. I won the fight, so help me God! The other girls were booing this big girl, and telling her they were going to throw her out of the club. I was ten and this girl was twelve years old, and I gave her a really good time, baby. I gave her a hard, hard time. Those girls never pick on me again. They started to talk to me and wait for me after school. They even started coming up to my house, and my mother would start making them cookies and giving them tea, coffee, ice cream—whatever they wanted. They became pretty good friends of mine, even the girl that I had the fight with.

I was married for five years and went on dope when I was twenty-one. It was after the second child was born. Sometimes Johnnie would come home from work happy, and sometimes he would start a fight with me. And since I always been a big man in the house, I'll answer him back, and he would hit me and I'll hit him back. Because that's one thing I never stood for, getting hit.

Sometimes we fought because Johnnie was very jealous. One week after I had my second child and came out of the hospital I went to work at a photo studio in order to help him out. He usually used to go to my work, to keep an eye on me. I don't know why he was jealous of me. He had no reason; I never went out with other mens. I went to work early and as soon as I finished I would come home to my childrens. My mother always had my oldest daughter; my first child my mother took. After my second child, I moved into Lillian Wald projects. I'll never forget it, because I had an apartment of my own for the first time in my life. That's why I went to work, to have everything that I needed— 'cause I have always wanted to have everything 'spensive and good for my own.

Johnnie one day accused me of making a date with a boy he saw me talking to in the street. The boy only wanted a job at the place where I work. I say, goddammit, Johnnie, you're always fighting, you're always jealous. Maybe if I was doing the wrong thing you'd be happy, right? Just because I said that he took his hand out and he slapped me in the face. And wow, baby, I let him have it! He got mad and he punched me in the stomach. I wasn't even forty days from having my baby, and I had to bend down, because I couldn't even breathe. When I got up, I kick him in the middle of the legs. He started screaming, and started throwing everything around the house. He broke off my clothes, so I had to run through the street in my slip to get to my father's house, four blocks away. I was bleeding from my stomach, cars were stopping, but I just kept on running.

When my father saw me, he went straight to my house. But Johnnie had ran away. He came three days later asking me for forgiveness. He came to my work—I came to work even though I had a black eye. I didn't even stay there for a whole year, because Johnnie made me lose my job. One day Johnnie came in and my boss was right there. Johnnie started slapping me around, so what does my boss tell me? Carmen, I'm sorry, this is a respectable place. You're a nice girl, you do your work clean, you're pretty fast with your work, but this has to be stopped. I have seen your husband stopping you outside the building, cursing you out. I cannot have this; I'll have to let you go.

My boss, Mr. G., told me, your husband is no good. Why don't you get a divorce from him? I told him, don't give me any advice, you know? I was very ignorant at the time. If I woulda listened to Mr. G., and if I had been very smart at the time, I would never have gotten into this drug business.

Everything went wrong. Johnnie and me started breaking up. I'll throw him out of the house, and he'll come back to the house. Then we got kicked out of the projects because of him. Not because of the drug, because of the fights. People started complaining.

We moved to 11th Street and Avenue B, to a 1½-room furnished apartment. Over there, Johnnie got into a fight with me again. Jealous business again. He came from work, and it was always because of a man. I was brought up with mens, but my father himself knows that I wouldn't do nothing with those mens, only friendship. They say hello, I say hello. This man was talking to me outside my door, to ask me if I would ask my father to get him a job on the waterfront. My husband came in and right away took his hand and started fighting with me. My third child then was three months old. I've never seen him like that—maybe he was on drugs. At that time I was also using it sometimes, behind his back. He took me by the neck and he had my head against the window sill, so the only way I had to defend myself was by making noise. I think fast and I punch the window glass with my hand, and I cut myself. The blood would not stop from bleeding; the blood kept on coming out, too much blood. Johnnie got scared and he ran. Then when I went downstairs, he said, don't you dare come downstairs! Go upstairs, I'm gonna call an ambulance! You're gonna die—oh God, what's gonna happen now—your father's gonna kill me!

It so happened when I was running to the drugstore, my father came around the corner in his car. He stopped the car right in the middle of the street and ran right upstairs to Johnnie. I got in a hysterical way—I couldn't stop from laughing. I said, you bastard, now you scared, you sissy, you faggot, oh boy my father's gonna give it to you, I'm so glad, ah ha ha ha ha! Look at you, you fucking punk, you!

I ran out and my father was coming up. He said, I can't take it any longer, Carmen, 'cause my face is full of shame.

Johnnie opened the door and the first thing my father did was Blah! he let Johnnie have it in the face with his hand open. He said, you've gone far enough. You're not going to put a hand on my daughter ever again.

And Johnnie did get nasty. He *dared* hit my father back! Yes, sir. And since that time, I start running away from him, I started using more drugs, I started double-crossing him, I started going to the movies with different mens. Maybe sometimes I would kiss the mens, yes, but I never laid down in bed with them—that's one thing I never did to Johnnie.

The fourth baby was six months old when I finally ran away from Johnnie. I had to go clean this lady's house way up in the Bronx. Johnnie had got in drunk the night before, and I had a hard time waking him up that Saturday morning. He said, go ahead, honey, I'll take care of the kids. I said, are you *sure* you'll take care of the kids, Johnnie? He said, don't worry. Go ahead.

I don't know what happened to me then. Instead of going straight to the subway—it was only a block from my house, we were living on 137th Street—I walk up to 138th Street, near the Puerto Rican movie. I had about six or four dollars on me, and I don't know what hit my mind. I say, Carmen, I think it's two or three days that I don't take off. I feel like getting a shot of drugs today. I feel good, and strong. It will be nice, Carmen, to be goofing in that nice beautiful house, where it's nice and quiet, the lady doesn't watch me or nothing, she goes upstairs to bed and she lets me take care of the house like if it was my own. Man, I feel good goofing around the place, you know, nodding, closing my eyes, scratching myself. I think I'll just do that.

And while I'm waiting for this boy to bring me the drug, who do I see coming down the block? Mr. Johnnie himself! I run up to the roof and he ran after me. He says, you son-of-a-bitch, I'm gonna kill you!

I started running up the stairs, and it's a good thing I had a loose skirt on, because I ran fast up them stairs, man. The first apartment that I found open, bloop! I ran in there and locked the door like I was the owner of the place. And there was these two girls and their mother sitting in the kitchen, eating breakfast. They said get out, but I said, shhh! Sit right there! My husband's gonna kill me! When they heard I was Puerto Rican, they quieted down. They thought I was a colored woman.

The girls they were shaking in the corner, two beautiful girls. And they said, why do you marry a man like that? I was shaking and crying and running to every window in the apartment. I saw Johnnie downstairs, cursing me out to the whole building.

You son-of-a-bitch! You bastard, you no-good drug addict! Because he was off the drugs at that time—I was on, but he was off. He says, you mother-fucker, I'd like to get my hands on you! You black bitch, I know you in there someplace! Come down! I'm gonna cut you up to pieces!

And I said to myself, yeah, baby? You gonna cut your ass in pieces; you ain't gonna get a hand on me again, baby. 'Cause this time I made up my mind you'll never see me, baby.

When he came out to look for me, Johnnie left my three kids alone in the apartment! Now before I ran away from him I got into some kind of trouble. I got picked out in the street at 123rd Street, and this man said that I have given him a holdup with two colored boys. I swear to God that I was not guilty. Johnnie left those kids to come after me, and the only way I could save my life was to run away, so I did. I never went back home. If I knew that I was gonna lose my kids, I would have let Johnnie kick me and cut me up. A week later I had to go back to court, and they found me guilty. Plus Johnnie had sent a letter into court, 'cause he knew that I was gonna be sentenced. He said that I have left my children alone, and that's a lie! Because he was the one babysitting; he was the one that left the children alone!

So the judge told me, Carmen, you're not guilty, and I was going to give you a break, 'cause I believe your story, I believe that you did not steal from this man. But young lady, since you cannot take care of your kids, and you left your children alone, I think you better go into the House of Detention. It's the best thing for you.

And I begged the judge. I told him the same story that I'm telling you people now. But the judge believed my husband instead.

So since I went to jail, my husband moved to Brooklyn with his mother. And instead of giving my children to my mother to keep for me, he told my mother to tell me that he was gonna put the kids away in a home. I told my mother, tell Johnnie I'll go back with him, but beg him not to put the kids in a home. 'Cause Johnnie was always crying for me to go back with him, and I never gave him a break. This time, I think I made the biggest mistake of my life. I should have at least told him, when I went to jail, wait for me, honey, I'll go back with you, forgive me for all the wrong I have done to you—even though I have done nothing to him. A week later my mother gave me the bad news: Carmen, Johnnie put the two girls in the home and he gave his mother the baby boy.

Now, tell me why a man put his own two little girls in a

home and give to his mother my baby boy, the one that I almost died giving birth to? (*Weeps.*) That's the thing that has broken my heart so much, and that's why I came back to using drugs. I had to even if I don't want to—I miss my children a lot. . . . (*Breaking down.*) I miss them, I miss them, please help me, please. . . .

I believe in God. I *know*, from my own good heart, that I did not leave my children alone. I know I'm going back to court as soon as I find out the address where Johnnie's staying with my child, and I'm going to take that child. I *know* I'm going to get him by the court's rights, I know it. That's why I want to break my drug habit. I'm tired of thinking already whether I should break my habit or not. I decided I'm going to break it for good; this time I mean it. I'm twenty-five years old and I made up my mind: never again! I'd rather get drunk, fall down in my face—but I never touch drugs again, so help me God! As long as I live! I'll be glad (*weeping*), I can't wait to get to the hospital. I'll be so glad!

You don't know what it is to be able to get up in the morning. I'll get up from the bed, and I'll get inside the bathroom, I'll be able to wash my face, wash my teeth, be able to sit in the kitchen and eat with my children and my mother. You know what that is? Now, that I'm in the habit, I cannot do those things. Why? Because if I don't get a shot of drug in these lousy veins that I have, I cannot wash my face, comb my hair, clean myself. I got to get a shot of drugs first—then I could get a bath. Ain't that something?

Without a habit, I could do anything. Sometimes I used to get up early in the morning singing in my house, and eat two or three plates of cornflakes, because I love cornflakes a lot. But now I can't eat until after I shoot up.

I was in the House of Detention five months. It wasn't hard to kick, because I didn't have a big habit at the time. I was taking goofballs, and instead of drinking them down, I was shooting them up in the vein.

Before that, before I left Johnnie, my father drove me down to Lexington, Kentucky. I was there nine days, and they shipped me back, because I was ready to have my baby. They didn't get the telegram my father send telling them, please don't send her back by herself—keep her there and wait for us to drive back and pick her up. When I got back to New York, instead of going from the subway to my mother's house, I went to Ridge Street to a basement, and there I was using drugs. I got my first shot as soon as I got there. I met this boy and he told me, man, you look sick. I said, me look sick? I kicked my habit. I was nine days in Lexington, Kentucky. So he says, you don't look it, man. I say, well, you got anything for me? He says, you know, baby, we got anything you need.

You know why they said that to me? Because they knew that I didn't have a big habit, and they wanted to start me on the habit again, so they could get my clothes, my jewels, money, things that I would have to steal. That's why they give it to me free. That's what they do to junkies. Sometimes we junkies are so stupid that we don't stop to think.

I stood out three days in the street, hiding. I was hiding in a basement, and somebody tip off the police. I was cleaning the needle, and that's how I got busted. My husband felt sorry for me, and he got me a lawyer, and the lawyer got me six months' suspended sentence. Mainly because I was nine months pregnant, and it was the very first time I was in that kind of trouble with the police.

So I was in jail three days, and I went straight from the court to my father's house. My husband and I were so happy we both started crying.

Two days later I woke up in bed and it felt like I was having a miscarriage. When I put my two feet on the floor, half of the afterbirth came out. I screamed, and I ran to my father, because I have more confidence with my father than with my own mother. How you like that? Instead of talking to my mother about things that are very personal, woman-to-woman, I talk to my father. He rushed me over to the hospital, and there they told him that I was gonna die. They asked him if he was sure that I had broken my habit.

In the hospital they were giving me a lot of medicines, liquids. They didn't give me no drugs, because I told them I did not want no drugs. They said, well don't you need it? I said, I got it in my mind to use it, but I don't want my baby to die. So I don't want no drug, please. If the baby comes out with a habit, then you give him what he deserve. Then you cut him off, slowly. But meantime, I don't want no stuff.

I stood in Bellevue Hospital for a week, then the doctor told me that the baby should have been born already, that he would die in the stomach unless he was taken out. And he said, we can not open you up, because you got varicose veins in your stomach. So they could not do nothing for me. They left me without food for two days, giving me the medicine to push the baby down.

They rushed me to the delivery room, but I had a hard time having the baby. I had labor pains, yes, but the baby wasn't coming out. The doctor starting pressing on my stomach and nothing happened.

Next thing I know a female doctor comes in. She put her whole hand inside where the baby has to come out, and she started *pulling* him out with her hand. Because she didn't want me to die: she says that the baby was dead, and there was no heartbeat.

She had a hard time pulling the baby out. She didn't use no forceps or nothing, she only used her hands. She finally got the baby out completely. Then the half of the afterbirth that I had left inside of me was pasted to my stomach. And boy she put her hand in there and she started scrubbing so I could feel her fingers on the inside of my stomach! I was kicking her so hard I knocked all the bottles on the floor.

But she's so strong, and I'm glad she was strong, that even though I was kicking her in the face, she kept on holding me with her left hand and the right hand was right inside my stomach and she brought all that out. She says, I know this is killing you, Carmen, but I got to do it: it's your life.

Meanwhile a Japanese female doctor was fighting for my son's life. My son was born dead, and they gave him life. She took blood from the cord, and gave him four shots, two shots in each leg—one shot in the big toe and one in each heel. The baby started moving a little bit, and that's when she put her mouth to his mouth, and she gave him life.

They brought me the priest, and they let my husband come into the delivery room. I was dying, so they let my husband come in to tell me the last words. Look how stupid he is: the doctors didn't tell me I was dying, so he tells me. You know what that stupid guy tells me? Aw, you ain't gonna die —stop making believe you're sick! Come on, come on, be a woman, be strong! He says, I begged them to let me come in here, because I heard you were dying.

I said, no, baby, I'm not gonna die. You're the one that's gonna die, not me.

Man, I fought for my life! They brought me the priest and he said blah blah blah blah, the last words, and they were gonna cover my face because I black out and they thought I was dead already.

So that's my life.

The prostitutes that don't use drugs, if they don't get a man to go out with them, it's easy; they go straight home. If the police is around, they go straight home. But we drug addicts that hustle, we have to stay in the street all night till we get our money.

Those girls that are not drug addicts that are prostitutes have an easier way of living than we drug addicts do. If they don't make no money, they can go right back to bed, with no complaints or nothing. Unless the pimps are bad, and are the kind of men that want their woman to get them a certain amount. Sometimes these girls that I know can't go home unless they get thirty-five or forty dollars a night. If they go back to their pimps with fifteen dollars, the pimps beat them up. They probably have to go out with six or seven mens.

Mostly all of them have pimps. The pimp does no work at all; he just sits in the restaurant, reading a comic book or a newspaper or talking to his friends. Or they'll stay in a bar, drinking the money that these womens are making. They have an easy life. If somebody wants to take the money away from the womens after they have laid down in the bed with them, the woman will start running to where the pimp is waiting, and he'll go out and get this man to give her the money, and if the man doesn't produce the money, he'll beat him up.

Sometimes I hear girls talking to each other, saying, man, I gotta get my husband forty-five dollars tonight, because if I don't get it, I cannot go home. No matter if I stay out till six in the morning, if I go home without it, he'll knock the shit out of me.

ELEVEN DAYS LATER, AFTER LEAVING HOSPITAL

I CAME out because of the changing of the rooms, the foods, and some of the girls. Last night, for instance, I was woken up by the noise that these two girls were making in the bed. They were having a sexual relationship with each other, and they woke me up. I was kept up all night, till four o'clock in the morning.

This bed was very close to mine. When they were moving, they were moving my bed also. They were trying to cover themselves, and they would put the covers on me, too.

It was the first night I was supposed to sleep in that room —I was sleeping in another room before. The girl next to me lent her bed to her Lesbian friend, and she was the lookout while her Lesbian friend was taking care of business with what they call "the woman." It must have been about one or two o'clock that they woke me up. At four o'clock, the one whose bed it was said, oh oh, the nurse is coming, and they all started combing their hair and they disappeared.

I get along with Lesbians fine. I know a couple of them. Matter of fact, I was the wife of one of them one time. It's terrible. No, no, no, I can't describe it. I don't even remember about it. It was so disgusting, you know, that I even took it out of my mind. It was only one or two days, that's all.

Another thing: they were using drugs in the hospital, so I figure if I'm going to be there to kick a habit and have drugs around me, I might as well go and kick in my house or go into another hospital. There's some teenage girls there, and older women, too—they stole a syringe from the doctors' room, and they also stole a needle. They make a phone call, and a girl would come in and bring stuff and works. They should examine the people before they come upstairs.

When I heard them talking about it, I said, look, baby, how can I get some stuff in here? She told me, I don't want to get this man in trouble, he's the one that gets it for me. She didn't want me to know who he was. She said, I don't want him to lose his job. After all, he's only mopping the floor.

This girl was named Julia. She told me he was one of her tricks, and she didn't want to lose him. The nurses in the daytime, they don't care what happens there. They just stay in the office, and the only time they come out is when somebody is arguing, or when somebody gets really sick and pass out on the floor. I have seen that when the man that mops goes in the side of the young girls' ward, one or two girls will come to the phone. Well, instead of talking to the phone, they're looking to the nurses' office, and if somebody gonna be coming this way, you know she'll say, Julia! And then a few minutes later, you'll see him making with his mop. He spends a great deal of time back there.

Instead of keeping an eye on the people, the nurses just sit all day in the office. You should see how filthy the girls keep the place! The nurses' aides are there to clean it, why can't they pick up the cups, ashtrays, everything on the floor? It's a very nasty place.

The food is cold, like a pig's food. The food you give a pig in Puerto Rico is better than the food you get over there. They think just because you're a drug addict you aren't used to eating good food.

I went home and I saw my mother ironing. I took the iron away from her and I started doing it. It was about three years that I didn't take an iron in my hands. I was ironing my daughter's bloomers, and she says, Mommy, what are you doing? You're doing it better than Mommy!

She says, how come you're doing this? You love me?

I say, I love you; that's the reason I'm doing it.

Tells me, that's good. And then, oh Mommy, how come you're here? Ain't you supposed to be in the hospital?

I say, I'm going back Monday. I came here to say good-bye, because I'm gonna stay in the hospital a long time this time.

She says, will you come to live with us? You gonna stay here tonight, Mommy?

I say, yes.

She started laughing, and she say, you're a good mommy if you stay here.

I came down to go to see you, and on my way I met Billy, the boy that I asked you to help him, and he went into the hospital, and yesterday he signed himself out. He said, Carmen, come over here—don't be mad because I signed out of the hospital!

I say, look, you put my word in the gutter with Mr. T. After all that he has done for you and me, you put my word on the floor, and make him waste his time for nothing.

As we were coming down Delancey Street, walking to see you, three detectives in a car looked at us, and I say, Billy, you got anything on you?

He says, no, Carmen. And then I see that he started shaking, and I say, I know; you got your works on you.

I didn't even say the last word when they thum! got off the car and said, come on, where you people going? What's your name?

One started speaking to me and two of them started speaking to him. Then I said, look, if you're gonna search my coat or something, take me in a hallway, please. There's too many people passing around here. And I don't got nothing on me.

But I didn't figure that they were going to take my brassiere off, and take all my clothes off in the hallway!

Two of them were talking to Billy, and the other one told me to take my shoes off and shake them. I say, you shake them. He tells me, don't get wise. Or else we'll take you to the precinct. I didn't want to go to no precinct, because I had to come to get these papers to get into the hospital. And since I wasn't doing nothing wrong and didn't have nothing on me, I told him, all right, go ahead.

He tells me, take your drawers off. He did that twice. First he made me take my panties off, and then he push me to the dark place in the hallway. So then he pull my panties down and he started searching. That's why I was so mad.

He says, why are you mad? You told us to search you!

I say, I didn't know you were gonna search me this way. Why don't you take me to the precinct?

He says, if I take you to the precinct, young lady, you gonna be locked up.

So I got scared. So I let them do anything they wanted. Plus I didn't want to get hurt, 'cause they were hitting Billy.

He undressed me entirely, piece by piece. He put his hands inside my brassiere, and touching my behind and all that, inside my shirt . . . oh God! I was fricking in that hallway! And they did the same thing to Billy. And when they found works on him, then they got more mad, and they started hitting him. That's when the other guy started searching me and wanted to take me to jail.

But one of the other guys says, look, you guys should be satisfied. You got him with a pair of works, right? Take the guy in, let the woman go. You know what she says, her kid's coming home. Why don't you give her a break? I can tell when a person's lying—I know she's not lying. And even the boy said she did not know he had the works on him.

I told him, thank you, and he said, don't let me catch you around this neighborhood, that's all. So I told him, what should I do? Jump in the river or something?

Henry Muller & Philip Kean

MULLER: My brother and I come up in a neighborhood where quite a few people smoked opium and thought it was smart. The way I got hooked was a madam put me on to smoke opium. It was outlawed, but they had quite a few smoking parlors in 1929, '30, and '31. Then it got to be real under-cover. But at the time, opium was quite popular.

At the time I'm talking about, most of the Oriental people were smoking opium. I don't believe I've ever met a Chinese person who was taking heroin. I've never smoked opium alone; it was always in the company of several fellas and girls. They used to sell it in what the Chinese call "toys." They'd give you a tin that was a little smaller than a tin of salve, and it weighed exactly twelve "fun." I think a fun is equivalent to a grain. Two or three of those tins would be enough for four or five people to smoke. In those years it was much cheaper than it is today. In the early 1930's it was three toys for five dollars.

KEAN: I started smoking opium in Miami, Florida, in 1933. Opium was not used by too many people at that time. When I started using it, it was just like a party. Instead of dancing we enjoyed ourselves just lying on the hip, and we'd have different sweets around. An opium party would take at least four hours. In the early 1930's it was inexpensive, and a pleasant evening. We'd pay three dollars for a small tin, and three people could smoke an evening. Later on, by 1936, there was a shortage of opium and the price went to six dollars a tin. Then during the war years opium was selling for about eighteen dollars a tin. It became hard to get opium in the United States, and the price continued to rise. When it got over twenty dollars, a lot of people couldn't afford it, and so they had to change either to morphine or heroin, which was plentiful at the time and much cheaper. As the years went on, the opium smokers kept diminishing. The last I heard, about three or four years ago, the price had risen to anywhere from thirty-five to fifty dollars for the tin we used to pay three for. So addicts had to find other methods that would be cheaper and less time-consuming.

Years ago we used to use a pipe made out of cherrywood. It was usually imported from the Orient, and the bowl was made out of clay. It was a whole process. There had to be somebody preparing it, and he was called the chef, and he would have to cook each pill individually over a flame, and then insert it in the center of the bowl. But it became dangerous to have a pipe around, because in case there was any trouble with the law, a pipe would be hard to destroy. They were practically unbreakable. So in order to insure ourselves, we used to make makeshift pipes out of a medicine bottle and a glass drinking tube.

Opium originally looks like dirt, but it's cooked down, and through a process the finished opium looks something like axle grease, but darker in color, a real dark brownish-black, with a gummy texture. To make a pill, you'd have to take a little bit on the end of a metal crochet needle and hold it over a flame. The flame would make it expand like bubble-gum, and finally it could be worked into a hard pellet which could be fitted into the pipe.

MULLER: Commissioner Anslinger says there's twenty to thirty thousand addicts in New York City. I don't think Mr. Anslinger knows what he's talking about. He took that census while he was asleep. Certain areas of six square blocks on the Lower East Side or in Harlem could fill his estimate up. There are probably fifty thousand addicts in colored Harlem alone. He's way off.

KEAN: The way I look at it, in order for a man to be a drug addict, you have to have the money to buy it. And most people, especially the youngsters, find it very hard to get a steady source of supply. Very few people today can get the supply and make the money to support a genuine habit. Most of these kids that Mr. Anslinger calls addicts are too young to be able to earn the money to be addicts—they're just users. And the heroin today is cut down so weak that it would take a whole lot of it to make an addict. In other words, I believe that maybe seven out of every ten individuals that Mr. Anslinger calls a drug addict have a *mind* addiction. I know that when I was using heroin, I had to have the same amount every day, which at today's prices would cost over thirty dollars a day and not be as strong as what I used to get for three dollars. So if a man buys only five dollars' worth at a time and doesn't know where his next five dollars is coming from, how can he be a drug addict? I would call it a man with a weak mind. It's mind over matter.

MULLER: Most of the kids who are addicted get their money by boosting from department stores. The department stores take quite a beating. We should get them interested in opening a clinic: it would save them maybe ten million dollars a year.

KEAN: But these characters that have to resort to petty thievery in order to support their habits cannot support them for any length of time, because they spend more time in jail than they do out. It doesn't make for a true drug addict, like there was twenty years ago. Before narcotics became so expensive.

The federal government has taken means now to make narcotics hard to get, which makes the price go up. Years ago, they did not have federal agents in other countries to try to stop the flow of narcotics. In fact the Treasury Department had very few agents on duty even in a big city like New York. But the latest reports that I know are that the Treasury Department has tripled or quadrupled its force within the last ten years. The city department used to have only forty men; today they have two hundred on a separate narcotics squad. And with the radio cars and walkie-talkies, they can take care of things much faster.

MULLER: Anslinger treats the addict as a criminal—that's his policy. He hasn't made one recommendation that agrees with any public health officer or doctor or churches or social workers or business people that have written him or gone to see him. He would never even look into the possibility that addicts might be looked on as alcoholics are. He's only interested in longer prison terms. All the articles he's written are inhuman, but the public is so unaware that they really believe a lot of the stories that he has come up with that have been utterly false. You wouldn't have enough tape on this recording to correct the false statements Anslinger has made.

KEAN: Mr. Anslinger treats addiction like a criminal problem instead of a health problem. He couldn't possibly treat it otherwise, because if it were treated like a health problem, there wouldn't be no need for Mr. Anslinger and his thousands of men! Drug addicts get stiffer sentences than other types of criminals. In fact, a bank robber doesn't get the sentence an addict would get if he was convicted a number of times with a reasonable amount of narcotics.

MULLER: Can you show me anything that has ever worked out when treated with brute force?

KEAN: When a man is incarcerated for a number of years, as I have been, you get to have a hatred towards the whole world. Far from helping the addict to get cured, prison builds up a resentment, and as soon as he gets out, the addict doesn't wait one day to use more narcotics.

I'm fifty years old and I've been on narcotics twenty-eight years. I've been arrested four or five times, and I probably spent a total of nine or ten years in prison. Which was totally uncalled-for. It didn't give me any help. The incarceration just built up a resentment, whereas if I had gotten psychiatric treatment in those nine or ten years, or hospitalization, it would have had far more effect. I was incarcerated with the toughest and roughest criminals in the country, people who were doing time for murder and major crimes, and the only thing I was guilty of was having a bottle of medicine. It was only through luck that I only did nine or ten years; if I wasn't able to pay high lawyers' fees, I probably would have had to do fifteen or twenty.

MULLER: I was last in The Tombs in 1953, and strange as it may seem, you was better off telling them you was not an addict. Then, if you did get a headache, you could get a couple of aspirins.

The Tombs are still quite vivid in my imagination. The first thing that happens when you get there is that you're told to take a shower, which I don't understand, because it's the filthiest place—it's a rat-hole. Now usually you were arrested the day before and you're already beginning to show withdrawal symptoms. After you take your shower, you see the doctor. You must stand eight to ten feet away from him. I don't know what he's afraid he'll catch from an addict, but he must be afraid of something. He prescribes no medication at all for you. His favorite expression is well, you'll come around soon; just lay down and get a lot of rest.

You were taken to a floor—either the fourth or the eighth. You're given a thorough searching, you receive two dirty blankets, and you're assigned to a cell. Each cell has one bunk and is assigned two men. One sleeps on the floor and one sleeps on the bunk. There's no mattress on the bunk, just a spring. If it's the dead of winter and you want to cover yourself with the blanket, you got to make that spring all night. If you want to use the blanket as a mattress, you go without covering.

The place is alive with mice. They run around in droves. It's not an uncommon sight to see fifty of them dash into your cell.

The average drug addict gets on the floor with the blankets, because you go into a horrible state of twitching when you kick cold turkey, with vomiting and diarrhea. You're afraid to lay on the bunk, because you might twitch right off the bunk and land on your head on the concrete floor. For someone who's really addicted, it's twenty to twenty-five days before he'll come around to where he realizes two or three hours' sleep at night. Your nerves are so taut that sleep is impossible, unless medication is given you. You lay anywhere from twelve to thirty days on the floor, mostly without food. Personally I once ate nothing for fifteen days, not even a drop of water. You don't even care to smoke a cigarette. You're sick.

When I was there, they got you out of your cell three hours a day. But it's pretty hard for a person sick to get out of his cell. And there's no place to sit; you have to stand up— that's how crowded it was.

Now the fourth floor of The Tombs, half of it is for drug addicts and half of it is for so-called alcoholics and bums— that's the term that they use. They pick them up and keep them there overnight and the next day they ship them to Riker's Island with their six-day sentences, ten-day sentences, or what have you. Try to picture this. There's two in a cell on the drug addicts' side, with one bunk, and one man on the floor and one in the bunk sleeping. Friday night is the general roundup that the police make in New York; on the East Side in Forsythe Street Park and Christie Street and The Bowery, they must pick up three thousand alcoholics and derelicts. They're brought to night court, they receive their sentences, and all these alcoholics and derelicts are brought to the fourth floor of The Tombs. They line them up on the tier and the guard pushes as many as he can into one cell— never less than four. So one makes it on the bed, one makes it underneath the bed, one on the terlet seat, one on the floor and maybe one on the table where they put the food. Now it's nothing for them to put six or seven in a cell. After they fill up all these cells on one side, which they usually do every weekend, they bring them over to the addicts' side. And they put three more in the cell where there's already two addicts.

So there's a man sick, suffering from withdrawal, and now he has three more men, usually dead drunk, coming out of a stupor or going into the DT's. Now I'm not against these men; in fact I feel sorry for them. But they derive a better break than the addict, because the addict can't even get an aspirin. But the derelict or the alcoholic can tell the doctor he's got the shakes and they'll give him a drink of paralde-hyde, which knocks him out for a few hours. The addict is not allowed this and he's not allowed anything.

I've been in The Tombs six and a half months, waiting for my case to come up in court. Sometimes you wait to get your charge reduced to a misdemeanor, or to get an understand-ing judge. Sometimes justice works very slow, and you have to spend a number of months there in order to save yourself a few years. You see, if you have over fifty-six grains it's a felony, because you're not just using, they think you're push-ing. But a judge ought to understand that almost any addict, if he has the money, would buy a little extra for himself on a weekend, say. With an addict, it's 365 days a year. There's no holiday. But you could get five to ten years for felonious possession, just because you tried to use common sense by buying more at one time and taking fewer chances on getting arrested. Now an understanding judge knows that having one-eighth of an ounce doesn't necessarily mean you're sell-ing. The average addict uses more than that each day, but he has to continually go to buy every few hours.

KEAN: As long as I'm fixed up, work is as normal as any-thing else. I've been on dilaudids now for three years. The heroin now is very weak and pretty expensive and it wears off faster. When the pushers get it they try to make a big profit by diluting it with so much sugar-milk that you need about five five-dollar bags to get high. To get high on dilaudids, it cost you maybe six dollars, seven dollars for four pills. I find that it's cheaper and much better. Yes, they have to be prescribed by a doctor, but you can get them on the black market from certain pushers who also handle heroin.

I used this vein once for two months and I thought it was starting to get infected. It started to pus up on me, so I put a little iodine on it. It'll probably leave a deep mark that will stay on a lifetime. What you see on my left arm is a vein that I haven't used for five years. It's dead now and can't be used anymore.

MULLER: This is quite funny. An addict has veins running all through his arms and legs and could hit anywhere, but he'll stick to one certain spot and never change. Now Phil here, as you can easily see, has all types of good veins. He hasn't even used his pit, which is what they call the original mainline to the heart and one of the best veins to hit. Even though it's near abscess, he'll stick to that same spot. For no reason—just that he's been hitting there. (*Laughs.*) That's his lucky spot.

Strange as it is, that's the way with most addicts. I've known addicts that leave a little blood-mark where they hit. They get a good hit, so they hit on the same spot. If they continually hit there, they'll eventually have a little scab, and they'll shoot right through it.

An addict is also in danger of getting infections from a dirty needle. They can get an abscess, which is quite painful. When the needle is not cleaned out good, and three-four people are shooting from the same needle, you can get a little bit of someone else's blood, and you'll go into a violent seizure of chills and shake all over. Then there's always the chance of catching yellow jaundice, or syphilis, or any disease of the blood.

About the various detoxification programs, let me state this for the record. I've been in the hospital in Lexington, Kentucky, the so-called hospital; I've been to private doctors and three-four different private sanitariums; and I can say that the detoxification program that they have right now at Manhattan General is the best program that I ever saw. Money couldn't get you a better program. Everyone tries to be helpful, from the porter up to the head doctor. They withdraw you very slowly, which is about the only chance the addict has of not tearing his nerves apart. They give you methadon four times at night, with a big dosage of sedation after the night shot, so you can sleep. And if you still can't sleep after you've tried, the nurse will give you more sedation. There's no such thing as leaving when you're still sick. The head doctor is a wonderful man; he'll go all the way with you. He doesn't worry how long you stay there. And they try to fix it so that an older person like myself will get a slow withdrawal, because the recuperative powers of a younger person are much stronger.

Why did I start taking narcotics? I believe I took it because I was bored. I really liked it in my younger days, but as you get older you realize there isn't anything to it; because once you're hooked, you're only taking it to be normal. Nobody today could afford the price to be high.

Mrs. Greenberg

I SIGNED him into the hospital and I told him he'll be all right there. But they took him off the drug and he lost himself altogether. He didn't know what he was doing; he fell outa bed two times. That was last month—when he had yellow jaundice. When we signed him into Bellevue Hospital.

When I came to visit him, he was crying and crying and crying and crying. He says, Ma, does it pay? Look at all the trouble I got for nothing. Does it pay?

I said, well, you wanted it that way. The way you wanted it, that's how you have it.

So the next visit I made with him, he was fine. He looked nice and clean. I says, I'm begging you, when you come home, you'll feel good, you're in the hospital—they try for you, you'll feel good, don't go back to this. Promise me, don't go back to this.

He says, oh, I never felt so good in my life. He gained a nice couple pounds.

I came to visit him again and he was fine, but I saw in his eyes that he wants to get out already. He wants to make his way out in the worst way. He was okay, but I see he was depressed already. He says, Ma, I'm gonna go home this week. I says, take your time. You had so much trouble. You just come waking up from a dream. Take your time. He says okay, okay.

The next day I was getting ready to visit him, and somebody ring the bell. I opened the door and almost fainted. I seen him coming in, and right away he had this dope already, in his body. He had a little radio, he sold it. Right away he was already not himself.

From then on, every single day. Every single day he wouldn't go away till I give him the five dollars. Otherwise he was looking something to sell from the house. I couldn't go down. I was so sick.

Then he went away and he came back late at night. He start off two times a day, three times a day. He came back and he couldn't walk on his feet. He was sitting in the bathroom and I ask him, what are you doing in there? I was afraid he's gonna fall down unconscious.

He says, Ma, you know what I do. I'm using the dope, he says. I'm using the dope. You know, you ought get used to it by this time.

I want to do this, he says. I feel good, I feel good. He says, you know, I'll go away soon. You wouldn't have me no more. I don't care what happens to me, he says. I want to forget what's gonna come over my head; I want to forget everything.

His eyes close completely; he could hardly talk. You can't understand. I ask him every time, what are you talking?

What are you talking? I don't understand one word you're talking! I don't know what's wrong with you!

He says, oh, you you you, you know what I'm talking about. But I couldn't understand one word. He was delirious, like. Sleeping and waking up and looking around and falling asleep again. He burned everything in the house: the floors, the tables, everything what's in the house he used to burn with cigarettes.

He wasn't sleeping; he was just dozing, like. He used to watch television, and everytime I used to shake him and say are you sleeping, he says no. He wouldn't go to bed till early in the morning. As soon as he woke up, before he ate anything yet, right away he went down to look for the dope. And that's the life he led. That's all.

I couldn't do nothing, I couldn't do nothing with him. Nothing. I talked, and I cried, and I tear my hair out from my head, I bang my head with the fists. I couldn't take it; I couldn't look on this boy. —What are you doing to yourself? Look what you're doing to me! Look what you're doing to your sister! Look how many times you went off, you can go right back; what's the matter with you? Nothing helped, nothing helped, nothing helped.

I went to Chicago and I saw what that boy did, I wanted to throw myself down fourteen floors. I started to cry. I says, why don't you do something about it? Because I'm going to kill myself. What happened to you? You live in a different world, you don't know your mother no more!

That was about three years ago. He went to Chicago to get away from it. He was trying for a little while. But after he came to New York for a little visit, he started all over again. When he went back to Chicago, he made his way to find it; he was riding around all over till he got it. Then he started off again, he started!

He was living with his brother, and his brother didn't

want to tell me anything about it. He didn't want to aggravate me. He said, Ma, everything is fine, he's working, he's making money, and he looks good and everything. But when I went out there and I saw what happened, I wanted to kill myself!

So he made a promise that he'll go for a cure. The boss didn't know. So my boy, the bigger one, told the boss what was happening. So the boss said, if you'll go for the cure, as your mother said, I'll take you back to work. So he went.

He got there, in Lexington, Kentucky, he was there about two days. He came back to Chicago. He came back and the boss wouldn't take him back no more to work. So he came home.

They liked him so much. They liked him, he was a good boy, he worked. But what good is it? He spent every nickel he made. His brother almost had consumption from him, the way he looked. He took money from his brother. He took money from everybody. His brother couldn't take it no more. So he sent him home to me. And since he's home, I got the troubles! *I* got it.

My husband gave him a job, to keep him occupied, but what did he do? He lend money from all the customers. He didn't return the money. He made such a mess that my husband had to give back every cent. And he had to go off the job.

My husband gets up twelve o'clock, one o'clock in the night and eighteen–twenty hours he works. He got my son a job where he worked. The bosses liked him, they did everything for him, to make him happy. But the more he earned, the more he spent. He used to go away with the truck to deliver, and he never showed up. They were losing customers. The customers would start to call in—where's the boy? Where's the chickens? We need to sell them and we haven't got the merchandise! They couldn't keep him no more.

So he made a promise he'd go to Kentucky last winter. So I sent him away to Kentucky, he was there three weeks, I had to send him a hundred dollars carfare to come back. When he came back, he couldn't work no more. Since he came back I supported him.

Some of the money disappeared from his job. He took $150 from my daughter to give back to the bosses, because he was afraid for his father's job. You know, they was missing the money. The customers said they paid him the bills, and the bills wasn't there.

He got worse—the more money he got, the more he used. If he didn't have the money, he used less. If he had money, he needed thirty dollars a day. From twenty to thirty dollars a day he needed the last coupla weeks. I don't care no more, he said. I don't care what happens to me. That's all.

Since he came out from Bellevue Hospital, he ate much better. He drank a lot of milk, and he ate ice cream, he ate cake, and sometimes he ate supper, and a sandwich or something. And he picked up a couple of bucks. And he dressed himself a little better. He has nice clothes—I had to hide his clothes! In a different house I put away his suits and the jackets; I hide his golden cuff-buttons; I hide everything from him, he shouldn't be able to sell it. But still he left me a couple of pawn tickets, I had to take it out.

I had a portable radio, he sold it. That's all, I think. I didn't give him the chance. I was watching. I didn't go out of the house, I was like a prisoner. Once I went out of the house, he came looking for me, he took the key. I was ashamed—I was sitting in the street, in the park, and I was ashamed to say to my own child, I don't want to give you the key. I gave him the key, but I had to pick myself up and run right back there, upstairs. So what do I find? I find a couple of friends, and they stick the needles in them! And that's what he did.

Sick sick sick, all the time I'm sick from that boy. I'm very sick. My condition is no good. I used to go to the doctor once in a while, but since I have him home, nothing, nothing matters. I don't care what happens to me. I don't go to no doctor, I don't check up, and now I'm sick! That's all, I don't care for nothing. I'm sick. Nothing matters. (*Weeping.*)

He wouldn't eat. I bought, I bought the best. Other children staying in the street, they would wish to have a home like he had! A beautiful house and nice food and I had steak for him and everything, but he didn't eat. The last couple of months I didn't even prepare for him. I used to prepare for him when he was working, but before you turned around he disappeared.

He only wanted to drink drink drink drink, sodas sodas soda, ice cream. It burned him and burned him and burned him—and he used to throw up a lots of times. And he used to have headaches, and he used to feel miserable, miserable. And toothaches—they pulled almost all his teeth out. He has no more teeth left. What a beautiful boy he was! What a beautiful boy! What happened to him, he lives in a different world. Nothing bothers him no more. Nothing bothers him. I could stretch out on the floor and drop dead. He wouldn't care, he wouldn't care!

Sometimes he used to say, Ma, forget about me, live your own life, forget about me. I'm dead to you. (*Bursts into tears.*) Take care of yourself. You got two children to live for, what do you need me? You got a grandson to take care of, what do you need me? Forget about me! (*She cries through this story.*)

Someday he says, Ma, you think I have no feelings? I have feelings, too, he says. But I can't help myself. I understand what you go through. But what can I do, what can I do?

I says, what are you doing to yourself? If it's so good let me try it, too!

He says, yeah? I'll cut your both arms off before you'll do it!

I says, you went through so much. Why don't you stop it? You went off it so many times.

He says, you wouldn't understand. You wouldn't understand this. You can't stop never, he says. Never. You can't stop this. It's like cancer! Could you cure cancer? That's how you can cure this.

So what can I do? I gave him my whole life already. Now I'm sick and broken and old. And that's what happened to me.

I don't know where I failed. I did everything I could for him. I cooked, I watched him, I gave him whatever he said. Whatever he want, I gave it to him. I don't know why he started this here.

He says, Ma, if I would know, he says, I don't know myself. Some children, they got control, they don't do this; and some children, they talk it into them. So they do it. He does it to show off, I think. Nothing missing to him, was nothing missing to him. Because he was the youngest and I gave him everything. Whatever he want, I bought him, I gave him. But I think he did it because he had it too good. That's the whole thing: he had it too good. That's why he did it.

You know, they say when you have it too good you slide on the ice and you break the leg. You don't know what to do with yourself.

He got on when they throw me out from the projects. I lived in the projects, and his brother started to work, and they said it's too much money, you have to move, you have to move. But I didn't have where to move, they didn't care, they throw me out from the projects. I had to move away in Brooklyn which I was never there in my life, and that boy was fifteen years old, and he was very much depressed. The neighborhood with his friends he missed, and they didn't care. He came running here to New York, and I didn't know where he was, and that's when he started it. I couldn't go after him—I was in Brooklyn and he was here. He was here all hours at night; I didn't know what he was doing here and that's what he was doing. When he used to live here, if I didn't see him I used to run out and look for him all over till I found him. He never stood away long; he used to come in, take something to eat, listen to the radio, he was sitting in the house: he was a happy boy! But when they threw me out of the projects, that's when he started it all!

My husband didn't butt in too much. He went his way, and I took care on the family. Whatever he gave me I was satisfied, and I made the best of it. The other children used to work part-time after school.

My husband didn't bother too much. He had his own business to tend; he didn't care too much. If I told him something, he started to beat them without a stop. He wasn't doing the right thing. He didn't go the right way about it. He never was friendly with them, never. He never talked to a child; he never was interested when they were sick; he never took interest in them. No. He worked hard, it was true—he came home, he went right to sleep. And that's all. He worked long hours and it didn't bother him nothing! Nothing bothered him. I did everything. I was a mother, I was a father, I was everything. I won't say it don't hurt him now—he's much older, he realizes what he did, and he would like to make it up to them. But it's too late.

The other one went away, he was nineteen years old. He didn't care no more for the house, he's not interested to come back any more. And my daughter is glad she got married. She met a very nice man, she's married, and she's out of the house. But naturally she's very depressed, because of the life I lead with the two of them. Between my husband and the boy, that's what kills her too. She's very run down with the shame; she has a lot of trouble from us. She has it very good for herself, but she has trouble from us. She begged me, she said, Ma, come to me, stay with me. I can't go, I have no strength to travel in. The husband wanted to pick me up with the car, but I couldn't go. I was there last week two days and I didn't close my eyes. I couldn't sleep in a strange house, even if it's my own child. She tried her best for me.

Now I live in the International, in the Co-op. I have a good apartment, but what good is it, if I have troubles like this? It's no good to me.

My husband, he made a hit. He gave me I should maybe invest it for a house. But I knew a house is no good for me; I'm a little older and I can't fix nothing, my husband don't fix nothing. I says I have a good place for this money. I'll invest it for rooms. Any time I move out, I can get my money back, and I'll have a nice apartment. Which he didn't care. He says do whatever you want. Whatever you do I'm satisfied.

He wanted the money back anyway, but I didn't care. I says if you want the money back, I won't live with you. If you want a divorce, I'll divorce you. But I wouldn't take the money out for all the money in the world.

I think he made the money in a crap game. He never gave me before, never. But he got crazy that night I guess, and he wanted to make it up to me. For all the times what he caused me miseries and troubles, he wanted to make it up. He says, I know you're not happy here, so it's better this way. He likes it too; it's a very nice apartment. I could have fixed it up like a palace with all the money that I spent for that boy. And now I can't.

I don't know what's gonna happen when he comes out. That's the whole thing. I wouldn't mind if he'd stay there at least three years, I don't know maybe the neighborhood will change. And maybe he'll come out, he'll get a little job, he'll be older, he'll realize. . . . But if he'll come out in one year, he'll go right back to it, I won't live through to see that.

The sentence is one to three years—it's according to how he'll behave. But I know he'll behave, he's a good child. He listens, he gets along with everybody, he's a very good boy. But as soon as he comes out. . . .

I had him off this here summer! Two and a half months he was off it! He gained about twenty-five pounds; he looked so beautiful. A girl fell in love with him in the country. She wanted to go, but you know, I couldn't butt in, I couldn't tell her nothing, he couldn't tell her nothing. He says, Ma, what's the use? I have to stand trial, he says. It's no sense getting involved with a girl. And everything was all right, and, when we came home from the country, soon as I walked off the car, before he walked upstairs he went to see his friends already, and he got a drug. Before he walked upstairs!

He says, Ma, I'm going to see my friends.

I says you could go, but come back the way you go. I trust you. You're a good boy, I know I could trust you. You know what it is to start off again.

He says, Ma, don't worry about it. I'll come right back.

So he came back, he was a different person.

In one minute he changes. Some boys you can't tell, but on him you could tell. He gets like delirious. He can hardly walk on his feet. His whole face, the eyes, the whole face changed, and the voice changed, everything. I don't understand, I don't understand.

When he came into that house and I saw him, I wanted to kill myself. I had a doctor that same night. They had to call the doctor! I almost collapsed. And how many times I had him by the doctor, it cost me sixty dollars a week, my whole pay I gave away, every single week! I gave away my pay, I took him private to the doctor. He cured him and everything.

I took him to Dr. G. It takes two weeks to cure him. Every single day. The doctor prescribed him capsules. I got them in the pharmacy where he send me. The treatment made him delirious. The first couple of nights he was scared, he was afraid, he didn't know what happened to him. It took a couple of days till he came to himself.

So what can you do? He was bad off, very bad off. He begged me, Ma, take me to the doctor. Ma, you'll see I'll stop. Ma, take me to the doctor. So we took him. I felt sorry for him. He says I'll go off it, I'll never go back on. I can't take it no more, he says. It's too much. It's time I should go off it.

So I took him. Soon as he fixed himself a little bit, he went right back to it. About three times I took him.

Now he's at Riker's Island for a sentence of one to three years. I can't tell you what he did, I can't tell you. I don't know myself, he wouldn't tell me the truth. I don't know. He got involved with some boys, I don't know what they did. And he takes the rap for the others. He's afraid, you know, and he takes it, he takes it.

He was picked up with stolen goods, but he didn't do it. The other boys did it. But he was the salesman. See, he's a good salesman; he was trying to sell it for them. He was carrying for somebody—it wasn't even his! He got a couple of dollars when he found a customer, but that's all.

So that's what happened. They took him. Maybe they took the others, too, but I don't know. He wouldn't tell me.

He called me from the police station where he was picked up, I should come to identify him. I couldn't find nothing to put on, I got so sick I didn't know what happened. So my husband finally went and identified him, and they sent him away to The Tombs here.

You know what happened then. I didn't want to bail him out, I wanted him to get off this here drug. I let him stay there for two weeks. Each time I went to see him, he banged his head on the wall. Take me out, take me out! Why you leave me here? —Where should I get the money to take you out? You think it's growing on the trees? He had $3500 bail. They wanted $175 to bond him. I didn't have the money, I told him. Naturally, I could have got it together, my daughter would have give me. But I didn't want to, I wanted him to get off the drug. So I made all kinds of excuses, and each time I went to see him I came home sick. They don't even give you an aspirin there—they let you suffer.

Finally he felt better, and I told him, on one condition I'll take you out, that you'll go with me to the country. He says okay, I'll do anything you say, but take me out.

So I took him out, and my son-in-law was waiting, the car was ready, and he didn't even pass the block. That was the week before the Fourth of July. I went out to the country to this here farmer. And he was okay there. He was all right, he ate, he gained a nice couple pounds. I gave him everything he wanted. He met the girl, he was very friendly, he went to the movies. My other boy came out for vacation from Chicago. He had the car, they went riding around together. They went out with girls and everything and he had a nice time.

So as soon as I came back, it started. The one week I came in for the trial, it started right away. Then I went back to the country, and he didn't want to stay there no more. We stood there another two weeks and then we came home. And he started all over again.

That's all. That's the end. What can I do? No way out, no way out. It's like cancer, like I said. You can't cure cancer, you can't cure that. I don't know, I don't know what it's gonna be when he comes out. I don't even want to think about it.

I'm so sick, I'm so sick. I feel he should stay there for at least three-four years. I know he's in good hands, they'll take care of him. I go to sleep, and I know I don't have to sit by the window and look. Every time he went down, I thought he'll never come back alive. I used to sit by the window till three-four o'clock and watch till I saw him alive come back home.

A couple of weeks ago, it was still hot and I was down in the street; my husband was sleeping. He had a key: I used to always take away the key from him; I don't know how he got a key. I don't know how he got into the house. He sat down on the couch, and he injected himself. I don't know what happened. He had a glass with him, and that glass fell down on the floor. And he fell right on top of it, and he was laying on the floor. And I didn't know—my husband was sleeping and I didn't know what happened—I wasn't in the house. Somebody came to the door and ringed the bell— the man who has the farm, he always come to my house. So he ringed it and ringed it and ringed it, and my husband came out and opened the door. My husband didn't know that the boy was laying on the living room floor, unconscious. So the man came in, he went into the living room, and he said, what happened here!

So my husband right away went in, and he started blowing into the mouth. He started to work on him until he brought him to it. But he had so much blood coming out from his forehead—he cut himself with the glass—so he was afraid to call an ambulance. He was afraid they gonna put him in jail. So he went in the druggist, he got it patched up. But he lost a lot of blood.

And that wasn't the first time. He was unconscious in the hallway, he was laying on the twentieth floor. He took an overdose and he wanted to go down. I don't know how he got upstairs—I live on the eighth floor. He got up in the morning and he says he's gonna go sign for the unemployments. And insteada going down, he went upstairs on the twentieth floor to inject himself in the hallway. And while he was ringing for the bell, the elevator came, he fell down half-way in the elevator, half-way in the hall. And the elevator door kept closing, back and forth, back and forth, back and forth. Then somebody came out and saw this and called the ambulance. The ambulance came, and they started working on him, and they brought him back to it.

And they ask him where he lives; he said, on the eighth floor. He came down; they carried him in the house, and I almost dropped dead. They said you're a lucky mother, you got your son back. If we didn't come, in a few minutes he would be dead. So I says, how lucky!—maybe I would be better off if he would be dead. So they took him to the hospital, and when we came down they thought I might be sick. I was so yellow till we got to the hospital they didn't know who was the patient.

So then they arrested him. . . . You know, they found in his possession the whole thing. They arrested him, but it wasn't too bad. We bailed him out, twenty-five dollars bail. We bailed him out, and they had a trial. Then they found him again, carrying in the pocket. But he was working, so he took a lawyer, and the lawyer saw that he just got a month. That's all. One month he got. Wasn't too bad—cost him three hundred and fifty dollars.

He wanted it this way. He don't want to live a normal life. The way he wanted, that's how he got it. I told him, I said get interested in a girl, you'll go out with her, you'll go to her house, you'll come to me, and you'll get a job, I'll try to help you pay out a car. But talk to the wall. Talk to the wall. That's all. It's no use.

I took him to a doctor, to a private doctor that's an uncle of my sister-in-law, in the Bronx. The doctor wanted to study him, look at him, he's like a psychiatrist. It didn't cost me anything; my brother took me there, last year. So he took him in, he talked to him, he talked to him and talked to him, and then he went out and he says, the mother should come in, I'll talk to the mother. I went in; he says, I'm very sorry to tell you, he says, your son don't want to be helped. He says, he don't care. He says, he thinks it's nothing, it's nothing to live a life like this. He don't absolutely care to cure himself. He's lost, he says. He never wants to help himself.

Now . . . I relax a little bit. But today I got very sick, I don't know what happened to me. My mind went away all of a sudden. I started to lose my memory. That happened to me before this way. My daughter called, and I started to cry, for no reason at all. She says, Ma, what happened to you? I says, I don't know what happened to me. I says, where was the boy? She says, you know he's in jail. I says, in jail? For what? He didn't do anything! Why should they send him to jail?

Then my sister-in-law called me and I told her the same story. And right away they start to call each other, and I was alone in the house, they got scared, my husband came running home, and my son-in-law came running home, and by the time they came, I came to already.

I went to see the doctor, and the doctor said, you're lucky you didn't get a stroke. He says, that's a very bad sign. You better take it easy. Take it easy, he says, you have a lot of pressure. Come back in two weeks. So he gave me a medicine, I went home. I can't last. I had to go down, wash my clothes. I came up, made my supper, I hung out the clothes, then I came here. I can't sit still—I got to do something.

I grow up in Poland, in a small little town. My parents came to this country, they left us in Europe. We were left in Europe, three children. And I couldn't go to school there, because they didn't let the Jewish children go into a Polish school. I came here, I was fifteen years old already. I couldn't go to school because I had to go to work and make a little for myself. My mother was sick, my father was sick, and they couldn't do nothing for me.

We lived on the East Side here. Since I've been in this country—forty years—we've lived around here. My mother had diabetes and she had TB, and both of them died when they were fifty-two years old. I worked dressing the models. I learned the language very quick, but I couldn't learn how to write and read.

My husband was born also in Russian Poland. I met him in a club; the immigrants made themselves clubs. But I didn't know that he likes to play. After I got married, I found out that he's a gambler. And he made my life miserable. But I tried my best. He liked me very much, he didn't want to leave me. He never wanted to leave me, never, never. No matter what I did to him, he was satisfied. He knows he's guilty, I'm always right, whatever I said to him.

As he got older, he started to give me a little money. He's getting better. He's old already, and he knows he needs me. Without me he's nothing worth. When I go away in a hospital or when I go away, he don't eat, he don't drink, he just don't know what to do with himself. He's very upset; he likes me always in the house. Even when he sleeps, he

likes I should stay in the house and watch television. He
never wants I should go away.

When I was sick, he sits and cries; there's nobody to take
care of him. When I was away in the country, he lost so
much weight and he lost money, too. For two months he
didn't give me no money. He lived it up here. He plays
cards, he plays dice, he owes everybody money, he took a
loan in the bank.

But he gives me money now. I don't know where he goes
to play, and I don't care. As long as he gives me. He buys
things for the house. He buys meat, he buys fish, he buys
potatoes, onions—he buys fifty pounds, a hundred pounds,
potatoes for the whole winter. He likes to bring up everything in the house. But money, he likes the money himself.

So everything is all right. But if the boy was home, he let
it out to me, he made my life miserable, he cursed me, he
hollered at me it's my fault. But now, everything is all right;
he keeps quiet. He relaxes, he looks a different person since
the boy is not at home.

Well, I'm a mother, it hurts me. I'm relaxed, I feel better,
but it hurts me. A child could live and laugh if he would
be normal. He could be married already. Look what he did
to his life. I don't know . . . I don't know what to do with
him.

Such a beautiful boy. . . . He's a nice character, he could
talk to people, good-looking, he has a good head on himself,
he knows everything before he went away. Ma, what do you
have to fix? I'll fix for you. Mama, what's broken? Tell me
what to do. For the Venetian blinds he made new straps—he
bought, he made it over. He says, what else, Ma? What can
I do? He fixed the fluorescent light—he bought it from
Chicago.

He's a very good child, I know. He likes me, too. I used
to hit him. I used to hit him, I used to curse him, and he used

to say, Ma, he says, I know you don't mean it. You just don't know what you're doing. He says, thank you. Thank you for doing this, thank you. Why didn't you hit me when I was small? Now it's too late. He didn't care, he didn't care what I do to him. He wouldn't hit me back, he wouldn't curse me back, nothing. Nothing. He just laid on the couch and talked to me, talked to me. That's all. Sometimes I couldn't even understand what he was saying.

It took hours till he got out of it. Couple hours, then he came to himself. He went to the kitchen, and he took a glass of milk with a piece of cake. But while he was in this position he didn't want nothing—he just wanted to lay, lay, and dozes off and dozes off.

That's what happened. Why it have to happen to me I don't know. I don't know why I failed; I always used to watch him. I used to go someplace, I took him with me. I bought him; I bought him ice cream, I bought him toys. I don't know why I failed. I don't know where I failed. I don't know what happened to him.

I says to him, why didn't you come to tell me, when they start giving you this here, why didn't you come to your mother, ask me?

He says, you don't ask a mother things like this. I thought, he says, I'll take it once in a while. It's nothing. And then, before I realize, I got in deeper and deeper, he says. And that's all.

Larry Greenberg

❖❖❖

IT seems that in the neighborhood there was just one age
group that stood together and became addicts. The fellas
before us didn't, and the fellas younger than us didn't. Aside
from our age group ninety per cent of the addiction in the
neighborhood is Negro and Puerto Rican, I'd say mostly
Puerto Rican.

I've been back home from Riker's Island about a month
now. My mother's well, but she has high blood pressure.
She works pretty hard taking care of the house. So she could
use the doctor once in a while, but nothing serious. She
worries about me. I try to tell her not to, because there's
nothing she can do anyway. But she worries anyway, and
she's got a very bad habit. Once she gets onto a subject,
she doesn't let it go. That's hard on her plus me, because
when I come home from work, naturally if I'm high, I hear
about it. And what am I doing this for, and what am I
doing that for. She has the attitude that I do all these things

187

just to hurt her. She doesn't understand that I don't. I'm not doing it to hurt anybody.

They say if you felt anything for us, you wouldn't do it. But it doesn't go like that. It has nothing to do with it. Because I wouldn't do anything to hurt them. It's not a matter of hurting you or not hurting you. It's something I do, I don't know why I do it, but I do.

I would do anything for them, but when they say, if you felt anything for us you wouldn't do it, it's not an honest reason. It's no reason to stop. Because I do care for them, but it just seems it hasn't anything to do with it.

There's always tension. They're always on my back to stop using or to cut down. Naturally I ask them for a couple of bucks once in a while, and they don't like that. I try to make do on my own money, but I don't contribute anything to the house, and I hear that too. I'm working for nothing; everything I make I spend, they say. I'm living in the house for nothing. I have a place to eat and a place to sleep and I don't do anything for it. They feel that everything I do is wasted. All my efforts at work and everywhere else—it just goes for narcotics.

I take a lot more drugs on weekends. All this copping keeps me busy most of the time—maybe at night I'll go to the movies. But just buying stuff and taking off and coming down and hanging around for a few hours, take off again— it's a whole day gone. And if you have to go out and raise additional money, it'll take up all your time.

When you have to steal or hustle for money, that's more work than working. It's a terrible feeling when you get up in the morning and you're sick and you have no money, to have to go scrambling around to raise money. I prefer working—I know I got something coming and I know it's going to be there. I don't like the idea of having to run around, maybe stealing, maybe borrowing. Especially in the winter-time.

I've taken a few overdoses. My first shot was an over-dose. I took one in Chicago and woke up in a hospital, not too far from death. Once or twice I had a friend to pull me out, and once or twice I was at home in my own bathroom. I'd taken a shot, and you don't know what happens, you just go out. My father or my mother or someone managed to get me up. I sure was lucky someone was there. I don't know if I woulda come out of it myself. That's something you don't know. Sometimes you just lay there for hours and you wake up, and sometimes you never wake up.

The time I got arrested was the worst. In my building, on the roof I took off. I'd taken off and I finished, and I went down to the elevator to go down—I was on the twentieth floor. I rang for the elevator and that was the last thing I remember. When I woke up the police were there with oxygen and everything, trying to wake me. I guess some woman came out into the hallway and found me laying there. They called the police and the ambulance, the police took me out of it and they found the works on me. And I was arrested.

I know three or four of my immediate friends who've not come out of it and died. In the neighborhood there must be a lot more.

ELEVEN MONTHS LATER

I'VE been on drugs now almost eight years. I've been arrested four times; I was convicted on three of the charges. Of the eight years I'd say I spent about two years in jail. In the past five years I haven't stayed a whole year out of jail. Since 1958 I've been continuously involved with the law or the court—arrested, out on bail, awaiting trial, or in jail.

I was arrested two months after we talked last April. On the new charge I did three months, and then I got six months for violation of parole. I was released two weeks ago; I've been living at home and haven't used anything since I've been out.

I've been arrested on four charges: 3305, possession of narcotics—which we had dismissed in court; 1747, possession of a hypodermic needle—which got me thirty days; burglary —I was convicted and sentenced to three years, and served ten months; possession of burglar tools—which got me this last term.

It seems I developed a knack for breaking and entering. I'm not the kind of person who can stand around all night begging for money; if you want money, you got to go out and make it. And it became easier and easier every time. You sort of get hooked on it. You get hooked on burglaries. You have good experiences with it, you've never been arrested, and you figure, well, you can go indefinitely. You also figure that you will get arrested eventually. But you don't think of the consequences at the time. Then you do get arrested and it's all over. You don't want to go back after you've lost your confidence. Getting caught isn't a matter of imagination any more.

I learned my burglary techniques from an older fella who wasn't a drug addict; he was a professional burglar. I used to go with him to different neighborhoods and he taught me how to open a door. You go up and ring the bell, make believe you're looking for somebody if someone answers, ring a couple of times to make sure no one's home, and then you just open the door and go in. Look around to see whatever was valuable—jewelry, cash—whatever it was, you took it. That was it. It was a very short procedure. The whole thing wouldn't take but fifteen minutes to a half hour, including five minutes to open the door.

This fella happened to go in for pretty classy apartments, and mostly they had steel doors. There's a type of pliers you use that will open these doors, take the lock right out. Just stick your finger in and open it up. We never worked any old buildings. In a lot of the old buildings there are wooden doors—guys just kick them in, just use a screwdriver to open them up. But in the newer apartments we figured we had a better chance of finding something.

You can't pry a steel door; you take the cylinder out, just like a locksmith would do. You take a lock out, find the mechanism and push it over, and open the door up. It takes only five minutes, and as you go along even less time; it doesn't make any noise, either.

I watched him and I learned how he did it by watching. A couple of months later he was arrested, and I just went out, walked in the hardware store and bought the tool. I walked over to a building, went upstairs, opened a door, walked inside, looked around, and the first drawer I opened I found about three-four hundred dollars in cash. It was so easy—in fact, they were all easy; I never had trouble but once or twice.

We weren't caught in the apartments, because when you take the lock out you just jam it back in and they can't open the door. If I heard people at the door, I went to the door and listened. They couldn't open the door—they thought it was jammed. One time it was a man and his wife; they weren't young, they were an elderly couple. I just opened the door and walked out. I guess they didn't know what happened; they were shocked. Well, I didn't really walk—I ran out. And I just walked away from the building.

There was no fire-escapes, and I was on the fifteenth floor. The only way out was through the door, and that's how I went.

This fellow used to have a car, and we would go out to Rego Park, Woodhaven—mostly out on Long Island. Later, when I worked alone, I didn't have a car and I would just work the better buildings here in the neighborhood. There were pretty big buildings out in Rego Park, some of them with fancy doormen. You just walk right in—that's one of the things, you act like you belong there. Just walk right in like you're looking for somebody. If you have any trouble, you just explain that you're in the wrong building and walk right out.

Most of these buildings have their own self-service elevators. Some of them have elevator operators, but you try to avoid that.

The first thing we look for is cash, the second jewelry: anything you can put in your pockets is preferable. But we went in for furs sometimes, and good silver sets, movie cameras, tape recorders—anything that you figure you can sell easily. We just walked out with them, take the elevator down like it was yours, walk out of the building. Just like the TV repairmen. In fact, once I was coming out of an apartment with a TV, and the next-door neighbor walked out and got in the elevator with me. It was on a Sunday, and she was looking at me like what am I doing with this TV? And I'll tell you the truth, I don't think she knew who lived next door to her. So I sort of explained to her that I was a TV repairman, and complained that I was working on Sundays; I got pretty friendly with her on the way down. And I just walked out with it.

You go back to the same building. Sometimes you can go back to the same building two or three times without even remembering you been there. But you try not to go to the same place day after day. You let it rest a while—there's a lot of buildings in Rego Park.

When it came to selling the stuff, he knew some people, I knew some people, depending on what the merchandise was. It wasn't any big problem getting rid of merchandise. A lot of people would be surprised who would buy stuff in this neighborhood, I mean the fences there are. Maybe they're not what you call really a fence: some people buy it and sell for a profit, but a lot of people buy because they really need it. Even though they know it isn't legitimate, they figure they're saving some money. Very legitimate people, too. People buy mink stoles for their wives, television for the kids, diamond rings, diamond watches for their wives.

We left it in the car. If I knew somebody I'd approach him and tell him, listen, I've got a mink stole for you. You want it? And if he wanted to see it, I'd go to the car and show it to him. And if he wanted it, he'd pay me for it. If not, I'd see somebody else. I used to know pretty well who wanted what. Or else we'd go as a last resort to a professional fence. He'd take anything; once I brought it up there it was as good as sold. He wouldn't pay as much, because he wasn't buying it for his own personal use. I guess when you need something for your personal use, you're willing to pay a good price for it. I got some pretty good prices; in fact, sometimes I think I got more than if they were buying new. People, you know, think like they're getting a bargain. Lot of times I sold television, radios for what you can buy 'em in the store.

I've taken things from one apartment and sold them to another in the same building. But if anyone asks me, it came from out of the neighborhood. 'Cause this is one thing they don't like—a lady walking down the street and another lady come over and say, that's my mink stole. So you try and avoid that. But it's been done. They might even be friends, for all you know.

I've never went to one-family houses or anything like this—strictly apartment houses. Say from middle class to upper class. I didn't go for any of these real rich places, because there you run into problems. People with a lot of things laying around the house, they watch 'em pretty good. Or maybe a burglar alarm, or a doorman. You try to avoid it. You go for the middle class, where maybe they might have some money laying around or some jewelry. No real rich places, Fifth Avenue or anything.

I developed a habit: I didn't like to get short of cash anymore. I used to keep a hundred dollars in cash in my pocket, which I didn't like to spend. When I got down to that hundred dollars, I would always go out and make fresh money. It was just as easy to go out and make it, because it only took a matter of minutes.

You become used to it. A detective once questioned me about an armed robbery, and I told him that's not my type of work. I don't go out with a gun, I don't stick up anybody: I'm strictly for burglaries. And he said, well, you feel it's easier to go into an apartment and rob somebody than to stick somebody up? And I do, 'cause you don't meet anybody. You don't meet anybody.

I would go into an apartment and I would stay there maybe a half hour or an hour if I had to. I would open up the refrigerator, take a bottle of soda out, sit down and try to figure out where to go. I never ripped the place apart, I never messed anything up: I just looked nice and easy, didn't make any noise, and never worried about anyone walking in. It just never occurred to me, maybe. Never happened.

No one could get in the door while I was in the apartment. I would take my time. Ninety per cent of the time I would work alone, because I prefer it that way. I found a lot of people get nervous. I've went with a lot of people they wanted to walk out before they walked in, and I was never like that. I worked alone because I figured I could work better that way.

Especially in the neighborhood I try not to tell anybody how I work or show anybody. It's bad, because especially now after I've been arrested, the police know my M.O.—*modus operandi*—in fact it's happened quite a few times that someone's been hitting the same apartments and using the same type of tools and I've been picked up about it. When too many people start doing it, they're liable to start looking for you even if you're not doing it.

The police know how you work; they have a whole file on you. They know what type of tool I use, how I enter apartments, etc. Even when I was in jail, I heard that people were doing the same thing. And I was glad that I was in jail, because at least now they know there are a few other people around doing the same thing. And maybe they won't bother me about it.

The tool costs about a dollar, dollar and a quarter. The cylinder is just like a nut; you just keep turning it like you would a nut and pull it out.

About twenty-four to thirty is the age group of the addicts in the neighborhood who've been on it eight-ten years. A lot of them just hang around, a lot of them go in for armed robberies. I don't know; I just could never do it. Standing on a corner, waiting for somebody. . . . I like to have the money in my pocket when I want it. That's really why I enjoyed the burglaries. It's like a job. When you go out with a gun you have to expect either to kill or be killed.

I have no record of assault or any acts of violence. Just narcotics and burglary, that's all. I guess there are quite a few addicts that are like me; but then again I guess there are quite a few who aren't. I think I know better. It may be upbringing, it may be family. I live in a nice home.

Maybe these people haven't had the same things. They just react differently. I won't say they're a different class of people, but they're different types. They're more used to it I'd say than I am. Even though I've lived in this neighborhood many years, I've never lived in a lot of these buildings —say, cold-water flats or anything—we lived in a cold-water flat when I was four years old and we moved out into a city project, which was decent, which was clean at least—my mother always keeps it clean.

I've gone up to houses of people who are addicts and the family knows about them. I've taken off with them; I've shot up with them in their own house. Now I know in my house, I'll say if I ever brought anybody in . . . it just wouldn't happen, my mother wouldn't let me bring anybody in. I have maybe once or twice, not very often, but I couldn't make a routine out of it. With them it's just a matter of fact; they accept it. The family allows it. They know what's going on and they don't feel as strongly about it. Never heard them yell at them for doing it—sometimes yes, sometimes no—but it seems like they'd gotten it a lot easier. Like sometimes I used to envy them, because they accepted them. Like, you know, the mother didn't say, well, why don't you stop using drugs? Or, don't bring anyone up to the house! Seemed more easy for them, but now I'm glad it's the other way around, that my mother did tell me to stop, because otherwise I probably never would.

There's a lot of things important in keeping me off. If I can find a job that I like . . . the job is important. Plus social life seems to be very important right now, finding something to do, finding a new set of acquaintances and friends —people that can accept me and I can accept, because actually I don't have too much in common with anybody, 'cause I been using drugs for so many years. I feel I could fit in in certain clubs, in certain circles, and that's what I'm trying to do. I figure I can find someplace where I can fit in, spend some time, and have less time on my hands to worry about other things.

Right now I'm trying not to get discouraged. I'm taking this pretty much on the selfish attitude that I'm not doing this for anybody but myself. I'm pretty tired of it, I feel that I do want to stop right now. Maybe this is the way I feel now, I can't say about a month from now. But I been looking for work about two weeks. I'm trying not to get discouraged; it isn't too easy to find anything. I finished high school while I was at Riker's Island last time; I feel this will be a help to find a job. I took a state exam and I passed it. To tell you the truth, I didn't do any studying for it.

I only lacked a year of graduating when I quit Seward Park High School. It was a little before I got on drugs. I quit when I was sixteen. I felt I wanted to go to work, I wanted to make money. I don't know why but I did. I'd say about six months, eight months later I started using drugs.

No one asked me to do it; I don't think anyone even mentioned it to me. There were two fellows using it and I asked them. There wasn't too much talk about it. We were pretty much a teenage crowd. We used to go to dances, and there was a crowd of girls staying with us. Just eventually —it didn't take too long—in six-eight months, everyone was using it.

I figured we knew what was going on and no one else did. We were really getting away with something. But no one actually did know about it for quite some time. But eventually it all came out, and I guess our group wasn't too select. A lot of people found out and a lot of events happened because of it.

It was a pretty good feeling. We used to come out from a dance on Friday night, and somebody used to go out and cop, we used to take off and go back up to the dance. We felt pretty good—I guess not everyone knew what was going on at that time. They didn't know what we were doing. Maybe they thought we were drunk, but no one actually knew what it was.

Many addicts feel cut off, but I don't think they worry too much about it. I don't think they worry too much about other people's opinions. They feel that it doesn't concern them what other people think, because as they say, you can't knock it if you haven't tried it. So you feel that a lot of people who are knocking it, they don't know how they would react if they were in the same situation. If they started using drugs they might like it themselves. You never know.

I don't know why I've gone back on in the past. You figure maybe because nothing has changed. You come out of jail and you figure, well, this is different. I'm gonna stop; this is a different time. But after you've been out two or three weeks, you're in exactly the same position as before you went in. There's nothing changed. There's nothing different happened to you, you get into the same routine, there's no different things around to do, so you're just about back where you started from.

I finish parole in about nine or ten months, and after that my time's up, I don't owe them anything. Actually maybe at first this has an effect, you're a little more careful. But after a while you don't even think about it, because the way it is now, I guess they don't have enough parole officers and too many people on parole. About the only time you see a parole officer is when you've been out to see him. Otherwise you don't even see him, and it's not that restricting. There's a lot of things you can do. You're supposed to be home at a certain time, but you don't keep up to it mostly. You do pretty much what you want, except for reporting.

Parole has nothing to do with whether you go back on

drugs. If you want to, you just go back and hope you don't get caught. In fact, a lot of times the parole officer does know that you're back on drugs. Their attitude, I feel, is that if you don't get in trouble, you're all right. Once you're in trouble, you're in trouble. You're going back. But if you don't get arrested or get in any trouble, they'll let you ride.

I'm not gonna look ahead too far, I'm just gonna take each day. I don't really want to look ahead, because I've seen people that have stayed off it a couple of years and gone back. So you can't tell anything, really. The first couple of years doesn't mean too much. If you completely forget about it, you have a pretty good chance. If you don't use it but you still have it on your mind, chances are you're gonna go back.

Ricky Garcia

❖❖❖

I'M twenty-one years old; I started with pot when I was fourteen. I used to go home from Junior High and get real high at lunchtime. I used to buy it from a man in the park. Pot keeps you cool. I used to eat a lot; I felt good. The man who sold it was a friend of mine, about twenty-four years old. There were a lot of dealers, but his pot was better. He didn't ask any of us to deal, because in pot only one dealer can make money.

In heroin it's much different. When you're using drugs it's really a dirty job, you know? When I was about sixteen I went to heroin. After about two weeks I wanted to use it every day. I started mainlining because I found that you get your high faster. But I can't explain it because it's too dirty. People don't care about their mothers.

I live with my mother and two younger sisters and a brother. My father's in Puerto Rico, he's been there all his life. My mother came here about fourteen years ago.

When you're sick you scream at your mother, you might beat her for her five dollars, you'd probably take everything she has. If she tries to take it back, you'd hit her. I know. I've taken my sister's ring, my mother's clothes . . . and I started breaking people's door. I used a crowbar.

One time I was going through the airshaft from one building to another, and when I was climbing in through a window a man was waiting, with a pipe. That was the biggest scare I got. If he had hit me. . . . I told him I was in the apartment in the other building, and somebody locked me inside. I was just trying to get out. He looked in my face and I don't know what he saw, but he let me go. I talked to him fifteen minutes; he gave me coffee and he made some toast. He said that I shouldn't be doing that 'cause I coulda got hurt. He didn't know what I was really up to.

The worst habit I had was about six weeks back. I was dealing for myself. I had about ten hundred dollars, and I went and bought me 127 spoons. You can get seven bags at the most out of a spoon. Usually it will cost you fifteen, and if you got a good connection he'll give it to you for twelve. I used to shoot up almost eight spoons a day. It amounted to almost two hundred dollars.

I was getting my supply on the East Side at 121st Street. They have good connections there. Most of the big connections are uptown.

The big connection was a friend of my father from Puerto Rico. He used to sell half a piece, a whole piece, two-three-four pieces. A piece would cost $350—you get thirty-six spoons, you might get thirty-eight. He's really a nice guy. If you would not be using drugs, you'd get rich within a month. I could have got there. I was shooting up too much dope, but I had seven guys dealing for me at the same time. He used to bring me seven-eight pieces. Every day I would collect from all seven people about two, three hundred dollars. I would get about two thousand dollars a day. I would never give it all to my connection—I would give him about eight hundred dollars. He used to meet me every day. We would get in a car and drive, and then he would bring me back.

My pushers were guys I knew and guys who could be trusted. My connection had plenty of stuff he wanted to get off, and he told me to get ten-fifteen-twenty people, it would make no difference. But you can't trust that much people. It would be too much dope out in the street.

Let's say I would give a pusher fifty bags. And I tell him to sell them at six dollars. On each bag he gave me four dollars—he would be making two dollars. He could make eighty dollars for himself within an hour. It might take him half an hour or a whole day. I would tell my pushers, don't be greedy; get off the streets by four-five o'clock, go to a movie at night and get nice and high. Mostly I would meet pushers at their houses. Because a guy who deals for you is always short: they want to shoot their part and your part too. So you got to keep on them, because you can't trust people that use dope. Sometimes you have to give it to them two-three times a day, and there's a big chance, because they're right out in the street and these are the people the cops are looking for.

I once swallowed eight bags when the cops were about to shake me down. They were in small envelopes like you use for stamp collecting. I swallowed them all the way down in my stomach, but when I threw them out afterwards, they were no good. They were all wet. I threw them out by drinking the soda. I wasn't high, I was straight—because when I was dealing I never liked to be goofing in the street where the cop could see me bending down below myself. I liked to keep myself alert. That way I would know if anybody's trying to take my stuff. Or if the man is watching me. You got to keep your eyes on three or four people. And the minute you take your eyes off your dope to look at anybody else, they gonna take it.

Junkies try to swallow their bags when the cops come, but a lot of times they don't get the chance. They really hit you. When you pull a stunt like that they get mad, 'cause they think you take them for a fool. I was pretty down once—used to shoot up only a bag or two a day—didn't have such a big habit. I was coming out of a Spanish candy store, and these two bulls jumped me. Before I could get it down they had me all over the floor, because they really hit you. The bag went on the floor. The two of them really worked me over. Since that day I say if I get a chance to swallow, I swallow. But with certain cops you can't do that, because they really whip the shit out of you.

The colored people that I see down here on Avenue C put their bags in balloons. That way a regular user can swallow it, reach his house and bring it back up again, and use it, shoot it up, without losing his money. They put it in the regular envelope and then they put it inside a balloon. You make it smaller than your pinky fingernail; you can hold twenty in your mouth at the same time. You put the bag in the balloon so it makes a perfect fit, then you cut off the extra balloon and tie it up.

We'd never cut at my house. I would have a room, or a friend of mine's house. Another junkie, you know? I'd say I'll give you a bag, get you straight, and he'd let me use his house. In my house I have my mother, my sisters—it's no good, 'cause anytime the cops will break in, they take everybody. They don't care whether you using it or not. Even though you're not a junkie, you're not free from reproach. So you get another place.

A four-to-one piece will cost you at this time nine hundred dollars, for a piece that makes thirty-eight spoons. A four-to-one piece means that you can cut it with quinine or sugar-milk or both of them together to get three more pieces out of the one that you got. You have four altogether— you can even make five. I test it by giving it to someone who's a user—like the man whose house we're cutting in. I let him shoot it up a little at a time and I watch him. I try to make it so it's the best stuff of anyone that's selling, but still cut it enough so I make more money.

The man that used to supply me ain't supplying nobody no more. He got caught in Canada with twenty-eight pounds of pure heroin. Twelve-to-one cut.

I went three times with him to Mexico. We were just flunkies, you know, working for somebody higher. I can't remember where we crossed the border. We went to a bar. We had fifteen-twenty thousand dollars. This man knew the place we were going; I was never there before. What I'm saying is I can't say the place. There's still two people on the outside that I might work for.

They have very young fellows working for them, and that's very stupid. 'Cause a detective catch you giving dope to sell to someone fourteen-fifteen-sixteen-seventeen, and he'll really flatten you out. He'll really hit you. I've seen it happen.

The supplies are coming into New York City every day. When they had that dock strike, you know . . . there was still enough stuff in New York to last for ten years. But in a way the strike caused a panic, because people was really hanging on to what they had. The more they hang onto it, the more a man like myself would have to pay. I was only a flunkie to the big man, and I was getting a five-to-one, six-to-one, ten-to-one cut, if I was getting that, for eight hundred dollars. That punk here would charge me twelve hundred dollars; he would raise up the price. Because he knows I aint gonna get it another place. I might get it, but it would cost me the same or more. Because they all one, you know.

The man I was working for is in jail now. But I can still work for the same people because his wife is outside, and she is a big connection. She's the one who sent him up there.

When the man pushing on the street has something weak, he'll be out there all night trying to sell it. When he's got something good, you can't hardly find him.

To tell you the truth, I came now to get into the hospital because I am sick. I look at my sister, you know, and she's fourteen. She goes with other kids, teen kids, you know? And I picture myself, the years back I wasted. I haven't danced I think in about five years. Or listened to a record. So I got talking with my mind, and she says, you should take something like a rest. It would do me good, you know, because I'm not really half the person I was.

I was down there with my father in Puerto Rico for about a year and four months. I used to work, but it all amounted to the same thing. Over there I used to shoot up less, but better stuff. You can find stuff anywhere in Puerto Rico. My father's in charge of a carnival, and I ran one of the games of chance. It's nice; you meet a lot of people—good people, bad people, all the kinds. But I didn't care; I just wanted the money.

I was at Warwick three months. When I got out I decided to see what it would be like hanging around with my father. So I went down there, and that's when I started getting more money, and that's when I started using more dope. So I got tired of that down there too, and I came back here. Here I have it worster, 'cause if you get a habit you got to quit your job and how you gonna support yourself? I have to break people's door, mug Chinese, do any kind of thing, you know?

Some people think that mugging a Chinese man is much easier than breaking a door. I think it's the other way around, because every guy that tries to mug people, you gotta kill them. 'Cause I know a lot of people, friends of mine, that are liable to get the chair now. You have to hurt a person.

Mostly they use a woman. The Chinaman will come and pick her up, and she'll be working with two more fellows, probably the brains of the house, her man, her old man, and probably the understudy. All three are in it. And when they get the man like up in his apartment, if they get the man right, they probably don't have to kill this stud. But you know sometimes they's people, they find themselves being attacked, and they get nervous, very nervous. They start blowing a whistle they got, like a police whistle, and you got to shut them up. A lot of people, they like to knife, like to cut people a lot. This leads to murder. And you can't get away with that.

You know they're gonna catch you. Two friends of mine —well, friends in a way, but in another way not, 'cause they're junkies—they just killed a Chink a week and a half back. I think it was eight hours before they got caught. They got caught right away. So I find that breaking doors is much easier than mugging Chinks.

Two or three guys will be sick, you know? And this here pusher, any pusher, will be on the street. So they walk up to the man and say, look man, we're sick. We ain't got no money—how about giving us two-three bags? If the man says no, they'll take him in a hallway, they'll whip him and take his dope too. Then he's gonna come crying to them, to give *him* two or three bags to get straight.

I wish I had had somebody to tell me not to do these things. I would help somebody else. Because it really tears you into nothing. You don't care about nobody but yourself, you just want to get straight. I would like to be pushing now, but I wouldn't be pushing to a kid.

TWO WEEKS LATER

My mother married again about nine years ago and my stepfather has got the same problem as me. He was on drugs when he married my mother. We were dealing together, but our habits kept getting bigger and that way we lost everything. That was just this June. We rented a room where we did the cutting.

We used to do most of the cutting at night, and be ready in the morning to do it to the pushers. That way we wouldn't be seen in the streets, 'cause they get hot fast. We would have a mirror, some sugar-milk or quinine, a teaspoon, a woman's stocking and a hanger. You take the quinine, measure out how many spoons you want for each spoon of heroin, then run 'em together through the woman's stocking out onto the mirror. You make a diamond-shape of the wire hanger and you stretch the stocking tight over that. You run a spoon through it and it falls right back on the mirror. You rake it back and forth with the spoon, and when it falls on the mirror it's mixed. From there you have a measure: like for a five-dollar bag, an eighth of a spoon. There's a measure for it. We just take it and put it in the bag. It's a special bag that they use mostly for stamp collecting. We could deck up two-three hundred in an evening's time. It all depends on how much you got and how fast you deck up.

Altogether I made about nine thousand dollars one time.

If I would count the man's money, I had twenty-five thousand dollars more that was his.

If you would be using your head, or if you had experience, you would have a can of water next to you while you're cutting, and have the water in the bathroom running good, so just in case anybody tries to break down that door you can throw it in the bathroom. Or you throw it in the pail of water. There's too much water, and that way when they take the pail down to the lab, they won't get no result on it. You would lose your money, but you'd get out of it.

I was walking down Clinton Street, and I met a friend of mine who wanted to cop two bags. But I didn't want to give it to him on that block, because that's where the precinct is. So I told him to keep walking up with me. When we got up to Henry Street, I gave him two bags, but there was somebody following us. He let my friend go and came after me. I was walking up the stairs when he got in the house. I was in the bathroom; I was going to take off. Knock on the door, Ma says, who is it? I heard, I heard, because the bathroom door is right next to the door where you come in. I knew it was a policeman, so I had to take everything and just dump it in. I lost about sixty-two bags.

My connection came to me. I was dealing for myself, and I knew this man, and he heard that I was pretty down. He came and talked to me, asked if I wanted to work. And he gave me down some money. At first he used to give me twenty-fifteen bags, then he let loose half a piece. I had to give him $150 back, and I made 450 out of it. But if I could have bought that half a piece myself, it would only cost me 120.

You don't find good stuff anymore. You can't cut it, you can't even touch it. You got to leave it just like it comes, or you'll be losing your money. People would buy off you the first time but not the second time.

But when I dealt for the man, he wasn't buying it from no other seller; he was getting it from the big man. He wasn't running it through no hands. When it runs through hands, each man takes out so many spoons of heroin and puts back sugar-milk. Say the man buy half a kilo. You probably get fifteen pieces—if it comes four-to-one cut, you can get fifteen times four out of it. Half a kilo you would take out fifteen whole pieces, and each piece would bring thirty to thirty-three spoons. Then you could cut it four times and you get your profit. The man could of had four-five thousand spoons out of a kilo. At least two thousand.

You get a kilo in any kind of paper . . . a small plastic bag, that's what they mostly use. I would call my connection to meet him. He would meet me near his house, say 84th and Amsterdam. I would have to wait for the man. He would come, stay a few minutes, and leave it right in my hand. I wouldn't pay him right when I got it; he trusted me. He trusted me in a way. He had plenty of people uptown, but he trusted me more than any of them. Because I knew him from my home town. He know my father, he know everybody in my family.

I have no idea how he got his stuff. I went with him a couple of times to Mexico. (*As questions about big connections persist, takes out switchblade knife and plays with it.*) I don't remember how I got there. I don't want to remember. It's no good. I'll be getting myself involved.

We went down by car: me, him, his wife and his kid.

We went . . . I don't want to say.

We didn't go to Mexico City.

(*Here Ricky broke off the interview.*)

Tommy Blake

I was thirteen years old when I had my first fix. I went directly mainline. I went with a guy, one of my friends —not really a friend but supposedly—we went down to the other end of the neighborhood to pick up something for some other kids. We got a free bag, and he asked me if I ever got off before. I said yes, so he said okay, let's split the bag. So we went up to the roof and that's where I got my first fix. It was 1953, the Saturday before Easter Sunday. Nine years and a week ago.

There was none of us over eighteen. I was hanging out with guys fifteen-sixteen and almost every one of us fooling around with narcotics in one form or another. Either they were smoking pot or snorting or skin-popping or mainlining. On account of the population explosion, different kids came down here from uptown and I guess they brought their habits with them. The kids I hung out with were all born in this neighborhood, but it must have come from out of

the neighborhood. Because it was something that was un-
heard-of before I was a teenager. The most the kids did
before then was drink. In the early part of the 1950's, that's
when drugs started coming down, and that's when the
neighborhood got really shot.

It affected the lives of almost everyone I hung out with.
Matter of fact, some of my best friends are dead now. They
all died of overdoses. I can remember three right offhand.

I had my second shot two months later, in the summer
sometime. I met someone, and we went down on East
Broadway. We went down in a cellar, and we split a three-
dollar bag. We started going on weekends, and before we
know it it was every night.

I was never really without it for the first three years,
because there was no problem with the police or anything
like that. There was nobody really too wise to it. But as it
grew and the problem grew, as more people started using
and more kids started using, the neighbors started getting
wise and started calling the cops. I got arrested in 1956
and that's when I found out I was really hooked. I kicked
cold turkey in The Tombs.

During that three-year period I could always get a dollar
and a half or three dollars. I had a part-time job. We would
take as much as we could get: if we could get four fixes a
day, we would take four fixes. If we only had one, we
would take one and we were satisfied with it.

When I was going to P.S. 12, I would have my fix after
school—about four or five o'clock in the afternoon. After
supper we would all come out in the street and pool our
money, and all go down in a group and get off again. I
don't think I ever nodded in school or anything like that.
To tell you the truth, I don't think I went to school very
much: I was always playing hookey. I think the most I ever
did, I came to school once drunk. I never nodded in class.

The majority of us met somewhere near school. We made appointments to meet and then we'd all chip in and go down to some movie house on 42nd Street. Most of us didn't go to school.

I worked with my uncle's father on a truck. I worked in the garment center and down on Spring Street. I worked pretty hard for a kid fourteen years old. I didn't make much except in the summer when I made about forty-five dollars a week. During school I made about twenty dollars, which is also a pretty penny for a boy fourteen years old. We went out and had good times with it: we went to dances and we'd throw parties and we'd all chip in.

I have no brothers and sisters. My mom and pop are still alive, and I guess they're both pretty good people, except for me. Nobody's ever had anything bad or wrong to say about my family. I guess I'm the black sheep.

My parents have been separated for quite a number of years. Right now my father is in Brooklyn Veterans Hospital. My mother lives downtown here. I was only about seven years old at the most when they separated. I've been raised by my mother. My father lived in the neighborhood with my grandmother, and I'd see him almost every day. He helped me out with a couple of dollars now and then, always tried to look out for my interests—you know, made sure I went to school, and told my mother if I don't do this just tell him and he'll take care of it. They both tried. I had good parents.

My mother worked in a factory, and then she went to school and studied psych and stuff, and now she works in an office. She's worked all her life.

I left home at the age of seventeen and got married. And that was it, as far as living at home goes. To be honest, I married a very good girl, a girl that, well, a drug addict doesn't deserve. She knew I had been taking drugs. You see,

I had just come out of Riverside Hospital. I did a cure, I stayed eight months and I was going to aftercare clinic, and I wasn't using drugs for a year almost. I was going steady with my wife, and I don't know what happened. But after I got married, I started fooling around again. She knew all about me, I mean there was nothing hidden. She knew I was arrested, and this and that.

The biggest problem was her family against me. Because they had money, and I had no money—I had a police record against me. She had a high school diploma and I didn't—they were really upset and against the marriage from the beginning. They lived on Avenue U in Brooklyn, and when we got married we got an apartment two blocks from theirs.

I met my wife in 1954. We were going down to Coney Island and we saw a bunch of girls, and we started kidding around. And I started going out with her. We went steady for about three months and then we broke up and we didn't see each other for quite some time. And then around the end of 1955 we saw each other again and we started going steady again. Then we broke up again—I got arrested and this and that, I went to Riverside and all. We wrote each other, and when I came home we really went steady, you know: I was working and taking her out to nightclubs and stuff like that. And then finally we decided we were gonna get married, and so we went to Mexico and got married. We just took off.

I married my wife on August 25, 1957. I'd been arrested May 10, 1956. We had just finished taking off, and I was at my house. A cop busted in, and I got caught with three sets of works. My mother wasn't home, she didn't know anything, and we used to go up there to get off. If my mother had known, I'd be dead now.

We had a clique. We had our friends, we had our own group. If one guy had a set of works, we all had a set of

works. There was no such thing as lend me your works and
I'll give you a taste. With this new generation of dope
addicts that's coming up, *everything* is changed—money,
drugs, and the ways of people.

That time when I first got arrested, the cop didn't have a
search warrant. Legally, if I could have had the money, I
think I could have beat the case. This was a neighborhood
cop who had seen us get out of a taxicab and go upstairs.
We had scored, and we went upstairs to shoot up. By the
time he came up, my three friends had left the house, and he
grabbed them in the hallway and made them come back to
the apartment and knock on the door. And then he come in
without a warrant and searched the house and found works
and confiscated the evidence. That's what actually happened.
It was Illegal Search and Seizure, but I didn't have the
money to fight it. If I had the money, I would never have got
three years' probation; I would have beat the case in court.

My mother was notified the day I was arrested; she came
down to the Seventh Precinct and wanted to know what it
was all about. She didn't know I was using it. She may have
suspected it, but she never let on. I don't know how she
took it when she found out; I don't remember. She didn't
get me out on bail or nothing. They told her, keep us in, it
will do us good. So she kept us in. She didn't do anything.

I was in The Tombs exactly two weeks, and I was sick
from the first day on. I just lay on the floor and kicked. They
don't give you no medication or nothing. Then the judge
remanded me there for two weeks before I went to Riverside.
When I went to Riverside I was really clean.

Was I helped at Riverside? How much could I have been
helped, if I went back to drugs? I did stay off for a year
afterwards, but perhaps it was a combination of not wanting
to be arrested, having my wife, and things like that. I might
not have been helped at Riverside. I refused all psychiatric

treatment. I didn't feel I needed it. I refused it, and I think I did pretty good without it.

Was I happy when I married my wife? I guess it was just like everything else. I don't know what's happy and what's not happy anymore. Ain't very much that's really happy. It was all right. We were having good times and all like that. What happened to my marriage? Drugs broke us up. I was married in August, I got arrested in October.

I was picked up with two guys, and we had three bags of stuff on us. I was on probation at the time, but they paroled me in my wife's custody. And the case ran two years, until 1959. Finally I was dismissed from probation favorably. But I was still using drugs.

I was seeing a probation officer all that time. I don't know how I fooled him. I had a job—I've always had a job, except now. He never looked at my arms. He asked me if I was taking dope and I told him no. He never bothered looking, 'cause he trusted me. And that was it. I didn't really fool him: I fooled myself.

The marriage broke up in 1959, after my case had been dismissed. We broke up on account of her family. They were bringing pressure to bear against her and against me. They constantly told her I was no good, and I'd never be any good. She finally went for it, and got divorced.

My mother disowned me. This happened just a few weeks ago. We don't talk, and I can't get in touch with her. It's the same thing with the rest of the family: they're all fed up with me. They went out of their way to help me. I did borrow money many a time, but times I paid 'em back and times I didn't. Very few times that I didn't—this way I could always borrow again.

I don't think they've been unfair. I think they've been very liberal, they've been very honest, and I love them all. I just wish that, well, with the help of God and somebody else, and with my own strength, that I'll stop using drugs and prove myself worthy of. . . . That's it. I mean, what more can I say about them? They've done what they did. They tried hard. They've gave me money, they've stood by me in court; they fed me, clothed me; they talked to me, pleaded with me; they've begged me; they hollered at me; they went from one extreme to another to help. It didn't do any good. They tried, they really did. I can't say anything bad about them, 'cause I've got a terrific family. Anything that happened to me, I brought it on myself. It's up to myself to get out of it.

I haven't had a shot in a couple of days, but I feel that maybe I need some, well, psychiatric help, or something like that, social work or something. Maybe I can find out more about myself and more about the problem. Maybe try and combat it. By getting a job and standing on my own two feet again, which I gotta do soon. Because I'll soon be standing on my two feet without shoes. It's rough.

Since 1956, when I quit vocational high school on my sixteenth birthday, I've belonged to the union—Printing Utilities Branch, No. 6. Long as you're paid up on your dues, you can get a job through the union one-two-three. I can get a job. I don't have to tell you why I haven't got a job right now. I'm behind on my union dues and I'm behind on everything. It's been six weeks since I've worked. I got fired. I got paid and I took off on a Thursday afternoon. I didn't come back to work in the afternoon—next thing I knew I'd lost my job. It was a pretty fair job—I was averaging 120 a week with overtime. I couldn't kick. But I just had to go down and get high, so I lost out.

I got paid before lunch, and I went down on my lunch hour. I figured I'd have forty-five minutes. Because it only takes six minutes down and six minutes back by cab, and I figured ten minutes to score and fifteen minutes to get off. I'd done it a couple of times before. But when I got down there I couldn't find anybody to score from, and I had to walk around and walk around and walk around and walk around, take a taxi here, take a taxi there. Before I knew it, three hours had gone by, and I couldn't go back then so I said the hell with it. When I went back the next day, I found out I got fired.

I usually try to get myself a furnished apartment—you know, two and a half rooms, something like that—because I don't like these dirty places. I usually go into a nice neighborhood and get a clean place. But right now it's the . . . it's the subway for me. I got no money, so I don't have no place to sleep or anything. But as I say, when I have money I go out and get a decent place, and I keep it clean, too. It's something that my mother always . . . always be clean. And that's the way I am. I go up to a friend's house every day and shave.

The general picture of a dope addict is being a dirty, nasty person, and I try not to be that way. Although the collar on my shirt is dirty . . . it's from sweat because it's real hot out today. But usually I'm not that way. I change my underwear and socks every day. If I possibly can.

The general picture of a drug addict is a person who is a vicious, low-life, scheming animal. They don't even consider him a person. And it's wrong, because he is a person. He has feelings. He knows what it is to love and be loved, and to like and dislike. They think the drug addict is the lowest form on earth, and it's not so. If the drug addict is given half a chance to—how can I say it?—to love someone or something, he does. You see, I'm all mixed up right now. It's hard to explain. But the image of a drug addict is wrong —it's entirely wrong. Because they're sick. They need not only psychological help, but medication. And after that there's a lot of things involved that I just can't put my fingers on. But it's not a problem where a person should be beaten or arrested and thrown into jail, like a common criminal that has no need for drugs, that just goes out to steal because he wants to steal, that he shouldn't work, that he should just steal to live.

The reason that the drug addict steals is that the public themselves force him in a way to do it. They disapprove of drugs: they disapprove of the drug addict. But while they're disapproving of it, they're making a market for the illicit sale of drugs. They're raising the prices—the public themselves are making the prices go higher—and that's making it harder for a drug addict to get stuff. Now if it were legal, what we spend five dollars for, we could go into a drugstore and get for maybe three cents. Now if you could go into a drugstore and get it for three cents, there would be no need to steal. Right? I mean the criminal element would be taken out of it.

All right, they say it's wrong, because you're hurting yourself. But so is an alcoholic hurting himself, yet he can walk into a store and buy a bottle of liquor. And the drug addict can't go out there and buy his shot. So I think the public makes a drug addict what he is.

Not that I'm blaming them—I think the drug addict should never have started using drugs in the first place. But they make him what he is, and then when they get something stolen from them, they holler.

And now there's a lot of people saying, let's help the drug addicts. What help? I went down to a hospital about two months ago, I went to Metropolitan to sign in, and what do they tell me? We'll give you a date. Two months ago they give me a date—May 10—to come back and kick a habit. I've already done it at home. I haven't been using drugs in a couple of days now. But if I had to wait till May 10—God knows what woulda happened!

I don't think that drug addicts are criminals—at least, not

the ones I know. We've all been raised by good families. Our families all got good names, good backgrounds. It's just the high cost of narcotics. They have to go somewhere, they have to do something to get money. That's the only reason they steal.

It's ruining our country. I'm a drug addict, but I'm still an American citizen and I'd gladly fight for my country. But it's really ruining the teenagers today. It's killing a lot of them off. I mean, it's no good.

ELEVEN MONTHS LATER

I GOT a job in a printing place, worked up until Christmas, bought a few presents for the family. I set type by hand, run a press, pick up type at other shops. The first job I ever had was in a print shop, and I stayed with it ever since. I've always worked, even though I used drugs. I've kept a steady job at all times.

I got arrested again: nothing new. On December 24, Christmas Eve, I went up to my mother's house and I stayed there until about three or four in the morning, celebrating Christmas. From there I went home, went to sleep, woke up the next day with a slightly large head. I had a few drinks at my mother's—I don't like to drink in bars, anyway—I just have a phobia, I guess. I woke up late, went out and took a walk. I went to call my mother, and the next thing I know I was arrested for interfering with a telephone. Telephone had been broken prior to my arrival; someone said they had seen me lift the coin-box off, or break it off, which I couldn'ta done, because I had no tools on me. This was brought out in court and it was in my favor, but my past record all went against me. I wound up getting convicted, and got sixty days.

I got a lawyer, cost me a hundred and a half, which is cheap. He come into court and defended me. Pretty good lawyer, but very young. He knows his law, but like I say, he's not too smart on court procedure, I guess. He can learn a lot.

Why didn't I get in touch with you? Well, it's my own bed, I gotta lay in it myself. Gave up a long time ago asking people to get me out of jail. So I figured I'd do it by myself.

I didn't want *anybody* to know, really. But I guess they knew because of the lapse of time I was gone. Then I told 'em anyway, when I come out. But I didn't feel I wanted to bother anybody with it, because, you know . . . such a meatball case . . . and I didn't want anybody down there.

I told my mother what happened. And she believed me. I wrote her a letter while I was in jail. That's how she found out.

We tried to get the case dismissed on the grounds of an illegal arrest, because there was three different arresting persons in the case. I should have been arrested by the first, but I wound up getting booked by the third. We tried to make a motion to have the case dismissed and the evidence suppressed and all, and they wouldn't go for it because the D.A. kept hollering, Your honor, he's a drug addict, he's a drug addict, he's got prior convictions, he's a drug addict! And that was it. Every time the judge heard I was a drug addict, they just put it into me a little further.

I didn't kick no habit in The Tombs; I didn't have a habit to kick. The Tombs is a drag anyway. It's a big bore, sitting in that cell, locking out, locking in, locking out. It's the same procedure, day in day out. It gets on your nerves. When I went in they asked me if I used narcotics, I told 'em yeah and they put me in on the ninth floor, which is reserved for drug addicts. It was ugly, deplorable! Guys sick all over the place! And they don't get nothing; they get thorazine, twenty-five milligrams of thorazine, which wouldn't calm an ant's nerves.

Most of the guys were kicking cold turkey. A guy died in the cell next to me, five days after I got there. Doctor comes up there every day, but I wouldn't call that an examination. He didn't die from drugs; he hung up, you know. . . . He had a real bad habit, they didn't treat him, he couldn't take it and he hung himself up. Hung himself! Belt, I guess. It was night, and I woke up with the commotion when they carried him out. And that was it: he was dead. No pity, no compassion, no nothing. He was just another inmate that was dead. The officer was mad because it happened on his shift: that was the only thing he felt. He said, couldn'ta happened on another shift, it had to happen on mine!

What happened with that telephone? I put a dime in the phone, I didn't get no dial tone, I hung up, but I didn't get no dime back. I pressed the coin return, but the phone was loose, it was at an angle, so I just lifted the top part up, with my hands. And I looked and I shook the phone to see if the dime would come out. It didn't come out, and . . . next thing I know I was getting arrested.

I had walked out of the phone booth. Someone had called the cops, said they had seen me tear the phone off the wall with my bare hands or a tool. They looked around the scene of the crime, or the supposed crime, and they didn't find no tools or anything. And I was pulled into the station house and booked. I was in The Tombs till January 16, when I went out on bail. I went back on February 10—I got remanded.

I served the rest of my time on Hart's Island. It's an island for petty crime—ninety-day bits, six months, a year I think is the most you can do there. Drug addicts everywhere. Any jail you go into, the main population is drug addicts. You always meet somebody you know.

I've lived in Rockaway, Queens, Brooklyn, New York—mainly below 14th Street. I live alone, mostly in a furnished room. I haven't got too many friends that don't use drugs. Occasionally I go out with them, or with myself, or my family. But I'm always out—there's always people around. You're never really alone. Can't be alone in this world. No, I don't walk the streets. I just come and go, I go home, I go to work, I go to my Mom's, or my aunt's, or I'll go out to a show every once in a while by myself. And that's about it.

I don't really have a social life. Not that I don't want to, it's just that activities are limited for a drug addict. Not much to talk about. You know the activities of a drug addict—it's been explained before. And like I say, I don't have very many friends who don't use drugs. I mean, I get along with people. I'm not anti-social, or anything like that. People like me and I like people. But sometimes I prefer to remain by myself.

The most dangerous time that I might go back on drugs? Any second, any minute, any day. Not necessarily a discouraging occasion—could be a happy occasion. It could happen any time. On the spur of the moment, without warning. I can't put my finger on any reason. If I could, I'd probably look out for that reason and not let it come. But there is no definite reason.

I come out of jail last Friday and I went back to work Monday. They knew I was arrested, but I told 'em I was arrested for drunk and disorderly. I told 'em I wanted my job, and I'm a good worker, and they held it for me. That's all there was to it. Same wage, same hours, same everything.

SIX DAYS LATER

I'M mixed up. (*Very upset.*) I'm mixed up and I don't know
where to turn. I'm looking for a lot of help. I don't know
what to do, honest, I don't know what to do.

I got paid Wednesday morning. At 4:15 in the morning
—that's the shift I'm on. That was just before lunchtime. I
got $39.37; we always get it in cash. I got paid, I had lunch,
I went and I worked through the rest of the night, I went
home that morning and I tried to sleep. I couldn't sleep: the
money was preying on my mind. I wound up going out and
I took a walk along the Avenue. In my heart I says I don't
want to score, but I did it anyway, I guess.

I live in a room, one room, with a bed, bureau, patched-up
walls, and cockroaches all over the place. It's not fit, really.
It's exceptionally poor. I have no friends in the building—
I try never to live with a friend or near a friend. I find the
only way you can stop is by getting away from them and
staying away.

I dozed off, but I woke up restless. I wasn't actually thinking of the money, but I guess psychologically, in my sub-
conscious, it was there. It kept pestering me. I got up, I took
a walk in the neighborhood, and I scored. I met this kid and
we went down and I copped two bags.

He went to the pusher's house. I told him to get two bags.
I gave him twelve dollars. We got his works, and we went
up to my room. And we got off.

I got off first, and that's all I remember until I got up,
I staggered out of the room, and I heard people hollering,
I heard someone hollering. I wasn't in my right mind. It was
my landlord. They started calling me a drug addict and this
and that, and I guess I said one word after another. She

threw me out, and I told them, take your room and shove it up . . . you know.

And I walked around. I didn't even go to work. Or nothing. I fell asleep on a subway or a bench or something, I don't know. I don't know because I was so high I wasn't myself, I just wasn't there. So it didn't make any difference where I fell asleep. I just fell right out.

It was an overdose. I never test it—just pick it up and shoot it in your arm and figure it's like always. This was the first fix in a couple of months. I guess the stuff was a little better than it usually is. And I went out.

When I woke up I was broke. And I had no room. That was it. And that's why I'm a louse. 'Cause I keep lousing up my life one step after another and I can't. . . . I don't know, I get so disgusted with myself.

My money went into somebody else's arm. I gather I was out for two hours, so anything coulda happened. We went up to the place about five; I woke up about seven downstairs on the cot. He wasn't there any more—he was gone and so was his works.

I went upstairs and sat in my room in a deep nod. And then the woman started. I walked out, and I just kept walking. I was so tired I don't know where I went—just sat down again and passed out. I woke up in the middle of the night sometime and I just walked. I always walk, I like to walk. I was just so muddled and in a mess I didn't know where to turn. I don't even know if I got a job.

I didn't even feel like coming back here. There's something wrong with me and I don't want to hurt nobody. I know everybody's helped me and everybody's been nice to me. I keep lousing up one step after another. I just keep lousing up.

I got to stop—it's not that I want to—I got to! I can't go

on living like this; I'm not even living, it's not even a life. I'm just one mess. . . .

Last Sunday I walked all over. I walked from the West Side, walked from the East Side to the West Side, through Washington Park. Watched them play on guitars and beat on bongo drums. Though there were very little bongo drums. Mainly guitars and banjos, singing folk songs. And I walked down, walked down along Sixth Avenue, all the way down to Broadway, down past City Hall, down to Battery Park. Stayed there and I watched the water a while. And people. Just listened to sounds, and watched the boat go back and forth to the Statue of Liberty. Just sitting, just alone, just thinking. Thinking how much I . . . I want to do good. Thinking how I failed so many times, and wondering if I'll ever do good. Listening to sounds: birds, people, wind, trees. All the little things in life . . . that somehow you don't pay attention to every day. Just when you're alone, and don't know where to turn, these things keep you company maybe. Maybe that's what they did to me.

There were lots of people. Washington Park was so packed you could hardly find leg-room. But I didn't pay too much attention to them. You know, a little—to the way they were dressed, to what they were doing. Sometimes I wonder— like I'd see a guy and girl, husband and wife, and I'd say, gee, look what I lost. I could be there like that, having someone to love, and someone to love me in return. That's all I really want. I don't know. I don't think it's too much to ask, but it's so hard to get.

I always feel that, walking down the street, I always feel people notice me. Like they say, look at that—he looks like a drug addict. I always feel that way. Always try to look good, but yet lately I haven't, I can't. I don't know.

Yesterday was my mother's birthday. I didn't go. I try not to forget her birthday, even though I don't buy her nothing big. A card . . . I didn't even send her a card. It's hard maybe for her to understand that I love her, and I don't want to hurt her. Maybe it's hard for people to understand that I love the human race.

I don't understand myself. Everybody tries to help me, and I take advantage, I louse myself up. That's why I didn't want to come back here tonight.

My aunt helps me. But some parts of the family feel I'm a lost cause, I'll just never be any good. Sometimes I hear it—mainly they don't tell you. No one likes to tell anybody anything, really.

Aunt Lena tells me anytime I want something to eat, I can just come on up to the house. But Jimmy don't even want me up there. Last Sunday I came up to get a cup of coffee, and I heard: What's the matter—ain't he working? Can't he afford his own coffee? Little things like that hurt. Maybe I deserve it, but nobody wants to hear things like that.

Sometimes things go smooth with my mother, but other times when maybe she ain't feeling good or maybe I'm depressed or something . . . maybe it's me, I don't know. Things just don't go right, that's all.

I can't, I can't steal. If I could steal I wouldn't ask people to help me out with money. I'd go out and rob my own. But I can't. It's hard. Like I say, I like the human race. People work hard for their money. I just can't go to somebody I don't know and take something off them, when they may have struggled for years to get just that little item. You can't do that. I can't do it, anyway. That's just the way I am.

I don't know, I guess addicts are lonely. 'Cause really you can't trust nobody. Like the friend who took my money. You can't trust nobody in this game. That's why mainly everybody stays by themselves. But some people are lucky enough they still have their family. Their families stay with them no matter what. They just, you know, they don't like what's going on, but they figure what can they do to help it, really. Except be nice to the party, and try their best to help him that way. 'Cause threats and all that other stuff, that don't help. They know it, so they figure just be nice to him. And help him out as much as they can. The ones that haven't got families . . . well, it's just that much lonelier.

I can't live with my mother. She's just a guest in the housing project herself—she lives with my grandmother. It's not that. I don't know, there's a lot of little things that I don't agree with my mother maybe, and my mother don't agree with me. I love her and all like that; I'd give her my two arms if they would help her. But it's always the drugs that come in our way. Come in my way to happiness every time, every time I try to do something good. To have people believe in me, to show people that I want to do good. It's always dope. Always something . . . there's something wrong with me. There's something so terrible wrong, I got to find out. And I don't even know if finding that will help. I just gotta do something, before I go completely nuts.

At times I feel I'm going nuts. And I'm not ashamed to say it. Not much to talk about. It's just that you feel so fed up that everything just hits in your head, just all at once. And you think of so many things all in one second, it just crams into your mind, you don't know where to turn, your nerves are all on edge. . . . I feel sometimes like getting out of the way, running away, just getting lost. Stop hurting people and stop hurting myself.

I don't feel like I'm like anybody: I'm just me. And I'm enough to contend with. I feel so ashamed of myself. Just sitting here talking to you, I feel so small. I don't know. I just want to beat my head up against a wall. Everything goes wrong. If I try to buy something I lose the money or something. . . . Maybe it just ain't meant for me to be normal.

Maybe I better go to an asylum. . . .

I just don't feel like myself. It just ain't me anymore. I'm a puppet.

Nothing gives me relief at a time like this. You take drugs, you still feel the same. At least I do, anyway. Right now a drug ain't gonna help me. 'Cause this is something that keeps eating away at me; everywhere I turn it's always there.

Can't blame it all on drugs, it's me, I gotta find out what's wrong with me.

To straighten me out, so I can be like other people. So I can be normal, or what they call normal. So I can converse, so I can get out to dances again. Like a shell—crack it, get out. Do something again, be normal. Do anything that everybody else does. I'm not that way anymore. I'm hidden away, I'm hiding myself away.

I was always social. And I still believe myself to be. But yet I have no friends, nothing to show for it.

I was just a little kid when I first came here. I remember how I advanced from the playroom to intermediate, and from intermediate into senior. You had one hell of a time to get us out of the building. I don't think any of the kids really wanted to leave. We really enjoyed ourselves here. I guess the kids today still do. We always had a good time at the Settlement. Even when we grew up. Except when we started fooling around with drugs, and the Settlement got lost in the background.

We had a club called the International Dukes. It was called that because we more or less had a person representing every race, every creed and nationality. Chinese, colored, Italian, Polish, Irish, Jewish, Puerto Rican, Filipino, and others that I forget offhand. We used to call the park the U.N., the United Nations. We had a girls' club—they used to call themselves the International Dukettes. And they were also the same way—interracial. We had a good time. When the Maros asked us to go down on another club, we went.

We were all friends in our club. We always stayed together —didn't make no difference who you went down on.

All of us were good guys. Almost every one of us turned out to use drugs. I don't think there's but about maybe two that didn't. So far two have kicked it—Jacky Stein and Rocky Rapello. Rocky's left it alone completely. And Jacky fools around every time he comes back to the city. They both live out in San Francisco. Rocky was gonna become a cop out there. I don't know what happened—something went wrong, he didn't make it. Everybody else except Solly —and the two Chinese guys—they all fool around. Solly never fools around. The Yang brothers did—only one of them did, Billy—and he's stopped now, from what I hear. But he goes once in a while. Denny Dickson never touched it; he's in the army now. I don't know how he had the will power, but he had it. I give him all the credit in the world. Jimmy Ruffo—he's had a rough time. Nick Abruzzi. My cousin Georgie. Dom Abruzzi. Allen Stanton—he never fooled around. Larry Greenberg, Frank Agostino. Dicky Shoemaker. Anderson. That's about it. The last guys I mentioned—every one of them uses dope. Oh yes, and Goldman was in the club, too. He's in Sing-Sing now. He was copping for somebody, and that somebody had a policeman with him. He used to be pretty good at numbers. He was a terrific gambler.

ONE MONTH LATER

My wife was the type girl that didn't really mind my using drugs—it was the idea that I kept lying to her. It was that I lied to her in a way so that I wouldn't want to hurt her, that I wouldn't want to tell her I was using drugs. Like I'd say, baby, I'm not using drugs, *believe me,* I'm not using drugs. And in the long run the lie would come out, and she would be more hurt in the end. That's the only trouble I really had with my wife. It wasn't the problem of using or getting money—just the idea that I lied to her.

Nobody wants to see another person hurt. And especially when they're causing the hurt. So naturally they're going to tell the other person a lie, so as not to hurt them. But in the long run the lie is exposed, the person is exposed to a double hurt, and, well, they're doubly mad. But even a drug addict has feelings for other people, doesn't want to see them hurt. So I feel that if the drug addict lies and says, well, I'm not using drugs, he's trying to be a little understanding and think of the other people's welfare, too. But I find now it's best to be honest and tell someone, yes, I am using. If they're going to be understanding, they will be; if not, if they're going to give you an argument and throw you out, it's best to have it right then and there.

You know how I am now: I'm as low as you can get right now. I was never without someplace where I could get money before. Never without my own money or a place to borrow money. But I think my chances of getting back on weekly salary are pretty good, as long as I keep looking. If I stop looking, then I'm worried. As long as I keep looking, there's a chance of me getting something. Thanks to you I have my union membership up to date. I'm going up to the union hiring hall every day—I been up there at eight-thirty every day so far, as soon as they open the doors.

In jail the addicts talk about narcotics every minute of the day. Every minute of the day. The main subject in the whole prison is narcotics. You could remember an instance where you almost got arrested, and you say yeah, remember we swallowed the bag and we beat the cop; could be another instance where you say, remember we went up in so-and-so's house, and the works clogged and we had a hassle; or remember the day so-and-so overdosed?—yeah, we had to work on him for hours; and then I was scoring over here on such-and-such a street, scoring over there on such-and-such a street, and I knew this guy and I knew that guy—oh yeah, he was a good guy, or he was a good connection. That's the main subject, every day. It's always drugs.

Drugs are more or less a password in jail. You use drugs, you hang out. That's mostly what you see in jail these days are drug addicts.

You meet people. You meet people in jail, you meet people in hospitals, you meet people in the streets. Everyone comes from a different neighborhood, but you know him. Say you're uptown and looking to score, and you meet someone who may be from a different neighborhood, and he'll put you on to someone to score, or he'll go with you. You stick pretty much to yourselves—pretty much one drug addict circle. As far as contacting people from the outside . . . well, you have very little to do with the rest of the world, because they have nothing in common with you. Matter of fact, they're going to put you down most of the time. So it's not you that's staying away from them, it's them that's staying away from you. If you want to look at it that way.

A WEEK LATER

I'M sick. There's no problem, just gotta go out and earn money. I got a job, but I didn't go to it in the past few days 'cause I didn't have a fix to go with. All there is to it.

I'm gonna lose my job if I don't go to work. I just got it a week ago, two weeks ago—how long can I stay away?

It's a printing place. I work on the floor, I make up ads, and that's it. It's just a regular printer's job. I don't run a machine right now, I'm setting type by hand. I make pages up. Right now I'm making eighty-seven dollars and change, to be exact—that's without the overtime. I got the job through the union. I borrowed money from you to pay my union dues.

I was hoping I wouldn't have to tell you I was back on the stuff again. Not that you wouldn't be able to tell, just that I wouldn't tell you. Thought maybe I would take off, stop, and straighten out. But things just ain't worked out that way right now.

Yes, I know, I've been coming in the past few months and asking you for money for food and rent. Well, most of the time it was legit—I used the money to rent a room, I got a job. It was legit; I was going out and getting money for fixes too, somewhere else. Tried my best, hustling around. But when I borrowed money for room rent, you could come with me and I'd prove to you I paid that money for rent. That's one thing I didn't do, is lie, about the rent. I told you, you're gonna get the money back. I got my work, I got my pay. And if I do get fired I got two weeks' pay. The first thing I do will be to go down and pay you. Part of it, any-way. Forty dollars—thirty dollars, I know, I gotta give you, I promised.

You ask me how I get along? I don't know; I just get along. It just comes. Doing people a favor or something. I don't know where it comes from, I don't know how it comes, but it comes. Every day, something new presents it-self. Maybe somebody wants to use my spike, or something like that.

I don't know anything about addicts living off prostitutes. Anybody knows there's prostitutes around here, but that's all I know. I don't bother with them, I don't want to bother with them, I don't want to know nothing about them either.

Using, that's all I know: using and myself.

No, not really, my mood hasn't changed. I'm not irritated. I'm sick. I haven't had a fix all day. And I *need* one.

I took my last fix yesterday night, about eleven o'clock. I had two bags. I gotta shoot 'em both up at once. They hold me long enough, 'cause I went to sleep. I took the shot and before I slept I read the papers. I woke up about two o'clock this afternoon.

I don't get high anymore. I just get straight; I take a cure. I'm just normal, that's all. You don't nod, you just act straight; you do things that you were meant to do. The way God meant you to be in the first place.

I'm getting nauseous, I got cold sweats, I'm nervous, I'm on edge. I'm soon gonna start vomiting. You get sick as hell and you can't walk anymore and you lay down and that's it, you don't want to move.

Every time I went to jail I kicked cold turkey.

Not right now! I'm hooked, I got to do something!

Yeah, but I'm not going to go in the hospital tonight. They're not going to take me.

Look at me now, look at me, I'm wringing wet. It's hot in this room, but I'm cold. I got the chills. There's no draught blowing and I got the chills. How do you get that unless you're sick?

When I get a fix I'll be straight. In seconds. Soon as you get it in your arm.

One bag's not enough to straighten me. I tried one bag and it don't even phase me. It don't even pin my eyes. I never go to work unless I'm straight. I need two bags every fifteen hours.

I'm asking you for money to cop two bags with. I'll have it back to you in the morning. That's my promise. I won't even sleep tonight. I'll be in tomorrow morning, I'll give you the money, then I'll probably have to go out and cop again, then I'll go home and go to sleep.

Sure, I want to go in the hospital—I want to kick. I went there once, but it didn't help. There was such a crowd there, and I don't know, they tell you wait, wait wait, wait wait. I didn't bother waiting; I left.

FIVE DAYS LATER

I NEVER use any other vein but the mainline vein inside my left elbow. All I have to do is put the needle on it and it falls right in, one two three—never have any trouble.

First thing you do is get your needle and your eye-dropper —which is a makeshift syringe—and your spoon, your cooker, and a piece of cotton for a filter. First I check to see if the needle is clean: I fill the eyedropper with water, and shoot the water out through the needle, and this way I know the needle is clean. Then I put the drug into the spoon or cooker—some people use a bottlecap—and add half an eye-dropper of water. I take a match or two and light it underneath the spoon or cooker and let it cook. When it cooks to a boil, I drop in the piece of cotton. Then I take the eye-dropper and I draw it up through the cotton. I put the spike on the eyedropper and I tie my arm up with a belt. I put the eyedropper and the spike in my right hand, and I hold the belt with my knee; then I just tap the spike in or push it in, depending on its sharpness. Then I get a hit. When the blood comes up through the eyedropper, you loosen up the belt and you shoot it in. Just to make sure you got a hit, you let go of the top of the eyedropper and the blood comes up. You shoot that in and you pull the needle out. Usually you bleed a little; you wipe the blood off your arm with a rag or some toilet paper or a handkerchief. Then you clean out your works, make sure all the blood is out. Some people shoot sterilizing alcohol through the spike. Once in a while, when I get a chance, I put the spike in a pot of boiling water. This way you don't get no yellow jaundice, or anything like that. If somebody else uses the needle besides myself, I always do that. I've never had yellow jaundice and I hope never to get it. After I make sure the works are clean, I wrap them up and put them away, so I can keep them clean. I put them in a pay envelope and I put them away someplace, so they can't be found.

I don't keep anything in my room. I usually hide my works behind a radiator, in a hallway, or under the stairs. Sometimes I keep them in the same place for a matter of weeks. But sometimes I might bring someone to use them with me, and he might see where I have them. So naturally I move them. I don't leave them there, because he'll be back to look for them to keep them for himself. So it's never in the same spot too long.

As long as we're leveling, I told you last Wednesday I was working at a print shop these past two weeks, which I really wasn't. It's just like, you know, maybe if I tell a man I work I'll be able to get something, and I can go out and use it for dope. And I did use it for dope, except when you did give me the rent money, I did pay my rent. Because to me having a roof over my head is much more important than having a fix in my arm. Because I can always go out and hustle a fix, but I can't hustle a room. Every time I told you I paid my rent, I did pay my rent. And I can prove it by taking you up to the man.

To get back to Wednesday night, I left you Wednesday after telling you I had a habit. I also told you I had money, which I didn't have; told you I had a job, which I didn't have.

Now you gave me ten dollars. With that ten dollars, I was going out to score two bags. But I met Roy, and Roy had dilaudid and dolophine. I told him I only had ten dollars, and he sold me eleven dolophine tablets, ten grains each. Now they help a drug addict kick better than anything I know of. With dolophine you don't have to stay in bed, you can walk around. So from Wednesday on I stayed up in my room and I kicked. I'm pretty well clean now—the only thing I have trouble with is sleeping at night. And right now I don't even have a bed to sleep in; the landlord locked me out of my room.

Roy had those pills because he had a doctor writing for him. But today I met someone who told me the doctor cut him loose; in other words, he's finished with him. I guess the federal government must be after him. Because this kid used to walk in every day and get a prescription for dolophine, dilaudid or demerol. Now you can't keep writing all three every day for the same man. Roy had kicked at K-Y [Lexington, Kentucky] but he started in again. And he's been getting this doctor to write for dilaudid at a sixteenth of a grain, and he writes for thirty pills at a time. And that's enough to get anybody hooked. Roy has been home for close to a month, and I guess he's using every day. He gets his money by selling what he doesn't use. He gets a dollar and a half for a sixteenth of a grain of dilaudid, and a dollar a pill for dolophine. Now he gave me eleven for ten dollars, so I got what you might call a break. They used to sell dolophine for fifty cents a tablet, so things have gone up.

Yes, I feel I've kicked. The only thing that will give me a hard time now is sleeping. But I'll tell you one thing I won't try, and that's sleeping pills. So I'll do without the sleeping. I took them once, and I almost fell off a train platform. I think that's worse than heroin. I'm just afraid of them—afraid of what I might do to myself. I might go to sleep with a cigarette in my hand, burn my house and burn myself to death. I just got a natural fear of them. Plus they make you crazy. You just keep using them and using them and after a while you go bugs. I'm talking about barbiturates—pheno barb, nembutal, seconal, nebutal, doriden. You just go crazy after a while. That's why they call those pills goofballs.

Some drug addicts get on goofballs in order to supplement the heroin—to bring up their high. The two of them work together because both of them are more or less depressants, I guess. But I won't try it. You can't take goofballs to kick heroin—you just get sick and vomit violently.

Last Friday I saw Howard and we got down on a bag together. I was already straight, so to split a bag would just add a little more. So we got off together, and he looked fine—you know, all in one piece, no scars, no scrapes or nothing. Then a few days later I saw him walking around and his nose had swelled terrific—looked like one of these Indian noses, but fat, gigantic. And it was all cut: his forehead was cut, his cheek was cut, and his whole nose was scraped, like the skin was just all taken off. And I says, Howard! What happened? And he says, oh, I got high on goofballs last night, and I fell on my face. And I saw him again and he asked me for fifty cents, but I told him, I don't have it, Howard; if I had it I'd give it to you. But Howard! Look at your face! Why don't you get off of them goofballs? And he told me, I'll have to, before I get hooked. They always tell you that. And today I seen him again. He fell down on his face again, and his face looks something pitiful. It looks like he fell on a grating of some kind, and it looks completely scraped—his forehead, head, chin, lips—everything cut and scabbed.

I looked at his face and I said to myself: Thank God, Tommy, that you don't use them goofballs. I was talking to myself now, and I said, Tommy, what is it? You get addicted to heroin, just like they do. But how come they let themselves go to such an extreme? How can a person do that to themselves? Don't they look in a mirror? Can't they see themselves?

What really loused Manny up was the goofballs. You know, I've known Manny since we both came here to the Settlement together when we were kids, and we went to school together, too. Well, Manny was a whole lot smarter than I was in school—although I had a pretty high I.Q. myself, which I never used to the right purposes. But Manny did use his I.Q. right, until he started hanging around with the wrong crowd. By now Manny's changed a whole lot since we went to school. He got slow mentally and slow in his movements, his talking, his thinking—everything slowed to a real lull. And I feel bad because Manny's a pretty bright guy. He still has enough sense to know it's gonna hurt and he's trying his best to get away. But it is a hard fight. He's got his brothers helping him once in a while, but when his mother died, in 1959, Manny went to pieces after that. The people in his family, mainly his father, blamed Manny for his mother's death. In that case you can't blame anyone: she died of cancer. You can't give anyone cancer. You can kill a person with heart failure or something like that, but you can't give them cancer. And they blame Manny?

How do I know? Well, you get high with a guy sometimes, and he lets out his innermost secrets. It's not really him talking, it's the drug. But he lets it out. I told him a lot of things, too: you know, about how I feel about my wife, and her family—things like that.

We get together sometimes, a lot of us, and we talk about how we'd all like to quit using drugs and we hope someday that there'll be a miracle cure and everyone would stop, and we'd all turn back to the way we were when we were kids— we were all smart kids. We'd use our experiences now to help someone else, and things like that. I mean, we're not really all bad, we haven't got all bad streaks in us. We'd like to do a lot of good, too, but, you know, like it's the dope. Anyway, we express ourselves to each other; we give a little more thought to each other.

The main topic is usually how we'd like to stop using drugs. Especially with Manny. I've helped Manny out a lot. Just the way you've helped me out. I'm not a social worker or anything like that, but I can honestly say—and God be my judge—that I've helped a lot of drug addicts down here on the Lower East Side.

I'll just take Manny for one example. One time Manny was living in the streets, and at that time I was a little lucky. I had left my wife and was living with my Aunt Lena. I was living up her house, and it happened to be Thanksgiving, 1959. I was using stuff, and I had just gotten rejected by the U.S. Army. If I'da gotten in, I think I would have been better off. Anyway, I was using stuff regular, and I met Manny that day on Norfolk Street and Manny was sick. He wasn't looking good, he wasn't eating right, and he was sleeping in the street. He was pretty damn miserable about it. So I got him high, took him with me and I got him straight; but it was Thanksgiving and he had no place to eat. I couldn't take him up to the house, because my Uncle Jimmy would have said, what is this, a relief home for addicts? He's like that—he's got a very nasty streak in him. So I did the next best thing I could: I got a big plate, and I cut white meat, dark meat, stuffing, sweet potatoes, mashed potatoes, cranberry sauce, gravy, and then I got him a little jar of wine and a bottle of cold soda. Then I took Manny up on the roof and he ate. We sat up there and I brought out knives, forks, glasses—everything you could think of. I even made myself a sandwich, so he wouldn't feel lonely. I didn't want him to feel funny, like I was standing there watching him eat. So I eat with him, you know, make everything on a social basis. I felt bad I couldn't bring him in the house. It's Thanksgiving and everything and he didn't have a home—I really felt lousy. And I gave him five dollars. I had money because I was working. I was using drugs regular, but not that regular.

So I got Manny, I gave him a pound, and I said, listen, Manny, you want to get a job? I'll get you a job in my shop. But you got to do me one favor: please don't come to work high. You'll blow my cool and blow your own. The boss will know that I'm associating with drug addicts, and naturally suspicion will fall on me. So I did get him a job, we got him a place to sleep, and all like that. He only lasted about three weeks. He was high—he used to nod out. We had him on the press; he couldn't run the press. He was too high, too slow. We took him off the press and put him on leads and slugs. Now this is simple—even children that are born half-wits can do this. All you gotta do is sort different leads in different sizes, separate the leads from the slugs. He couldn't do that. He used to stand there and nod out. He'd wake up and go back and shoot a little, and the boss couldn't take it. Now I knew Manny knew how to run a press, because both Manny and I worked on a printing job when I started out and was straight. So I told the boss Manny could run a press and Manny got up there and ruined a plate! He was lucky the plate cost only four hundred dollars—some plates run into thousands. You can imagine the impression that made. Thank God I know my job or I would have got fired, too.

I got home from Riverside in February, 1957, and took three shots in two days. Then the next day I had a date with my wife, and I never touched it after that until October. I don't remember what caused me to take off again. Maybe I don't want to remember. But I remember how I got arrested. I had gotten off already only twice, and the third time I went to get off I got arrested. I was walking down and I saw Gene and Al. They were both sniveling and sick; it was chilly out, but they were sick. They tell me they just got beat for their money, somebody just beat them. They went to score and somebody took their money and never came back—played a bomb on them. I was going to take out my wife and I had twelve dollars in my pocket. So I says, okay, you guys are sick. Now I'm not hooked or anything, so I'll do you a favor. So I went to cop two five-dollar bags for them. All I need for myself is just a wee bit, because I'm clean. We were walking up towards Delancey Street and boom! they grabbed us. Four of them. Four narcos—four narcotic squad men from downtown. They pounced on us. I don't know what happened, it happened so fast. Al made a run for it; he threw the bags over a fence. But they seen what he done: they got him and picked up the bags. So they take us to the station, and Al, he's gotta go back upstate because he's on parole, so he says, look officer: why take these three guys when I can take the rap? But they wouldn't hear it; they said no, everybody's going. And I was on probation, so I made the same offer. But they said no good; everybody's going.

At the time I was seventeen and they were all over twenty-one. So they stayed in The Tombs and I went to Brooklyn. I went to court two weeks later, and I figured they're gonna send me away. But it was Judge C., a very good judge. And I had Father P. with me, and my mother, and my wife. Father P. told the legal aide that I was a steady worker and I had just got married. Then there was my probation officer. He was terrific; he'd give a guy a break where he deserved it. And he knew I had just got married and I was off drugs. Anyway, he sent in a very favorable report to the court. I hadn't done anything wrong

—the only wrong thing I had done was to get married without telling him—and I hadn't missed a reporting date. And he wrote this all up. He even wrote that he knew about my marriage. So anyway the judge postponed the case. And the judge says, I'm paroling you, son, in your wife's custody. You'll be back in court in two weeks. Well, I was so happy I nearly collapsed in court, with joy. And I cried all the way out the door, which is something I had never done in court. I was just so happy to be with my wife once more.

I went back to court two weeks later, and he postponed the case again. He postponed it a couple of months, gave me a break. To make a long story short, every time I went back to court I went back with a different suit on, always dressed well, I gained weight, looked good, had a watch on my wrist that was worth a hundred and fifty dollars. Put it this way: when my wife and I walked into court, there wasn't an eye that didn't turn to look at us. We were a very attractive couple, believe me. This went on for two years, until we were both nineteen. But we looked older—we were much more mature. We carried ourselves as an older person would. We were very well dressed—my suit cost me no less than a hundred and a quarter. We went back to court approximately every three or four months.

Now all these other guys that were caught with me—three of them—they all had their cases dismissed, don't ask me why or how. Mine was the only case that lasted for two years. Everyone else beat the case. And they went right back to drugs.

As for me, I used every day almost. And I got away with it. Only once did I get caught. Me and this guy Dom Abruzzi, we went early in the morning to cop in Brooklyn. Now what happens is that these cops see us copping. Like I'm sitting on the stoop, and the pusher lives underneath in the basement apartment. Well, he's reaching up and putting the bag on the steps, and all of a sudden these two narcos come running down the block. They don't bother me and Dom—they go running right into the pusher's house. So I pick up the bag and I put it in my mouth sideways, so if I do get away with it, it wouldn't get wet. But when we'd walked about twenty feet, they said, Hey! Where you two going? So Dom and I walked in separate directions, and they said, Stop or we'll shoot! So I thought the hell with this, I gotta swallow it. So I swallowed it before I turned around. We went back and we got the heck kicked out of us. We really got hurt. They took us inside the hall, and while they beat us they said, you were copping off him, right? And we said, no, no!

They searched the guy's house and they found fifteen ten-dollar bags and ten twenty-five dollar bags. I figured like whoops, me and Dom are going! 'Cause like Dom is on probation and I still have that case in court. But they had nothing on us, nothing at all. So they took us to the police station, scaring us and everything, trying to make us say that he was dealing to us. But we wouldn't say that. So finally the Puerto Rican, the kid that was dealing, said the hell with it! 'Cause they had him up tight: they had him on two sales already, plus a burglary and an armed robbery. What more could you want? Just the possession was enough—he had far more than the fifty-three grains it takes to make a felony. So he said, I was gonna sell 'em a bag, but then I seen you, and I didn't sell 'em. So he cut us loose. I felt bad for the guy.

Anyway, we were out. As soon as we got out of the station we went to the frankfurter stand on the corner, I bought Dom and me a soda, and I threw up. I threw up and the first thing that come out of my mouth was the bag. Well, we ran down to the subway so fast, and got out of

Brooklyn so fast . . . I think we beat the train. I was in the front car pushing.

So after that we kept going back to court, my wife and I. And every time we went we were dressed to kill. And finally the judge says to me, he says, son, you've made a man out of yourself. I don't know how I did it. I gained weight and we stayed in clothes and everything. I maintained my job, went to my probation officer, and supported my wife.

My probation officer never looked at my arm. He knew I was working and all that. And sometimes I didn't report, because I was high and couldn't go. So I'd call up and I'd tell him, and he'd say, next week, if you can't come, don't waste a dime on a call. Just send a letter, spend three cents on a postcard.

The fact that I was married, that I was working, and that I invited him over to my house made the difference. I never missed a reporting date and if I did I called or wrote, like you were supposed to. I always did what he told me to do. I invited him over many a time, him and his wife, to have dinner with us. Because my wife and myself, we had a doll house. We had a house that people were afraid to sit down in, because they were afraid of wrinkling the couch. And that's the truth. My wife used to keep it spotless. She was terrific.

In-laws ruined the marriage. In-laws and dope. They always downgraded me in front of my wife. That's something they always did; they never failed. I don't know whether that contributed to my taking dope, but I know it made a difference between me and my wife. If I would have put my foot down and said stay away from them, I think we would still be married today. But I was brought up to be a respectful son. I paid them all kinds of respect, right to the end.

TWO DAYS LATER

I PROMISED you I'd bring the works down, because that would be the only way of showing you that I'd really kicked: that I don't need the works anymore. I promised to come down last night but I took sick. I don't feel good tonight, but I promised you I'd be down and I'm down.

I took a bus to get here so I'd only have one block to walk in the neighborhood. I don't like to walk over there by Delancey Street. I'm scared because of . . . you know, the cops, the people. . . . I just don't walk there anymore. One of the detectives over there arrested me twice, and every time he sees me he shakes me down. Sometimes he just says, hello, and I say, how ya doin, Mr. N.?, because I treat him with respect, like I treat everyone. And if he asks me if I'm using it, to him I don't lie, because he'll only make me go in a hallway, roll up my sleeves, and look and see if I got fresh blood or marks. And he says, how ya doin? Ya using it? and I tell him, yeah, once in a while. And that way he don't bother me. He asks me if I got anything on me, and I say no, and if he feels in the mood he takes me and searches me. And then usually, as we say goodbye, he says, don't worry, Blake, I'm gonna get you again. You're going back to jail. And he says, I'm going to frame you, put something on you—but he don't mean it. That's one thing I can say about the man—I never heard him put one thing on anyone. He's gotta catch you right.

Excuse me, but I feel like I'm gonna vomit. . . . I'm doing myself a great deal of good, getting rid of these works. Less temptation. Long as I got them around, I can always get a fix—no need for money, I can always go out and see if anybody needs a set of works.

I feel I've stopped. I want to stop, I've got to stop. There's no choice in the matter. God knows what's gonna happen next week, but right now I know I gotta stop.

Right now I went to a couple of places to look for jobs, and things look pretty tight. A lot of shops tell me they're laying off.

I could use something to eat—I didn't eat all day yesterday. Today I think I got a fever, but right now my head feels cool. My mouth is completely dry. I've kicked a couple of habits, and usually after each one you get some sort of relapse. Sometimes it comes out in a cold, sometimes you just get nauseous, like I feel now. I feel that all the energy in me has just been drained out; I feel tired, listless. Just like that commercial—tired blood. That's what I feel like: beat.

But it will subside. It'll last a couple of days, until you rest and eat, and everything usually works out all right. The only thing that usually lasts is a cold.

I think it would be better if you didn't try to get in touch with my mother. She's got a lot of worries now, and why put an extra burden on her shoulders until I'm sure I've kicked? Until everything is perfect. Until I'm normal, I'm healthy, I'm working, and things are going along smooth. Let's just give it a try that way: I don't want to break her back any more than I have already.

I go over once a day to eat at my Aunt Lena's. Yesterday and today I didn't go over, but I usually go and I get one meal, and I go. Sometimes it's substantial and sometimes it's not, because she don't always cook right, because she don't always feel right. Practically all her stomach is gone from cancer; she finds it difficult walking and she has a lot of pain. The only reason why she's staying out and fighting as much as she is is because she wants to go to my cousin's wedding in August. The kid's more like a sister to me, 'cause Aunt Lena is my godmother and I'm practically her son. Another reason she fights is, well, she's worried about me. You know, she never knows where I'm gonna sleep, where I'm gonna eat, and what I'm gonna do. Right now she can't help me too much because my Uncle Jimmy put his foot down. He says no more money to the kid, no more nothing. I'm not even supposed to go up there to eat. But she tells me to come up while he's at work. I go up, I get a meal, and that's it.

Jimmy is like that because of the years I been fooling around with drugs. I always try, and I always fall back. They all get the same way.

We had a little difficulty when I got married. My uncle's funny; it's very hard to say but I think the man is over-sexed. There was a couple of times there when he made wrong passes at my wife. Even though I understand that my aunt is sick, and a man can't have anything to do with her, still, if you love your wife—as I loved mine—you stand by them no matter what kind of hell they're in. You don't look for other women, no matter how bad off you are. Not unless—God forbid!—God should take your wife. Then it's understandable. He made the wrong kind of passes not only at my wife, but at my mother. And I told him where to get off. And that led to a lot of the conflict. Although the rest of the family knows I'm right, they told me I should ignore him.

I can't ignore a man like that. I told him to just keep his mouth shut. If you want to do something like that, just go out to the Bowery or Delancey Street and pick up one of them two-fifty jobs. Don't come over here bothering respectable people. Especially after your wife loved you all these years and gave you herself. My mother's coming up here out of the goodness of her heart to help her sister and to clean your house, and my wife comes to help, and you've got to come out with something as nasty as that.

He never got along with me after that. Before, he was always inviting my wife and me over to the house—mainly, I think, just so he could have his look. He was funny that way—every time my wife went through the door he wanted a kiss. Of course I let my wife kiss him on the cheek, because it's something that they do regularly, in her family. Italians always believe in kissing, which is something I don't believe in. Not as a greeting. Men should shake hands like men. In my wife's family, even the men kiss when they meet. That's not an Irish custom.

My wife is very good-looking, I mean *very* good-looking. It never fails: a drug addict always seems to get himself a good-looking girl.

As far as my aunt's concerned, I'm still her son. You know, I always was her son. Because my mother always worked. My aunt looked after me. I was about seven when my parents separated. My father didn't live that much at home for me to recollect anything. He was always out. Mainly I used to see him standing on the corner. After he'd come home from work he'd be standing on the corner with his friends, or else I used to go up and see him at my grandmother's house.

When I was real young my mother was a factory worker —she worked at all kinds of factories, didn't make no difference. Any way to make an honest dollar. And I think when I was about nine or ten—no, I'm lying, I was a little older than that, about thirteen or fourteen—she got a job in an office, and she's been working there ever since.

My father is home now living with my grandmother. He's been in and out of the hospital since 1955. He's got a cerebral hemorrhage, anybody can get it. Blood clot on the brain, that's all it is. Well, he *was* a heavy user of alcohol, but not any more. He can't.

Last time I saw my father was 1958, I think. Up in Metropolitan. I went up to the hospital with my wife and introduced them. But he was incoherent, you know, with that brain damage. I don't think he even remembers I'm married.

As a father I don't know him too much. As far as him being considerate, there were times when he was and times when he wasn't. I guess everybody's like that, but a little more so with him because of the drink. As far as living a useful life, well, I don't know about useful, but he did serve in the war. That's what really ruined him. When he went to war he came back a real alcoholic. It really ruined him. He seen all these kids getting killed in action and all like that, and he used to think that he's got a son home and just thank God that it ain't his kid over there getting his belly blown out. The war really loused him up, really turned him into a real alcoholic. 'Cause he used to hold onto a job before he went into the war. He drank every once in a while, but not to the extent that he did later.

Before the war he was married and he had a job. He was always a truck driver. But I think in the worst way he wanted to become an electrician. He was good—he could wire a whole house up, but he never went to school, he could never get a license. So he stayed with truck driving. He used to always want me to become an electrician. An electrical engineer.

Like I say, he wasn't around too much for me to know about him. There was a couple of years before the war, and then when he came back he didn't live home that long. He was like a father away from home, something like that. That was it.

I don't know how my mother feels about my father. I

mean, nothing was said. What I told you was what she told me, about the war and like that.

I used to have a key to the apartment when I was in the third grade. When I was in the fifth grade I stayed out of school for three months without anyone knowing. A lot of us used to cut school. We'd go up to Dom Abruzzi's house, then we'd go to my house, then someone else's house. I mean, everything gets boring after a while. We would keep moving around. I'd sleep late till eleven o'clock, and then maybe Dom would call me and we'd go somewhere. We used to go up to 42nd Street, and for thirty-five cents we'd see three movies. I looked older than my age—I used to get away with a lot of things. We all used to act older. We were all about the same age group—only Dom is about four years older than me.

My grades weren't bad, but I always had bad conduct in school. I never got along with teachers too well. I didn't care for school anyway. What I learned I put in my head— I never kept a notebook. I know now if I woulda kept a notebook and all like that I guess I would have been a helluva lot smarter.

I quit school on the exact day I was sixteen. The Dean of Boys told me I had no choice—I had to quit. School wasn't doing me no good, so the best thing was to get me out. I was hooked; I was using already two and a half years.

I was thrown out of one junior high school for truanting and things like that . . . having fist-fights with teachers. I was more or less a nonconformist. See, I was wrong, because sometimes I seen the teacher picking on somebody they shouldn't of been picked on. So I tell the teacher, what are you picking on him for? The teacher told me mind your own business, and that would start it off. Next thing I know I'm in the principal's office, and I'm telling my story and she's telling hers. So naturally who do they believe but the teacher?

Ever since I started junior high—I don't know whether the kids respected me because I was a fighter, and I was pretty smart—I was always elected some class officer. In high school I was auditor, you know, I made speeches. Anyway, when I went to P.S. 614 I was head of the monitors, head of the safety patrol, head of everything. I was it; in 614 I was the boss. In the year and a half I was there I had two fights, and both fights were with the killers. They were supposed to be the roughest guys in the school; they were the bosses. I beat the both of them, so I became undisputed boss of 614 and I reigned for a year and a half. The teachers knew it and the kids knew it. That was it. I was like the ultimate.

We had our share of fights, and I had my reputation. Matter of fact, I got stabbed down here, when I fought the Puerto Ricans. It was in the papers. I was with seven guys; they all ran. And I fought them alone in the park for about twenty minutes. And I was beating them: they wanted to make peace. I went to make peace, and I got stabbed eight times.

It was stupid, but I wanted respect. Lot of good respect did me.

Our gangfighting didn't last too long. It's common sense: anybody that's gonna get hurt at something is not gonna keep it up for too long. You got more of a chance of getting killed in a gangfight than you do with taking drugs. So naturally guys settled down, they got girls, they got started on dope. In them days it was play, it was like a kick; nowadays it's more serious. They used to take dope, go with their girls and sit down in a corner. Mainly at the Settlement on a Friday night, we used to sit down and nod out, dance once in a while and that was it. Drugs was more relaxing; it took your mind off of things. And, you know, you didn't bother nobody.

We fought the Puerto Ricans when they first came into the neighborhood, but we all use dope together now. Matter of fact, one of the guys that stabbed me is one of my best friends now. He just got back from upstate again, and he hasn't used for four months. So I always tell him when I see him, I wish you luck, Louie! So he says, yeah, same here, I wish *you'd* dig yourself!

When we first started, instead of drinking alcohol, we went out and got high. And there was less fights. Nobody got into arguments with each other. Everybody had a good time. There was nobody really hooked. It was mainly operated on a weekend basis. It seems funny that when the cops came in to break it up, that's when everybody started getting hooked, and trouble started to begin all over again.

I just went along with the guys and we all used and that's it. Almost everyone in our club had a spike in their hand at one time. Everyone except Jack Lessing. Jack Lessing never had a stick of pot in his hand. Everybody said he was stupid, but he was the smartest one of all. Though Jack always was slow; there's something mentally wrong with him. He's retarded. The smartest retarded person that I know.

Henry Brown refused it every bit of the way. He had to go over to Korea to get hooked, and come home to die. I remember one Christmas Eve we offered it to him. He waited downstairs for us to get off. When we came down, he went off drinking with us. We were drinking, too, even with the stuff, though we didn't drink very much. We had to keep up a front. If we had some whisky our walking and our manner of scratching and our throwing up would be covered up.

Brown would refuse it, until he went away. Then he

come home, and I remember that Saturday morning, his mother woke me up with a phone call. Tommy, Henry's dead. Never forget him, I'll never forget him. The guy was like my brother. I mean, so what, he was colored—he was still like my brother. My mother treated him like a son, and his mother treated me like a son. All our club members were the same way; we were all the same way. Every one of us. Italian, Jewish, Irish, Polish, colored, Puerto Rican, Chinese—everything. Everybody was the same; everybody's mother treated everybody as if they were her son. And if there was something one mother could do to help another, she'd do it.

Those were the good old days and it was a good old club. It's no more like that; everybody's out for themselves. (*In a whisper:*) That's life.

I don't know. If it's a crutch, it's an unwanted crutch. At least by myself. But you always turn back. And when you say fall, you do fall. You fall from the heights—heaven —to the lowest hell.

I don't know what to say. I mean, who am I? I'm a guy who wants to give up something he shouldn't have started in the first place, just like a whole lot of other people. The question is will I? Can I? Sure, I got a whole lot of living to do. But will I do it with drugs or without it? All I know is I gotta try, I gotta make an effort. Without the effort I'm lost. When there's no hope, there's nothing to live for. I hope there's still some kind of hope.

I'm using dope ten years: ten years is an awful long time. I'm young in age, and I'm old in experience. I don't know. I'm alone a lot of the times. Sometimes I find it hard even where to begin to make friends.

Don't get me wrong—I'm not anti-social. I like friends. But sometimes I . . . I don't know. I don't get along with them. I don't agree with new friends or something . . . I don't know. It's hard. There's something wrong somewhere. I don't trust a lot of people. A lot of people I should trust, I don't. I really don't know why. Honest, I have no idea. That's why I say it's hard; it's really hard.

ONE MONTH LATER

THEY say every drug addict has a different problem. Maybe the reason a guy or girl turns to drugs in the first place is because at home or somewhere along the line they didn't receive the affection or understanding that they needed. So they hung out with a group, or a gang, or a club. And, you know, the club does things—maybe it will lead into drug addiction.

Now this person might have a feeling of not being wanted, or being wanted only when he's with this group, or being high on narcotics to hide from reality. Well, maybe someday they meet someone, and they fall desperately in love, really in love, really really in love with this person. And when you're in love with someone, you'll do anything to help them.

But it don't help everybody. Sometimes a person is really too far gone. Sometimes a girl straightens out a fella, and sometimes a fella straightens out a girl. But usually it's the girl who straightens out a fella. Because when a girl's been addicted, she's been around, and there's very few fellas who want her. To break it down into simple language: who wants second-hand merchandise? You know what I mean? Although sometimes the heart plays funny tricks and it doesn't matter. Sometimes it helps.

I've known guys who've gotten married and have stopped

using drugs for a little while, and then returned. And finally the marriage ends in divorce or annulment. Sometimes in marriage the drug addict turns his wife onto drugs, or the girl turns on her husband—so that she won't be alone. Mainly I think this is done because of a feeling of guilt. Because they're using drugs and their husband is not—and they know that they're hurting their husband and all like that. They introduce their husband to it, and he's just as guilty as they are. So it eases their tension, it eases their mind.

Then there are other cases where the girl has completely saved the drug addict, has taken him away from everything. And he devotes his life for her and, if he has children, his kids. This is pretty rare, but it happens.

I know cases of all three types. In my own club I know one, two, three, four . . . four definite people who were just as hooked as anyone else in the crowd at that time, because they started when everybody started and they kept using. The girl changed them entirely, changed their personality, everything.

I know also of a marriage where a guy turned his wife on. Of course, this never happened in our club. But it has happened. There are a lot of motives for starting a wife. You know this case in the papers where this kid was killed in Brooklyn just recently? Well, he had an old lady; they lived together common-law. She hustled for him and he hustled for her. I knew them both well. I met her back in 1956, on my first trip to Riverside.

She's a white girl, and she divorced her first husband. Her first husband stopped using narcotics completely; he's doing terrific in construction work. As a matter of fact, he turned her on. Now this is a funny case: the first husband turned his wife on—now he's stopped and she's using. When they went to Riverside, he had already stopped, and she was making it with a whole bunch of colored guys. She was selling her body, more or less, to the colored people. Of course, that didn't go over too well, but it's all forgotten in the drug world. One thing happens one day, and it's forgotten the next. Unless you rat. A rat is never forgotten. Or unless you beat somebody out of a very large amount of money. Those are the two things that are never forgotten in the drug world. Other things are remembered, but nothing is said.

That's how she started going out with these white guys again, and that's how she met this guy. She hustled for him and he hustled for her. Now he's dead and she's still hustling. He ratted. He sent somebody to jail—he ratted him out, and was getting paid for it by the cops. He sent some big people away. He set them up, and that's how the order went out to kill him. That's all there is to it.

That's one thing that never becomes known. It's too high up for us—we're only kids on the corner. These are big people. All I know is what I read in the papers, that he got shot six times. The only thing that did come down is that he is a rat. As far as anything else goes, you can't get no higher. A drug addict is never trusted with information like that.

You never see a drug addict getting high up; none of them ever get higher than a street-corner pusher. Even the people that supply these street-corner pushers use dope, but above that, that's it. You stop right then and there, because there's too much money involved. There are a lot of legitimate people involved, I guess, and they just don't want their names scandalized.

The pusher is the only guy I know, and that's the only guy I want to know. If I know too much, that might not be healthy.

And if I'm not using dope, well, I'm much better off,

like I am now. See, I'm getting a pot-belly! I'm feeling very good, I'm healthy again, I'm working and so far I'm doing very good, with the help of God, and you, and I gotta say my Aunt Lena is still with me.

That policeman who got shot by addicts? They were trying to get away—that's why they shot him. No one wants to do time in jail. By all rights, addicts are really not violent people. There are some that are violent, but they have been violent prior to addiction. They have arrests for assault—they show their aggressiveness before the use of narcotics. But most of us really do not want to hurt people. You'll find that a drug addict will find the quickest and easiest way to make money, without hurting anybody physically.

It's common sense that when you go to hit somebody, you might get arrested. And a drug addict doesn't want to get caught, for one reason: he doesn't want to kick cold turkey in jail. He hates jail. It's the worst thing in the world to kick in jail. Because the guards have no human compassion. They treat you like a dog in a cage. If you can't stand up for their count, they'll come in and beat the shit out of you to make you stand up. That's exactly what they do; I've had it done. And you know what a drug addict goes through when he withdraws—it's something pathetic. If he isn't dead at a certain time, and they don't like it, they'll throw a bucket of ice water all over him. And that's one thing a drug addict can do without, is ice water, because he's got enough damn chills and fever and pain and everything wracking his body all at once. And these nasty louses throw ice water on him! That's why a drug addict tries to do something non-violent, like boosting or passing a rubber check or conning or selling a television that's not there or stealing hubcaps. But very seldom a stickup. A guy that would have a gun in his hands would have it even if he weren't on drugs.

They say that because addicts are afraid of being locked up, this deters them from taking drugs. But if that method were any good, do you think that they would return as often as they do? At least ninety-five per cent of the people in jail are drug addicts or pushers. If this is such a good deterrent, why hasn't it worked yet? I can't name one guy that stopped using drugs just because he was in jail and got beat up. But there are a few you can name that when they were treated like decent human beings maybe didn't give it up, but remained at a certain level that was acceptable to society. At this level nobody knew that they used drugs. They just remained there, happy, and everybody else was happy.

We're all human. We're all under one God. Why should one man hit another because he has a weak will power and uses drugs?

Does someone take a club and beat that hack in The Tombs because he drinks? There are a great number of guards that smoke marijuana. There are a great many that drink to excess. But does anybody beat them up? No, because they got a badge. They're untouchable. There are definitely guards that blow pot. They talk about it openly in front of prisoners.

The only way is to make drugs legal, and to distribute them with an IBM card that can only be punched once. If a man is really incurable, the hell with him! Let him get high! Let him pay two or three cents a shot, where he's paying thirty dollars now. Let him have a job—he can hold a job. Cut his shot down, offer psychiatric treatment. Don't demand it, offer it. And you'll be surprised how many would be willing to accept it. And to stop. Try, always try. But don't force; try.

Don't forget, there's a lot of money lost in this city every year through drug addiction. It fattens the wallets of a lot of people. If they made it legal, these people wouldn't have that fat bank account anymore.

There are so many good reasons for legalization. An addict could get his drug cheap and pure, with no danger of overdose. He could hold a job and pay taxes, where now he's robbing and causing the other people to pay heavier taxes. He could lighten the load.

You could stop the crime—cut New York City crime at least fifty per cent. You could stop it overnight. Even if a person don't want to work, he could go to any trashcan in the city and pick up two five-cent soda bottles. He could go in and cash them and have enough money for a fix. Because that's how cheap drugs are on a legal market, and you know it! But illicitly, you know that they'll never get it with just two soda bottles, unless they use one of the bottles to split someone's head and rob him.

And if you make it legal, you're not killing the man. That man's gonna live just as long as you or me or anyone else. The only thing that's killing this poor guy is the ingredients that's put into this narcotics that he's copping on the street corner—the milk sugar, the quinine, the benita, the rat poison, the powder. That's what hurting him, hurting his liver, his mind, his whole body chemistry.

Harry Anslinger's not in there now. But he's been fighting a damn vicious war against narcotic using, peddling and smuggling. Right? What did he get? He raised jail penalties, did everything. Where did he get? What did he do? He didn't get *nothing!* Because there's still dope coming in, there's still the pusher, and there's still the user. And as long as it's pushed there's always the chance of some innocent kid getting stuck. And once he gets stuck, he's a new market; so the market will never die out. It will always be in demand. And these smugglers are geniuses. If they put their mind to the right thing, they'd be fantastic in the financial world.

Make it legal. Give an addict half a break—to work, to have a family, to live like a human being is supposed to live. And not in a crummy dump like I live in. Although, soon as I straighten out with my pay, I'm gonna move out.

So far I haven't slept on a roof. I've slept in subway cars, I've slept sitting up in a hallway, but never laid my head down on a roof. But there are people that have to do it every night. And in order to get up in the morning without being sick they gotta steal. It's lonely, it's miserable, and it's rotten. It just stinks—it stinks to high heaven!

If these people could get their drugs, they wouldn't be anti-social. They'd be very sociable. Because they're just human beings. They just have one weakness—narcotics. So give it to 'em. The United States will not become a nation of hopheads, just because it's legal.

I haven't seen my mother since last week. You know my Mom is mad at me. So purposely I walked over to Grand Street to see if I could see her. I wanted to see how mad she was, because she said she disowned me. Said she wouldn't talk to me even if she saw me in the street. I knew she was in Bingo, because they have a booster, and she only goes the first of the month to see who won the thousand dollars. So I'm walking back and forth for a half-hour or an hour, waiting to get a glimpse of her. Another reason I went was to set her mind at ease, to show her I was still living and all right. Because even though she says she's mad at me, it counts a lot that I'm okay. So anyway, I was looking in the window of the food store, and I turn my head and I seen her walking. She walked right past me—I looked directly into her eyes, and she looked directly into mine—and she just kept walking. She turned her head like as if she had snubbed someone. She kept going down Grand Street, going home. And I walked home with a tear in my eye.

Why do I go back? I don't know. I told you, if I had the answer to that, I'd never go back. I don't want it. I know it's hell. I don't want to fall back. It's murder on the people I love. It's murder on me. I really don't want it. But I don't know why I do.

If I could answer those questions, then I'd know myself. I'd know what I want and I'd know how to get it. But I can't answer those questions.

SIX WEEKS LATER

THE last time I was here I believe I asked you to loan me some money, and said that I would return and pay you. I said I was working. And the truth of the matter is I only worked one day on the job. Never went back.

I was using drugs. It was a brand-new job. The first day I was working, I told the boss I needed money for rent, and he loaned me the money for one day's work in advance. I put in the time, so he didn't give me anything I didn't earn. On lunch hour I took a cab, came downtown and copped. I got high, I went back to work and completed my work, and I just never went back. Just walked home and never came back. I didn't know why; I still don't know. I just never went back. I don't know what happened—all I know is that it's the first time that I never went back to a job.

And then the reason I didn't come back here was that I didn't have the money to pay you . . . felt like a damn fool.

This week I'm supposed to pay fourteen dollars back rent. My mother's going to give me seven dollars for one week's rent, and I got to think of a story to tell the landlady about the other seven.

My mother's been giving me some, and my Aunt Lena comes across when she can. Sometimes I get money from my family, sometimes I get money here, sometimes I don't know where it comes from. It just comes. I'm not a thief; I have no steady hustle. Yesterday I got money for my fix from my Aunt Lena. The day before I got it from my ex-wife. She happened to call up my Aunt Lena, like she always does. I was there and talked to her on the phone. Told her I was sick and she gave me fifteen dollars. This was the first time I've seen her in God knows how long. I met her around the corner from where she lives, picked up the money and left. She felt sorry. I think she still loves me. I love her—that I know.

I don't know what I did to get money. I know I beat a couple of people a few weeks back. They were creeps. These were a certain type of people that beat other people, all the time. I told them I'd get it for them, they said okay, they gave me the money, I went away, and I never came back. They just trusted me with the money, and I walked away.

There's a certain type of people, they like to beat other people. So I just figured I'd teach them a lesson, because I usually don't beat nobody. I don't like to do that, because I know what it is to be sick. I just figured I'd teach these certain people a lesson, and they learned, because so far they haven't been back. They found somewhere else to cop. And maybe they say to themselves, now I know what it feels like when I beat somebody.

Don't get me wrong, I'm no slickster. I got beat myself many a times. But it's been a long time. You always got to put your faith in somebody, and somebody always louses it up. You just got to know the connection—you know the guy who's dealing and you go to him. If you don't know the guy who's dealing, don't rush into anything—just take your time and watch. Sit down and watch, no matter how sick you are. You'll find out soon enough who's got and who ain't got.

Anyone can sit on a street corner and find out who's selling dope and who isn't. Just like you can see who's taking number and who isn't. You can be standing all alone on a corner, all of a sudden one guy walks over to you, walks away; another guy walks over, then two guys walk over; and each time you're giving something, taking something. I know one thing: you're not buying. You got to be selling. Right? You're the man with the stuff. All these people are not getting beat. Otherwise you're not gonna be standing there. 'Cause once you beat one party you're gonna go. So you got to have stuff. I go over and I cop. I make it.

I haven't had sexual intercourse in eight months. A guy without drugs, maybe he'd go out looking for it; a guy with drugs, he don't give a damn. If it comes along, it comes along. You can always find a girl. But to me, I want one person, and that's just the way I feel. I got no feelings for anybody else. I love my wife, and she's the only one I really really want. We had a normal sexual life, even when I was hooked. We both enjoyed it. I know I satisfied her. She can tell you that herself.

I'm trying to be truthful, and tell you just how things go. But I'm on edge. I ain't even got a cigarette to smoke. I need a fix.

I see lots of teenagers taking dope—it's increasing. They do the same thing we used to do—get high just for kicks.

We used to get high and go out, go to a movie or a dance. Then after a while the kick is gone, and it becomes an obsession. That's how I started (*whisper:*) just for the kicks.

THE NEXT DAY

LAST night I took the six dollars you gave me and I went out and I copped. There's nothing to say.

(*Irritated:*) Most likely I'll get a job, why not? I'm no cripple. I don't know, I'm not gonna count on nothing till I get out of the hospital. Right now, I'm not thinking too far ahead, except to the hospital. That's as far as I can think. That's all I want to think.

How will I get stuff till then? I don't know. I have no ideas in mind—believe me when I tell you I don't! I don't have no idea in mind!

Mrs. Blake

✤✤✤

I'M not only supporting myself, I have to support a drug
addict. When I come home to eat supper, I see him sitting across the table half-asleep. He can't eat, he has pains
in his stomach, his eyes are droopy, and when you talk to
him he's so dull and lifeless. It's no fun when you see a
boy dying from dope.

When he was fifteen, how nice and handsome he looked!
Now he's drawn and thin—his sizes are much smaller than
they used to be. It was a pleasure to walk with him then.
Now I'm ashamed to walk with him, 'cause everybody
knows he's a drug addict. But I make sure that he's kept
clean; he has clean clothes on, his body is clean, his hair
cut, and he's shaved. He's always out not for food—that
isn't good enough for them, healthy meals like he used to
eat—all he needs is his fix. And that's the only food he
wants. His stomach hurts him, his back hurts him, he can't
see so good—it ruins them.

You try so hard to go someplace. Go to who? You don't know where to go. You're afraid. And especially where I work, you can't tell people. There's no place to go, no one to talk to; you got to keep it to yourself. Just go to church and pray. I've been lighting candles every week for my son. I pray, I offer masses and communions—not for him but for many others. Maybe someday God will hear my prayers. I don't know whether he's gonna live or whether he's gonna die. He's gotten so bad that food don't mean a thing to him anymore.

And he keeps coming up. I give him seven, I give him ten. My take-home pay is only fifty dollars a week. I take care of a mother and myself and my son.

Tommy has a father—he was in the service. When he came home I don't know whether he was jealous of the boy or what. The boy wanted to learn how to read I remember once, and he asked his father. His father says, don't bother me. Couldn't be bothered. The only thing he was interested in was his friends in the bar and grill. Then his father had malaria, and he wouldn't go to the hospital. He wanted me to take care of him. Then he lost his job, but I had to continue working. I'm working twenty years. Then Tommy's father got worse; he used to come in at three in the morning and leave at three in the afternoon. At that time my salary was only twenty-one dollars, but we managed to get by. Then I couldn't take it anymore. The boy was ashamed of his father, 'cause he drank. But I always told Tommy, that's your father. Always love him, never hate him. And if your dad doesn't know where he belongs, pick him up and take him home.

And Tommy always done that. But still, Tommy would not go to his father, because there wasn't the feeling of fathership there. He went to mother.

Then Tommy began to go to dances, and I wasn't aware

of what was going on. I never thought of such a thing. One day when Tommy was thirteen I was cleaning his room and I happened to hit against his coat. There was a bulk in the coat, and I found it—a hypo needle, a spoon, and a handkerchief. I was so excited I didn't know what to do. I called one of his friends, Henry Brown—he's dead today from it. I told him, and he explained to me; and he did away with it. The next morning Tommy was wild; he hollered at me and everything else. But I didn't answer him, and he went to school. I found out later he was absent from school.

One day I come marching down the block with the boxes of Mother's Day gifts. I come into my apartment, my apartment was all upset. All the neighbors were looking at me and pernting their fingers at me. I didn't know what it was all about. Then a knock on the door and a policeman tells me my son is arrested for heroin.

When we got before the judge, a mother besides each child, the judge asked each child why did they do such a thing? My boy's words were, a kick. And the judge said, you have no reason. You have everything: clothes, money, clean home and love.

But it was kicks. So Tommy was sent to Riverside Hospital for a cure. I kept him there a little longer than usual, because I thought six months wasn't enough. He stayed there nine months. He went to the after-care clinic, he was doing fine. He had a job, he made very good money. I never got it: he always kept it for himself.

He met a nice girl, he kept company. We talked it over; we always sat down and talked things over. I always told him it was nice to have a nice wedding, nice home—something to always remember and bring your children up to. Tommy ran away and got married. And that was another shock.

He come back, I put him in a beautiful home. I didn't have the money, but I managed. Gave him the best. He had a nice girl—it was wonderful. But he had in-laws that didn't like the nationality, which is prejudiced. We don't believe in that; we believe we're all human, and God made us. And that's the way Tommy was raised. I very seldom went over there, because I didn't want Tommy to have in-law trouble, like I had. I wanted Tommy to have a happy life, 'cause when he's happy, I'm happy.

Well, it didn't turn out that way. He had a father-in-law to tell him how to live. His father-in-law didn't believe he made so much money, but Tommy worked very hard. They got along wonderful, but then Tommy broke out again: he couldn't take it. Then her family was causing them to get a divorce. It was a shock: after two years, the home was broke up. I couldn't get over it.

Then Tommy would work, but he never wanted to live home. He says, no, Mother. You live alone, because you can't live my life.

It's true; nobody can live nobody's life. Tommy lived in one beautiful apartment after another. He made the money, he worked, and yet he always used the stuff. He'd get arrested and I'd have to clean out the place. I'd find the needle. Take his clothes home, get them cleaned up, pay his bills for him, straighten him out.

Last place I sent him was Kentucky. With all my vacation money, sent him there to be cured. He didn't last very long. He ran away from it, and he went to Florida. With the help of my sister we sent him checks twice a week. He finally got back, we put him up in a place, and then he got in a mess again. Now he isn't in a mess, but my sister and I pay his room rent. He hasn't been working since March, and it's gotten to be more money and more money and more money.

I'm at the bottom of the barrel. Tommy wants to be cured, but Tommy is so far gone. It's gonna be so hard for him to get well again. If he gets well, we only make him well for a while. After a month, make him healthy, he'll go back on again, whether he's in this neighborhood or any other neighborhood. It's all around us, so don't blame the neighborhood. It's got to be up to the self, just like a drunk. I've had them both.

Sometimes you haven't got the money. You give him the last change you got, and I've seen myself go to work on a Monday with just three dollars to my name for the whole week. I do without, so that he will not hurt nobody. I'd rather see my son dead before he steals or before he hurts anybody.

Where do we go from here? No one knows. We just sit and wait for someone to help us, only with their mouths and not their hearts.

I notice Tommy's complexion is not a very healthy one, and his lips are blue. His teeth have been pulled out one by one. All his upper teeth are gone now. I got him an upper plate, so he wouldn't look bad. I used to get some bill from the teeth. He wouldn't get them pulled by injections, like any normal person. It used to be gas, and you know how much gas costs. His eyesight is very poor from the use of drugs. Drugs affect the whole body. My boy was a nice-built boy, and when I used to see him dressed, it was something to look at. He loved clothes and he always had clothes. Now, he just wears his T-shirt and pants, and his clothes look like they're hanging on a hanger.

He was a happy child. He always sang. We were always happy. We loved music, but now we don't feel it no more. He loved football, baseball, dancing; he was very active in the clubs. We look at each other opposite the table, and his head is drooped and he's half-asleep. He says he's fine, he won't complain. You can see him rub his stomach, and his face is all drawn in. Instead of beautiful blue eyes shining, they just hang drowsy. That's the dope. And when they haven't got it, they're very nervous; they walk the floor, they sniffle, they can't sit down or talk, and if they do talk it's very dull.

Tommy told me he wanted to cure himself by taking certain pills that cost eight dollars. Well, you're green, you don't know what it's all about, so you say all right. You're so happy over it, and you think he can do it. So I give him eight and my sister gives him eight, and two days later you see Tommy the same as before. What are you doing here? you ask him. You said you were going to stay in your room and really break it!

Friday night I seen him, and I knew he was looking for money. So he says, I wrote you a letter. Did you get it?

I gave him money that night, and today I got the letter:

July 26

Dearest Mom,

Here it is morning. The pills I bought don't seem to be doing what they're supposed to do. Because it's four A.M. and I am sick, and I mean sick!

Mom: call me what you will, but it hurts. I guess maybe I am a weakling or a punk, just as everyone says, but I really can't help it, I am sick and it hurts. I am sorry, but I can't do it by myself.

Please, I can't help it if I'm weak. Mom, the whole thing is murder. I really didn't think I was using this much. I am sorry but the only way I am going to beat this is by going in a hospital.

Please believe me when I say it hurts and that I am sick. Because I am, Mom, I really want to stop, but I can't do it by myself. I am sorry to put you in the middle, because you are right, and you don't deserve this, by me or anyone.

Sorry. That's me, always too late!

Love,
Tommy

You can see the boy just wasting away; I don't know whether there's a possibility of a cure. I think he's all et up; I think his kidneys and liver are affected. And he's very very thin; I'm not fat, but I make two of Tommy.

I hope he can get in the hospital, and that there is a possible cure. I don't know if he'll be finished. I doubt it; I've seen Tommy go away for two cures. And I've seen him sent away for nine months because he didn't stay in Kentucky. And as soon as he came out, he only lasted two days and he was right back on the stuff again.

I don't know where he buys the stuff or who he buys it from. Believe me, I wish God would strike them dead. Or if they have children, maybe, God forbid, they might be one of them. Let them feel how we feel; let them be hurt like we're hurt; let them feel sick like we feel sick.

When I'm in bed at night, if a phone rings, I wonder if my Tommy's dead. I had very bad pains today, and I was afraid to eat, and I had a funny feeling Tommy wasn't at the hospital at nine this morning—which turned out to be true. I'll be very glad to go to the hospital with Tommy tomorrow, if he's willing. Because if it keeps going, it's going to be too late. Maybe that phone call will come through—and it's a funny feeling, you always get that feeling—it's going to be Tommy next. There's so many of them going; that's all you hear. And no one likes to hear their loved ones died, especially when they're young. They got a full life ahead of them. And life's so beautiful, if you'd only look around. You may not have a lot of money, but there's a lot of beautiful things to see. And I'd love to see those boys see those things.

(*Weeping:*) I wish somebody could help them. God knows how they suffer! Why can't we do something? Nobody wants to help them: they only talk talk talk. Politicians as well as the rest—they sit and talk, but they don't have it in their own backyard and know what it is. Then they'll tell you, well, it's not our fault your children are like that. Yet they want voters, but they don't want to help them. God forgive them.

I don't know if there's ever going to be help. I have a drug addict son—that is my cross. I have my mother to support, and I have my sister that's sick and can die any day. I haven't seen my husband in eight years—since the last time he took a stroke. Somebody notified me and I went up and I gave him a pint of blood and I helped to feed him. Until his people started intervening—and I left, minding my own business. I don't know where they live; they don't want to tell me what hospital he's in. I don't ask because I have my own cross to bear. He don't know what's wrong with his son; I don't tell. He has his own burden; he's very sick and they don't know how long he'll last. So why should he suffer? God has made me a little stronger, and He's been good to me so I can take care of it myself.

His family always called me stuck-up. I didn't care to hang in bars and grills. I believe in staying home, keeping my home clean, cook the good food. I don't believe in standing on corners and gossip. Tearing other people apart I don't like, because none of us have a clean backyard. So that's why maybe I wasn't very liked. I don't know if it's bad or good, but that's my life. If I can help you, nurse you to health, or feed you, I'm always there. I'm not afraid and I'm not ashamed. I like to do voluntary work. I don't believe people should have too much idle time. There's a lot of people need help and you can go out and help them. I did that until my sister took sick, and then I had to give it up. It's nice to make other people happy; it don't cost no money.

When Tommy was arrested, I happened to be coming back from the hospital, and I happened to see a couple of women talking. I was walking and I turned around and I seen them pernt a finger at me. I says to myself, oh, what a foolish woman; she never knows when you pernt a finger at others it falls on yourself. I told my sister and she says her daughter and son don't even live with their husband and wife! But I beared it, and I didn't care what they said, as long as my conscience was clean and I was doing right by sending my boy away to be cured. And then I thought another thing. They don't pay my rent. I don't live on charity; I work. I don't ask for nothing from nobody. So I kept walking; I kept my going to church and coming home and taking care of my sister and mother and working, and it didn't bother me no more.

The tenants in the project where we live now don't know nothing about my son. My son doesn't raise no disturbance because he knows his grandmother is seventy-four years old and has never had a black mark against her name since she was born. None of us did; we always kept our name clean. Tommy comes right up, and eats, and goes right out of the building. Never disturbs nobody, never asks questions. They know he's my son, but that's as far as it goes. He does not hold conversations with no one. And that's where we want to keep it. Because I would never hurt a hair on my mother's head.

My mother's only retired about six years. She was a char-woman and she worked hard. My sister Lena has helped me since Tommy's been born; she loves him devotedly.

She's the godmother and she actually raised him; when Tommy was three I went to work. She'd give her life for him.

No, none of us is married a second time. We're all with one husband. That's the way we believe. Even though I'm separated from my husband, I have never thought of marrying again. It never occurs to me; my hands are filled with Tommy. If Tommy wasn't what he is, I think we would be a very happy family. We used to go out together to the beaches; we used to visit each other and we had a table it was like a banquet; we used to sing. It was always a holiday, and now it's no more. When Christmas comes around now, I want to be by myself. No more singing or laughing.

I got to be with Tommy. Wherever he is, I got to meet. . . . (*Weeping:*) My sister has been operated on three times; her cancer is getting worse. Whenever she comes out of the anesthetic, she asks for Tommy. He's her baby. She prays for him; she has the priest pray for him.

So where's it gonna land us? What's gonna happen? (*Bitterly:*) Nobody knows. Let 'em be dead rotten stuff. Who's gonna help? Nobody finds out how to help. There's no cure. We kid ourselves. We keep saying yes, maybe. But they can't—it's too much. What can we do to help them? Nobody knows, only God knows. We leave it to Him.

Believe me, Tommy's too sick to work. And I know Tommy: he's not ashamed to work, he'd scrub floors. But he's too sick. In fact, if he doesn't get taken to the hospital, the undertaker's gonna take him.

Tommy at thirteen got a job, so he'd stay off corners. And he liked work. He'd work from seven in the morning till seven at night. He saved that money all up and bought clothes for himself. He worked after school and when summer came he worked full time. And then when he left school he left as a printer. Even at home: he painted his apartment and fixed it up beautifully. I loved the place. Tommy even helped his father-in-law. He paints, fix electrician, anything. It isn't that he was lazy—he was never lazy. He was an active boy and he loved it. But not now —he's going down and down.

I used to be so sick from going to pay his rent. I'd have to lay in bed and I'd get terrific pains in the head. And about two days later I'd get black and blue marks break out in some parts of my arms and legs and the pain would go away. If you seen the places! I used to feel so sick that Tommy wound up in such places. With the place he came from, the boy he was, and what he dressed! It would really nauseate you—you wouldn't want to eat no more.

When Tommy showed me that green paper, knowing he was going in the hospital, it gave me a happy feeling, but yet I had an awful disillusion. I don't know why, I'm sorry to say it, but I don't know: I think Tommy's afraid. He hasn't said it—he's happy, he acts happy. But yesterday he acted very morbid. He sat in a room by himself and he didn't want to be bothered into conversation whatsoever. But very morbid; I couldn't look at him. He was so down.

A lot of Tommy's friends made good. Denny Dickson made good. But Brown didn't. He didn't get on drugs here, but he got on in Korea. When he came out of service, I used to meet him, and I used to say, there's nothing around here, Brown; go back in service. Please. Because he came from a very good father and mother. I says, you're gonna get in trouble. Then I noticed Brown stopped saying hello to me. And I remarked it, because that boy never passed me up without saying hello, Mom. I said there's something wrong with Brown, I told my son: Brown is taking it. And it was true. One day he passed me fast; he said hello,

Mom, real fast, without looking. And that's the last I seen of him.

Dom Abruzzi? He's still on it. Thank God his brother is saved. I heard he's going to try to become a minister. Tommy told me. And when I meet Nick Abruzzi, we talk. I'm very proud of him; it makes you feel good. He'll pray for his brother's soul.

We have no right to condemn nobody, 'cause even ourselves could be easily addicted by taking drugs through medication. Like these things that they have for cough medicine, or these tranquilizers. I don't take no tranquilizers; I don't believe in it. I take a Bromo Seltzer or once in a while a Bufferin for headaches. But otherwise I don't take anything without a doctor's prescription. And if I find out it's drugs, believe me I don't take it. I'm afraid of it. Because I do not want to become addicted.

I had two other children I lost, and it took me five years in order to have this boy. And I was lucky I had him alive. I used to take a month off from work in the wintertime, because Tommy could not stand the cold weather. I love children, and how I would have loved to be a real mother! I always called myself a part-time mother, and that's a hard, cold word.

Tommy grew up without a father. When Tommy was small, he always used to play he was a father with a lot of children. He turned around and he looked at me, and he said, gee, Ma, why don't you get a divorce and get married and get me a new daddy? Well, he didn't understand. So I said, your Mommy and Daddy are Catholics; we cannot get divorced. What God joins together stays together. But he didn't understand that so much. But then as he got older, he had friends that had a lot of "uncles." He didn't understand that, either. So I let things ride till he got older, and he learned himself. But my son always wanted a father, and never got one.

I had to be father and mother. I often blame myself. But they say drug addicts tend to feel that way, that you failed in every way, no matter even if you turned the world upside-down. You're always wrong and they're always right. Because they're sick, and they tell you, you don't understand. But I try to understand. I don't know. My mother was left a widow with four of us children and one coming. I was nine. My mother went to work and she supported us. There was no such a thing as home relief. But we all had our chores. We had clean clothes, plenty of food; we were never neglected. My mother was father and mother. And we love her. If we did something wrong, she'd take a broomstick to us. And we were scared stiff. She'd say, I'll put you in a home! That's all we needed to hear and we'd kiss her feet. And we turned out all right. I can't understand this. Why didn't we go wrong?

You got to be laugh clown laugh. Nobody wants to know that you're crying inside, because they're only going to mock it. And condemn it. So you always pretend everything's all right.

Tommy Blake

❖❖❖

I WAS afraid when I heard that you were talking to my
mother. I was afraid that it would come to a head and
she'd find out about the lies I been living. I was afraid both
ways—that she'd tell you and you'd tell her. And being
that I live in a world of lies, I didn't want them exposed.
That's how I get my drugs—I lie.

With my mother and my aunt I used to tell them I was
going out and getting a job or something. Now I just tell
them I'm sick and need the money, that's all. Or I'd tell
one I needed the rent money when I'd already got it from
the other and spent it for dope. But most of the time I
worked and had my own money. It's just been recently that
it's been getting bad. I don't know why. I have no idea.

I haven't had a fix since last night.

It's going to end either one way or another. Either
I straighten up or I end up in a coffin. I'm not talking about

suicide. I'm fading away to nothing. It will only take one pallbearer to carry me.

I just gotta stop, that's all there is to it. It's just not normal, you're not human using dope. I'm tired of living lies. Every day it's the same thing: I'm tired, I just want to stop.

My mother's stayed with me—stayed a lot longer than some drug addicts' mothers I know. Most drug addicts break with their families. But it's not really the mother; it's always the father. It's always the father that throws the guy out of the house. The mother usually says let him stay, let him stay; the father says no, it's either him or me. So what's the woman gonna say? He's my bread-and-butter, he's not; so boom! let him go. It's the old man that throws them out.

I'm getting sick. I can't sleep, eat, do anything. I got pains in my stomach. I get nauseous. And I get these migraine headaches so bad I want to beat my head against the wall. I'm just uncomfortable right now.

I wanted to kick by myself, and my mother gave me some money for it. But it didn't work—the four walls just closed in on me. I don't know. I just wanted somebody to come up once in a while. I asked her recently, and she didn't want to go for it. So I didn't kick. I was willing to do that to go to my cousin's wedding. All I wanted was someone to come up every once in a while to see how I was, bring me food or something, though I wouldn't eat it maybe. Because I can't keep food up there. I wanted somebody to come up and check on me, see if I was okay or if I needed anything. Or if I really got too sick, you know, maybe they could help me go out to get a shot to straighten up. But they didn't go for it. Nobody wanted to come up. I didn't kick.

I bought a bag of heroin and some dolophine pills. Just before you get sick you take the dolophines and they help you out. You keep cutting down each day on the dolophines until you cut yourself off. Then towards the end, when you're cutting down on the dolophines, you take a sleeping pill maybe, to go to sleep with. A goofball, but you don't use them to goof on, you use them to sleep with. Then you stop; you kick.

I've had friends kick with dolophine, but they had their family with them. Or they went away to the country somewhere.

Altogether I bought sixteen dolophine bills, and I paid about sixteen dollars to a pusher. I don't know how they get them. I don't ask questions. I took the bag of heroin, and I took four dolophines when I started to get sick. A few hours later I took two, then I took one. I took a sleeping pill and I went to sleep. The next day I took three, then two, then took half a pill. Then I took another sleeping pill and went to sleep. I couldn't do it after that; I just left the house.

I just couldn't stay at the house, the house was closing in, it was lonely. There was nothing to do. Nothing to read, nothing to do. I got tired, I walked out. I didn't prepare reading material or nothing, I just got the pills. I had no extra money for nothing; they wouldn't give me extra money. I didn't have nothing, I had nobody coming up, I had no extra food in the house; all I had was the pills. That's all I had. If I asked them for any more they'd blow their top. There just wasn't enough help.

I don't know, I'm just afraid, that's all. Afraid of my mother coming here . . . I don't know, afraid of the lies I been living, the life I been leading. Going to the hospital . . . I don't know what it is, I'm just afraid, that's all. I don't know, I can't tell you. It's somewhere in the back somewhere. I don't know what it is, why I feel that way, but I *feel* that way! That's the only thing I can express at this time.

No, I don't feel security because my aunt and mother help me. Let me put it to you this way. They give me the money. I suffer for it, too. What do they think, I just ask and they give me the money? They don't. I argue with them, I con, I fight. I'm tired of it. I don't want to fight people for money anymore. I don't want to hear it no more. I'm gonna go out and make my own, and I just don't want to bother no more. People think just because you go out and get high you got a bed of roses. They feel, we're giving you the money, you're going out and having a good time. I'm not having a good time. Yeah, when I first started out I had a good time; I'm not having a good time now.

I'm tired of it, I'm tired, that's why I want to go to the hospital, to get away from it all. Things like this: I should be out like them other guys in the street, normal, back with my wife. I should never make a recording like this. I'll tell you the truth; I don't like the idea of making recordings like this just to get enough money to go out and get a fix. I'm going to be very frank. I hate it. I despise it. If you want some, I'd like to give you a tape-recording. But I'd like to give it to you in my own way. Not answering question after question after question, because sometimes these questions are repeated; they just keep coming up and coming up and coming up. And I can't answer them. They just keep coming and I beat my brains out and I can't answer them. And it hurts, Mr T., it hurts. I don't like to feel that way, I don't like to feel at a loss. If I want to give you something, I just want to put it down, tell you how I feel. I'll tell you how I feel, but as far as answering question after question, I don't like it. I don't like making recordings like this, just to know I'm getting fix money behind it. I really hate it; I'll tell you the truth, I hate it.

It reminds me of my old man, like when he used to give me questions. I used to answer the same thing over and over and over and over. I hate that; I can't stand that from anybody.

I told you how I'd like to make a recording! Someday I'd just like to just sit down, maybe up at my own house with my own tape recorder, somewhere I'm relaxed, and maybe when I'm high and I let out my inhibitions, my feelings. I can just sit there and talk and talk—not even talk, think out loud. This way I know I'd tell you exactly what you want to know. Because it wouldn't be answering questions, it'd be just telling the story.

I'm not alert now. My mind is somewhere else, it's not on the subject. What is it on? Getting a fix! If I'd come down here high like I wanted to, if I'd been able to get money to get high, I would have been able to talk, I'da been relaxed. But now . . . it's hell.

THE NEXT DAY

I'M not high, but I'm not sick. I'm more or less normal, the way God put everybody on this earth. Right now, in order for me to be normal, I have to have this drug. After Thursday, if I go into the hospital, I hope I'll be able to kick the physical part of it. After that, it's up to me, and partly I guess the people around me. I don't know if I'm going to stay away. Because only God knows what's gonna happen. He knows at the beginning when the end is gonna come, so He knows all. All I can say is that I'm gonna try. I'm gonna put everything I can into it. Every resource that I can find.

Every time I get money from somebody by lying, I feel guilty, and, I don't know, sometimes I tell myself I got a complex because of it. And because of this complex, I continue on, and I just make it worse for myself. I know I'm making it worse, yet I continue and I keep continuing. Just keep going and going and going. I can't make any wild promises, because I'm still a junkie. But I hope to pay everybody back. 'Cause maybe if I do, I'll help myself to get away from this guilty feeling I have about taking money from people.

When you take a shot, you may feel a rush immediately, or it may come upon you slowly, even though you took it mainline. It depends on the stuff you have and what it's cut with. Sometimes you might think you got garbage, but it comes slow and keeps building, and you wind up with a pretty good head. I really can't explain what I mean by a "good head." Most of the time now I just need the drugs to feel normal, but if I had enough of it I'd feel high. I'm not much on nodding or scratching when I'm high. I walk around. I like to walk when I'm high, I really do. I like to look at things, see things. Maybe I fall back to when I was a kid, because back then I liked to see things too. I liked to go out on trips. Matter of fact, when I played at the Settlement we formed a Trip Club. I always enjoyed it and I still do. I may have seen the Statue of Liberty four times, and every time I go it's a new thrill, it's a new kick. And going to 42nd Street, it's a new thing to me every time I go, because I always find something new to interest me. There are a lot of interesting things in the Museum of Natural History, too. Or just maybe walking in the park and enjoying life.

Sometimes when I'm high I may go to my mother's, watch a little television, have something to eat. When I'm high and go to my mother's, we always get along well, because I never give her any reason to argue with me. The only time my mother does argue with me is when I ask her for money. She always gets aggravated, always gets mad, flies off the handle and that's when I got my trouble. But what can I do? I don't want to go out and steal it. I got no choice. Even though I know I'm breaking her heart. But maybe I'm wrong and maybe she's right, I don't know, but I feel that sometimes it's better to give. I'm looking at it from my point of view now, maybe I'm jealous, but I've got a hard enough time to go out and cop, get straight without getting beat, getting caught, dying from an overdose, or stealing to get it.

I think my Mom loves me, and I love her too. But I put my Mom through hell. She's a good woman, she works hard. But it's hard for her to walk down the street and have people say, there goes Mrs. Blake, her son's a drug addict. These things you don't do to a mother. I get her nervous, and she has to take it out on somebody. She's worked hard all her life and she doesn't deserve this.

My father never really bothered. Like the only time he ever opened his mouth would be if my mother told him I was playing hookey and he'd come over and start: what're ya playing hookey for? Don't you know you got to go to school? He never raised his hand to me. He'd tell me, you try and do your best and pah-pah-pah we'll see if we can do this for you, help you out. But I always knowed that after a while it would be forgotten. He was drinking, but not all the time. When he come up to see me, he wouldn't drink. I don't know out of respect for who, but he never came up drunk.

No, I never took him home when he was drunk. Never. Never.

No, I never had longings for a father, 'cause I knew I'd always find him on the corner. I knew if I needed something, I got it. Used to walk over and ask him for a dollar to go to the show with my friends, and he'd give it to me. One time he was working in the Pitt Street pool for the summer—provisional help, city department of parks. And all that summer we went swimming for nothing, me and all my friends. He used to let us in the park any hour of the day or night. We used to go in ahead of all the crowds and everything. He treated me pretty good, you know? Except that he didn't live with us.

He used to talk and tell me, treat your mother good, she's a good woman, and this and that. Then there's a lot of times he used to be drunk and he'd maybe tell me that he was sorry that he was a drinker, and this and that. Sometimes he'd be drunk and think about the war, and run down about how he'd seen kids get killed and he'd think of me at home. He used to say, thank God my son's only a baby, he can't be over here to get his belly shot open like these other kids.

I was working up in the country this summer and I met this girl Jenny. She was very skinny and she had for her age a very stupid personality. Though she was twenty-eight, she was still in her childhood. When I lost my job I couldn't pay for dates, or anything like that, so Jenny started paying for them. I was only going out with her as a favor to my friend Charlie, who was going out with a married girl who was a friend of Jenny's and needed her for an alibi so she could see Charlie. That fall, Jenny's friend left her husband, and Charlie left his wife, and they moved into the city. Now Jenny lives in the city—she was only vacationing up there. So I continued seeing Jenny in the city. Mainly I borrowed her car a lot; I used to go down and cop with it, things like that. As soon as I got back to the city I started using dope again. Then I took an O.D., and they came home and seen me in bed, 'cause I was living with them at the time. Well, Charlie and Nelly thought I was sick, so Jenny thought I was sick. So I told Jenny I needed money for the doctor, and Jenny came across. So I worked on it from there. Every time I needed money, I'd go to Jenny and tell her I'm sick. One time I told her I was supposed to go in for an operation and borrowed four hundred dollars off her.

I kept borrowing money and borrowing money, and finally I said I'm just ruining this kid, so I made her break up with me. I told her I was using drugs, and different things like that. I told her, remember when I was sick? Well, the doctor was giving me morphine to kill the pain. I got hooked on morphine; I'm hooked, so I'm using dope now. So I ain't got time to do this, and I ain't got time to do that. Then I told her once I'm going away for a cure. I didn't go—I took more money off her. Then I said, I can't be doing this no more. I just stopped calling her. She wrote me a couple letters, and then I never heard from her again. That's it.

That was the only girl I've ever gotten money from. When I was with my wife, I got all the money I used for dope from working. I made sure my house came first and my dope came second. My wife was still with me even after I went to Lexington, left there and got arrested in Florida, and came back. Finally I got arrested in May of 1961, and her family talked and talked and talked and talked and finally got her to get a divorce. By the time I got out of jail, she was remarried.

She got a quickie divorce in Alabama. Matter of fact, they're being investigated to see whether it's legal or not. Anyway, she didn't get a divorce in the eyes of God and the Church. I'm a Catholic; so is she. In the eyes of God, we're still married, and she's living a life of adultery with this other guy. So I still think by the Church, that we're still married. I still think of her as my wife, though I refer to her as my ex-wife, out of respect for her.

If you find an in you work it: that's what I've been doing. It comes along; it just comes. You just get to know people, and you just know the right moment. You just try. But I'm tired of it. I'm tired of begging people for money, because I know it belittles me. And really, I'm the last person in the world that wants to be belittled. Because I always try to act above somebody else, which is wrong. When my Aunt Lena got sick and needed a hundred dollars for an operation, I was just seventeen, right after I was married, but I said here, take it. If you need more, just ask.

I've got that hundred back more times. . . . But I felt good then, when I was able to give. When I used to go out and buy presents for my mother. . . .

Now I feel like a real idiot, to have to go up and beg people for money. It's no more like I was a kid and I say, Ma, give me some money, I want to go to a movie. It's different. What a change! Maybe I've lied to fill that gap. Like maybe I think that I'm putting something over on somebody else. And while I'm thinking that, I'm covering up my own feelings of belittling myself—of me myself being the fool, instead of the other person who's giving me the money out of the kindness of their heart. Maybe that's why I do these things—to cover up. Because I really am a fool. And these lies help me hide the fear, help me hide the truth from myself.

Half of the kids today, they know what they want. Or they *think* they know what they want, like I thought. They think that they're wise, that the world owes them a living, and that things should come fast. Not slow but fast. They don't believe that you got to work and save and put your mind and your back to something. The same guys that think this way, they hang out with a crowd, and one guy will say, I want to get high. And the next guy will say, I want to go along. With me, it was a big kick. I was doing something that nobody else was doing. Now, after all these years, you learn that you didn't do anything. You only put yourself back ten years.

I should be so far ahead of myself! I should have so much money in the bank, I should have so much clothes, a wife ... I should have a beautiful home now. I've made money. I've made good money, honest. And it all went into somebody else's arm; it went to put a pusher behind the wheel of a Cadillac; it went to put somebody up in a penthouse. And me: I gotta roll around in dirt, suffer pain, go to hospitals, beat people for money, lie.

I would tell kids today don't go near it. And don't ever think you're the one that can beat it. Because nobody beats it. Everybody says, not me, I'll beat it. Don't ever think that, because you'll be the first one hooked. Everybody's said the same thing. Even after kicking, guys I know will say, I'm not gonna get hooked now—I can use on weekends. And they're hooked in two weeks. I know, because it was me. I've done it.

I wish they'd wipe narcotics off the face of the earth.